THE URBANISM OF METABOLISM

This edited book explores and promotes reflection on how the lessons of Metabolism experience can inform current debate on city making and future practice in architectural design and urban planning. More than sixty years after the Metabolist manifesto was published, the author's original contributions highlight the persistent links between present and past that can help to re-imagine new urban futures as well as the design of innovative intra-urban relationships and spaces.

The essays are written by experienced scholars and renowned academics from Japan, Australia, Europe, South Korea and the United States and expose Metabolism's special merits in promoting new urban models and evaluate the current legacy of its architectural projects and urban design lessons. They offer a critical, intellectual, and up-to-date account of the Metabolism projects and ideas with regard to the current evolution of architectural and urbanism discourse in a global context.

The collection of cross-disciplinary contributions in this volume will be of great interest to architects, architectural and urban historians, as well as academics, scholars and students in built environment disciplines and Japanese cultural studies.

Raffaele Pernice is an Italian architect and Senior Lecturer in Architecture and Urbanism at the University of New South Wales, Sydney, Australia. He holds a Ph.D. in Architecture from Waseda University in Tokyo and a M.Arch. from the University IUAV of Venice in Italy. He has extensive research and teaching experience in Australia, East Asia, and the Middle East, and his interests and activities lie at the nexus of architecture and urbanism, ranging from design practice through to the theory and history of architecture and city planning, with a focus on the evolution of the cities of Japan and the Asia-Pacific region. He has been the recipient of scholarships and grants from universities and national and international institutions, such as the Japanese Ministry of Education (MEXT), the Italian Ministry of Foreign Affairs, the Japan Foundation, the Australian Department of Foreign Affairs and Trade (DFAT), and the Japan Society for the Promotion of Science (JSPS).

"Rising from the ashes of the Pacific War, a new generation of Japanese architects sought radical new ways to solve the challenges of social change and material destitution in their devastated cities. In fusing native tradition and radical modernity, they created a movement which was to influence the architecture of the twentieth century. Through a compilation of scholarly essays and personal narratives this valuable English language collection provides a cohesive evaluation of the Metabolist movement in both its domestic and international contexts. It is a comprehensive reference for both the professional and the general reader."

Peter Armstrong (University of Sydney) studied under Yosizaka Takamasa and worked for Kiyonori Kikutake from 1969 to 1973

"What can we learn today from the radical visions and thinking of Japanese Metabolism of the 1960s? In this indispensable book, the best international scholars critically interpret Metabolism as an avant-garde movement, at the same time deeply anchored in the Japanese reality and a transnational phenomenon with great critical success, but also as a symptom of a condition of environmental and urban crisis to which architects must respond as a priority commitment: today as yesterday."

Pierre Alain Croset, *Department of Architecture and Urban Studies (DAStU), Politecnico di Milano, Italy*

"Among the merits of this publication, there is the effort to present a fresh and broader new look at Metabolism by means of a series of contributions by high-calibre experts in disciplines which do not belong only to architecture. For everyone interested in Japan, this book is full of useful insights to understand modern Japanese history from the point of view of urbanism and architectural forms."

Masaki Koiwa, *Department of Architecture, Waseda University, Tokyo, Japan*

"This book, edited by Dr. Raffaele Pernice, has as obvious feature in that the authors are all independent writers, and someone experienced the Metabolist movement in Japan in the 1960s. The scholars explore pioneering issues related to climate change and social identity worldwide which were affected by Metabolism. Besides, this book is also an engaging incipient index of Japanese modern architectural masters and their practices."

Xiaoming Zhu, *College of Architecture and Urban Planning, Tongji University, Shanghai, China*

"A much-needed rediscovery of a significant cultural and design movement that still influences the development of global cities. The book sheds light from multiple perspectives on what Manfredo Tafuri defined as an 'academy of the utopian': a group of visionaries that, with their bold proposals, introduced in the global debate ideas that are still relevant today, tracing clear paths for the further developments of design disciplines."

Benno Albrecht, *Rector Università IUAV di Venezia, Italy*

THE URBANISM OF METABOLISM

Visions, Scenarios and Models for the Mutant City of Tomorrow

Edited by
Raffaele Pernice

LONDON AND NEW YORK

Cover image: 3D rendering of Kiyonori Kikutake's unbuilt Marine City 1962–1963, created by Antxon Canovas.

First published 2022
by Routledge
4 Park Square, Milton Park, Abingdon, Oxon OX14 4RN

and by Routledge
605 Third Avenue, New York, NY 10158

Routledge is an imprint of the Taylor & Francis Group, an informa business

© 2022 selection and editorial matter, Raffaele Pernice; individual chapters, the contributors

The right of Raffaele Pernice to be identified as the author of the editorial material, and of the authors for their individual chapters, has been asserted in accordance with sections 77 and 78 of the Copyright, Designs and Patents Act 1988.

All rights reserved. No part of this book may be reprinted or reproduced or utilised in any form or by any electronic, mechanical, or other means, now known or hereafter invented, including photocopying and recording, or in any information storage or retrieval system, without permission in writing from the publishers.

Trademark notice: Product or corporate names may be trademarks or registered trademarks, and are used only for identification and explanation without intent to infringe.

British Library Cataloguing-in-Publication Data
A catalogue record for this book is available from the British Library

Library of Congress Cataloging-in-Publication Data
A catalog record has been requested for this book

ISBN: 978-1-032-03071-5 (hbk)
ISBN: 978-1-032-03073-9 (pbk)
ISBN: 978-1-003-18654-0 (ebk)

DOI: 10.4324/9781003186540

Typeset in Times New Roman
by codeMantra

CONTENTS

List of figures	*vii*
List of contributors	*xiii*
Acknowledgments	*xvii*
Foreword: The Logic of Metabolism	*xix*
Toyo Ito	

Introduction   1
Raffaele Pernice

1 Back from Behind the Curtain of Oblivion: Metabolism
and the Postwar Actuality of Japan   8
Hajime Yatsuka

2 The Aesthetics and/or Formalism of Change: Paradoxes and
Contradictions in the Metabolist Movement   22
Botond Bognar

3 Engineering a Poetic Techno-urbanism: The Metabolists'
Visionary City in Postwar Japan   45
Raffaele Pernice

4 The Metabolists in Context   61
Jon Lang

5 The Infrastructure of Care: Metabolist Architecture
as a Social Catalyst   73
Peter Šenk

vi Contents

6 "Sunday Carpenter" Metabolism: Artificial-Land
   Housing and Resident Decision-Making 84
   Casey Mack

7 Maki and Dutch Team X: Step towards Group Form 101
   Kiwa Matsushita

8 Kiyonori Kikutake circa 2011: Sustaining
   Life through Metabolism 114
   Ken Tadashi Oshima

9 Metabolism as Survival Architecture 131
   Hyunjung Cho

10 Metabolism Adventure: A Personal View 142
   Philip Drew

11 This is Your City: The Pop Future Foretold by Metabolism 160
   Yasutaka Tsuji

12 Spaceship Earth: Metabolist Capsules,
   the Petro-economy, and Geoengineering 173
   Yuriko Furuhata

13 An Eternal Return? Considering the Temporality and
   Historicity of Metabolism 184
   Julian Worrall

Afterword *195*
Gevork Hartoonian
Bibliography *199*
Index *209*

FIGURES

1.1   Sketch of Kiyonori Kikutake's Sky House, 1958. Image: collection of the architect's family   10

1.2   Digital reproduction of Koto ward project by Kiyonori Kikutake, 1959. Image: author's collection   11

1.3   Section of Kiyonori Kikutake's Marine City, revised version 1968. Image: public domain   12

1.4   Digital reproduction of Kisho Kurokawa's Agricultural City, 1960. Image: author's collection   13

1.5   Sketch of Kisho Kurokawa's Kasumigaura Lake Project. Image: public domain   14

1.6   Masato Otaka's Motomachi Apartments Project in Hiroshima, initiated in 1968. Image: courtesy Botond Bognar   17

1.7   The residential complex of Sakaide in Shikoku Island, designed by Masato Otaka in 1968. Image: author's collection   18

2.1   Kiyonori Kikutake: Marine City project, 1958. Drawing courtesy of K. Kikutake   23

2.2   Kenzo Tange: Plan for Tokyo 1960. Photo courtesy of K. Tange   24

2.3   Arata Isozaki: Joint Core System. Drawing courtesy of A. Isozaki   25

2.4   Kiyonori Kikutake: Sky House, Tokyo, 1958. a) Drawings. Courtesy of K. Kikutake; b) Interior. Photo by B. Bognar; c) Interior, on the left is Kikutake and on the right is Toyo Ito in August 1980. Photo by B. Bognar   26

2.5   Kiyonori Kikutake: Office Building of Izumo Shrine, Izumo, 1963. Photo by B. Bognar   28

2.6   Kiyonori Kikutake: Hotel Tokoen, Yonago, 1964. Photo by B. Bognar   28

2.7   Masato Otaka: Tochigi Prefectural Conference Center, Utsunomiya, 1969. Photo by B. Bognar   29

2.8   Kenzo Tange: Yamanashi Radio and TV Headquarters, Kofu, 1966 and 1974. a) Photo of the complex after its extension in 1974. Photo by B. Bognar; b) Section and 1F plan of the building. Courtesy of K. Tange   30

viii Figures

2.9   Kenzo Tange: Yamanashi Radio and TV Headquarters,
Kofu, 1966, showing the original building before extension.
Photo courtesy of K. Tange   32

2.10 Kenzo Tange: Fiera District Redevelopment project, Bologna,
Italy, 1982. Photo by B. Bognar   32

2.11 Kenzo Tange: Yamanashi Radio and TV Headquarters, Kofu,
1966 and 1974, detail. Photo by B. Bognar   34

2.12 Kisho Kurokawa, Odakyu Drive-in Restaurant, Hakone,
1969. Photo by B. Bognar   35

2.13 Kisho Kurokawa, Capsule for Living, Osaka Expo, 1970. a) The
Capsule suspended in the Space Frame over the Festival Plaza by
K. Tange. The Space Frame acted as a "City in the Air". Photo by
B. Bognar; b) Close-up view of Kurokawa's Capsule in the Space
Frame. Photo by B. Bognar; c) Kurokawa's Capsule for Living seen
from below. Photo by B. Bognar; d) Floor plan of the Capsule.
Courtesy of K. Kurokawa   36

2.14 Kisho Kurokawa, Nakagin Capsule Tower, Tokyo, 1972. a) Exterior
of the building suggestive of what Kurokawa characterized as "the
aesthetic of time". Photo by B. Bognar; b) Interior of one capsule
residence. Photo by B. Bognar; c) General floor plan of the Nakagin
Capsule Tower. Courtesy of K. Kurokawa   39

3.1   Bomb damage in Tokyo in 1945. Japanese photo depicting the
aftermath of American air raids near Hisamatsu, part of what is now
the Tokyo Metropolis. The Sumida River can be seen in the right
portion of the photograph. Image credit: Wikimedia Commons/
Public domain   47

3.2   Chart depicting the share of immigration into the three main
urbanized areas of Japan (Tokyo, Osaka, and Nagoya) in
1954–1987. Urban immigration peaked by early 1960s. Source:
Fujita Kuniko and Richard C. Hill (eds), *Japanese Cities in the World
Economy* (Philadelphia: Temple University Press, 1993)   49

3.3   Cover of Luis J. Sert's *Can Our Cities Survive?* (1942). Image credit:
Public domain   52

3.4   Destruction and floods in South Japan caused by Typhon Vera,
September 1959. Image credit: Wikimedia Commons/Public domain   55

3.5   Expo Tower, Osaka, Japan. Designed by Kiyonori Kikutake for
the World Expo 1970 in Osaka. Image credit: Kirakirameister via
Wikimedia Commons   56

3.6   The Takara Group, Beautilian Pavilion, designed by Kisho
Kurokawa, at the World Expo 1970 in Osaka. Image credit:
m-louis/Wikimedia Commons   57

3.7   3D rendering based on Kiyonori Kikutakes's Marine City, which was
originally conceived in 1958. Images created by Antxon Canovas
(image published with permission of the author)   58

4.1   The Constructivist City: Hammer and Sickle, 1933 by Iakov
Chernikov. Digital image 2021, Museum of Modern Art,
New York/Scala, Florence   62

4.2	José Luis Sert and CIAM's view of the future city: a design for Barcelona set against Ildefons Cerda's *Eixample.* Source: Sert and CIAM (1944) and Lang (2021). Courtesy of the Frances Loeb Library Fine Arts Library, GSD, Harvard University	63
4.3	Yona Friedman's 'Spatial City' concept. Source: Friedman (1959) and Lang (2021). Courtesy of Le Fonds des Dotation Denise y Yona Friedman	64
4.4	Arcosanti. Drawing by Tomaki Tanmiura. Courtesy of the Cosanti Foundation	65
4.5	Skyrise for Harlem. Drawing by Shoji Sadao. Courtesy of the Estate of Buckminster Fuller	66
4.6	Salzburg Superpolis, 1965–1967. Source: Justus Dahinden, *Urban Structures for the Future*, trans. Gerald Ohm (New York: Praeger, 1972, 22). Collection of Jon Lang	67
4.7	Urban designs for 2045: the mile-tall Sky Mile for Tokyo (left) and the proposal for the smart city of Rublyovo-Arkangelskoye, near Moscow (right). Image courtesy of Kohn Pedersen Fox, architects (left) and a rendering courtesy of Flying-Architecture (right)	70
5.1	1) Taoist yin and yang; 2) and 3) traditional Japanese crests (featured on the cover of *Architectural Design* magazine in May 1967); 4) Metabolism symbol designed by Kyoshi Awazu; 5), 6), and 7) *sustainism* symbols, designed by Joost Elffers (Source: Michiel Schwarz and Joost Elffers, *Sustainism is the New Modernism: A Cultural Manifesto for the Sustainist Era* (New York: Distributed Art Publishers, 2010)); 8) recycling symbol	75
5.2	Metabolic infrastructure: vertical megastructural form. Artificial ground (ag) with program (capsule) units. Plan and elevation. Adapted from Šenk, 2013	79
5.3	Metabolic infrastructure: horizontal megastructural/group form. Artificial ground (ag) with program (capsule) units. Plan and elevation. Adapted from Šenk, 2013	80
6.1	Takamasa Yosizaka, artificial land sketch, 1954	85
6.2	Kisho Kurokawa in the Nakagin Capsule Tower, Tokyo, circa 1972. Image credit: Tomio Ohashi	86
6.3	Le Corbusier visiting Yosizaka at his artificial land house in Shinjuku, Tokyo, 1955	87
6.4	Wajiro Kon, sketches of barracks after the Great Kanto earthquake, 1923	88
6.5	Takamasa Yosizaka, artificial land house frame (left) and enclosed with infill (right), circa 1955	89
6.6	Kunio Maekawa, Harumi Apartments, Tokyo, 1958. Image credit: Chuji Hirayama	90
6.7	Kunio Maekawa, Harumi's *minka* inspiration, 1957	90
6.8	Kenzo Tange/MIT proposal, community for 25,000 people over Boston Bay, 1959	91
6.9	Kiyonori Kikutake et al., Stratiform Structure Module, 1977	92
6.10	Yositika Utida, comparison of *kyo-ma* (left) and *inaka-ma* (right) measurement systems, 1977	94

x Figures

6.11 Yositika Utida et al., NEXT21 Experimental Housing, Osaka, 1993. Photo taken in 2010 ... 96

6.12 Shu-Koh-Sha Architecture and Urban Design Studio, NEXT21 floor plans, circa 1993 ... 97

7.1 The town of Hydra, Greece. Image credit: Fumihiko Maki ... 102

7.2 Three paradigms of Collective Form (from left to right): compositional form, megaform, and group form. Image credit: Fumihiko Maki ... 104

7.3 Letter from Bakema to Maki, August 28, 1961. Het Nieuwe Instituut/BAKE_g122-12-1 ... 105

7.4 Housing with Walls (1962), a collaborative work with Otaka. Het Nieuwe Instituut/BAKE_ph61-10a ... 108

7.5 The competition designs for the Prix de Rome (1962) by Piet Blom, an example of configurative design. Het Nieuwe Instituut/BLOM_17-10 ... 109

7.6 Three models of the exterior-interior spatial correlation. Image credit: Fumihiko Maki ... 110

7.7 Aerial view of Daikanyama, with buildings of Hillside Terrace highlighted. Photo credit: ASPI, and Hillside Terrace overview; image: Fumihiko Maki ... 111

8.1 "Metabolism: The City of the Future," Mori Art Museum, 2011 ... 115

8.2 Chikugo River, Kurume, Fukuoka Prefecture. Photo by Ken Tadashi Oshima ... 117

8.3 Itsukushima Shrine, Hiroshima. Photo by Ken Tadashi Oshima ... 118

8.4 Eifukuji Kindergarten, Kurume, 1956. Courtesy of Kikutake Architects ... 119

8.5 Kikutake, Sky House. Source: Oscar Newman, *CIAM '59 in Otterlo* (Stuttgart: Karl Krämer, 1961), 184 ... 120

8.6 "Ideas for the Reorganization of Tokyo City, Kikutake Kiyonori," in Oscar Newman, *CIAM '59 in Otterlo* (Stuttgart: Karl Krämer, 1961), 185 ... 122

8.7 Hotel Tōkōen, Yonago, Tottori Prefecture, 1964. Photo by Ken Tadashi Oshima ... 123

8.8 Pasadena Heights, Shizuoka Prefecture, 1974. Photo by Ken Tadashi Oshima ... 125

8.9 Kiyonori Kikutake, *Kaijō toshi no hanashi* (Tokyo: NHK Books, 1975) ... 127

9.1 Kiyonori Kikutake's Aquapolis floating platform built for the Okinawa Ocean Expo 1975 (model). Image credit: Wikimedia Commons ... 136

9.2 Plastic Ski Lodge capsule designed by Ekuan Kenji and GK Design Company Inc. in 1962. Image courtesy of GK Design Company Inc. Tokyo ... 137

9.3 The Hills Side Terrace residential complex designed by Fumihiko Maki. Image credit: Wikimedia Commons ... 139

10.1 Unlike monumental masonry in the West, Japanese architecture is a post-and-beam carpentry tradition, insulated from earthquakes by an elaborate shock absorbing bracket system, resulting in an open flexible lightweight architectural aesthetic. Photo by Philip Drew ... 144

10.2 Le Corbusier. National Museum of Western Art, Ueno, Tokyo, 1957–1959. The stay of Juzo Sakakura and Kunio Sakakura as assistants in Le Corbusier's Paris studio (Sakakura for many years) ensured an authentic interpretation from the source filtered through their Japanese sensibility. Photo by Frank Martin ... 145

10.3	Kenzo Tange and Yoshikatsu Tsuboi, National Olympic Gymnasium No. 1 (Swimming), Yoyogi, Tokyo, 1964. The roof adopted the same ridge tent form as Saarinen's earlier Yale Hockey Rink supported on two masts and anchored at either end above the entrances, unlike Gymnasium No. 2 which is supported on a single mast that repeats the traditional symbolism of the central post. Photo by Philip Drew. ID: 4662	146
10.4	Sachio Otani, Kyoto Conference Centre (ICC Kyoto), 1966. Its distinctive trapezoidal cross-section responded to the variety of large and small interior spaces, which like the Izumo-Taisha administrative building was at once evocative of the past and Futuristic in its Baroque imagery. Photo by Frank Martin	147
10.5	Kenzo Tange. Shizuoka Press and Broadcasting Centre, Shimbashi, Tokyo, 1966–1967. Tange adapted the symbolism of the sacred central post to the requirement for flexibility of Metabolism by leaving spaces for additional cantilevered bracket-floors. Photo by Philip Drew. ID: 4681	149
10.6	The October–November 1977 issue of *Japan Architect* examined trends post-1970 and posed the question of who would succeed Kenzo Tange (hidden top right in a darkened sky of clouds) with the rise of a new post-Metabolist generation. Arata Isozaki (upper left) and Kisho Kurokawa (upper right) hover below Tange, and below them a group of young samurai is seen rising (*Japan Architect*, no. 247 (October–November 1977), 12 and 13)	150
10.7	View of the Central Alps, Honshu. Many outstanding examples of *Minka* are found there, including spectacular A-frame Gassho-style houses at Kamitaira Village, Toyama Prefecture, which were the model for Kenzo Tange's 1960 Tokyo Bay Proposal. Photo by Philip Drew. ID: 4804	151
10.8	Yoshijima House, Takayama, twentieth century. The combination of primary and secondary posts is both functional as well as highly symbolic. The posts carry the entire load of the heavy roof, yet are symbolic, as evidenced in the sacred post of the famous Kasuga Shrine in Kyoto Prefecture. Photo by Philip Drew. ID: 4837	152
10.9	Kiomizu-dera Temple, Kyoto. The huge timber post-and-beam supports under the veranda deck presaged Tange's core-node structure of the Yamanashi Building. Photo by Philip Drew. ID: 4951	153
10.10	Kenzo Tange, Yamanashi Press and Broadcasting Centre, Kofu, 1966. Too small to qualify as a megastructure, the Yamanashi structure is Tange's frozen manifesto for the Metabolist vison of a remade world. Photo by Philip Drew. ID: 4718	153
10.11	Arata Isozaki: Oita Prefectural Library, Oita, Kyushu, 1966. Isozaki began with post-and-beam Japanese carpentry, hollowed out and enlarged the Library beams, then further enlarged them to the point of extreme giantism for the Kitakyushu Museum of Art, 1974. Photo by Philip Drew. ID: 5452	155
10.12	Garden of the "Blissful Mountain" at the Zuho-in Zen Monastery, Kyoto. At its best, the Japanese capacity to emote with nature set it apart from the West's need to dominate and exploit nature. Photo by Philip Drew. ID: 5493	157

xii Figures

11.1 Frederick Kiesler, Endless House, 1947–1960. MoMA Exhibition Records, 670.11. MoMA Archives. © 2021. Digital image: MoMA, New York/SCALA, Florence 162

11.2 Kisho Kurokawa, Agricultural City, 1960. Photograph by George Barrows. International Council and International Program Records, I.A.1082. MoMA Archives, New York. © 2021. Digital image: MoMA, New York/SCALA, Florence. Yasutaka Tsuji, *Postwar Japan as Dullness: A History of Art Movements and Exhibition Installations* (Tokyo: Suisei-sha, 2021): 161 164

11.3 The Plan of "Visionary Architecture." MoMA Exhibition Records, 670.11. MoMA Archives, New York. © 2021. Digital image: MoMA, New York/SCALA, Florence. Yasutaka Tsuji, *Postwar Japan as Dullness: A History of Art Movements and Exhibition Installations* (Tokyo: Suisei-sha, 2021): 162 165

11.4 "This is Your City: Urban Planning and Urban Life," Seibu Department Store, Ikebukuro, October 12–17, 1962. Photo: © Osamu Murai 167

11.5 "This is Your City: Urban Planning and Urban Life," Seibu Department Store, Ikebukuro, October 12–17, 1962. Photo: © Osamu Murai. Yasutaka Tsuji, *Postwar Japan as Dullness: A History of Art Movements and Exhibition Installations* (Tokyo: Suisei-sha, 2021): 165 168

11.6 Murals by Hiroshi Manabe. Photo: © Osamu Murai 169

12.1 Kisho Kurokawa manifesto, "Capsule Declaration 1969." Published in the journal *Space Design – SD* (March 1969), 50 178

13.1 Rem Koolhaas presenting his book *Project Japan. Metabolism Talks* to an audience of professors and students at the University of Tokyo, 2011. Image: Julian Worrall 191

CONTRIBUTORS

Botond Bognar is Professor and Edgar A. Tafel Endowed Chair in Architecture at the University of Illinois Urbana-Champaign (UIUC), USA. He received his B.Arch and M.Arch degrees at the Technical University of Budapest and his M.A. in Architecture and Urban Planning at the University of California, Los Angeles. With a Japanese Ministry of Education (Mombusho) Scholarship, he conducted research at the Tokyo Institute of Technology for two years. As a licensed architect, he practiced architecture in both Hungary and Japan, where he lived for several years. He is an internationally renowned scholar of the history and theories of contemporary Japanese architecture and urbanism, and has published over 20 books and monographs, numerous chapters in volumes, and many essays and articles. He has also lectured all around the world. He is the recipient of a Japan Foundation Fellowship, the Architectural Institute of Japan (AIJ) Cultural Appreciation Prize, two Graham Foundation Fellowships, the William and Flora Hewlett Fellowship, the Social Science Research Council Fellowship, the Asian Cultural Council Fellowship, and the title of University Scholar at UIUC.

Hyunjung Cho is Associate Professor in the School of Humanities and Social Sciences at KAIST (Korean Advanced Institute of Science and Technology) in South Korea. She received her Ph.D. in art history from the University of Southern California in 2011, with a specialization in Kenzo Tange and the Metabolist Movement. Her research topics include Korean and Japanese architecture, with an emphasis on the intersection between art and architecture. Her articles on this topic were published in *Journal of Architecture*, *Journal of Architectural Education*, and *Architectural Research Quarterly*.

Philip Drew is an internationally regarded authority on the architectural careers of Jørn Utzon, Frei Otto, Harry Seidler, Glenn Murcutt, and Sydney Opera House. A graduate of the University of New South Wales (B.Arch), he holds a master's degree from the University of Sydney and recently completed a doctorate on the Victorian architectural sculptor T.V. Wran, which opened up a new field of study into the critical expressive and aesthetic role performed by sculpture not only in nineteenth-century Victorian architecture, but also in contemporary architecture. He has published important monographs on Arata Isozaki, including *The Architecture of Arata Isozaki* (Harper & Row, 1982) and *The Museum of Modern Art, Gunma. Arata Isozaki. Architecture in Detail* (Phaidon, 1996), as well as Tadao Ando, *Church of the Light, Church on Water, Tadao Ando. Architecture in Detail* (Phaidon, 1996). Following his graduation in 1966, he backpacked around Japan staying in youth hostels, an experience which led to a lifelong fascination with its people, culture, art, and architecture.

Yuriko Furuhata is Associate Professor and William Dawson Scholar of Cinema and Media History in the Department of East Asian Studies, and an associate member of the Department of Art History and Communication Studies at McGill University, Canada. She is the author of *Cinema of Actuality: Japanese Avant-Garde Filmmaking in the Season of Image Politics* (Duke University Press, 2013). Her second monograph, *Climatic Media: Transpacific Experiments in Atmospheric Control* (Duke University Press, 2022) traces the technological, institutional, and geopolitical connections between Japan and the USA that led to the development of artificial fog, weather control, cybernetic environments, metabolic architecture, and networked computing during the Cold War period.

Gevork Hartoonian is Professor Emeritus at the University of Canberra, Australia, and holds a Ph.D. from the University of Pennsylvania, USA. He has taught in American universities, including the Pratt Institute and Columbia University. He was previously Visiting Professor of Architectural History at Tongji University, Shanghai, 2013 and 2016. During these visits, he also delivered lectures at the Southeast University, Nanjing, and at the China Academy of Arts, Hangzhou. He is the author of *Time, History and Architecture: Essays on Critical Historiography* (Routledge, 2018) and *Global Perspectives on Critical Architecture* (Routledge, 2015). His previous publications include, among others, *Architecture and Spectacle: A Critique* (Routledge, 2016) and *The Mental Life of the Architectural Historian* (Cambridge Scholars Publishing, 2013). His forthcoming books include *Reading Kenneth Frampton: A Commentary on "Modern Architecture" 1980* (Anthem Press, 2022) and *The Visibility of Modernization in Architecture: A Debate* (editor, Routledge, 2022).

Toyo Ito is an architect and founder of Toyo Ito & Associates, Architects in Japan. After graduating from the University of Tokyo in 1965, he worked in the office of Kiyonori Kikutake until 1969. His representative projects include Sendai Mediatheque (Japan), Serpentine Gallery Pavilion 2002 (UK), Tama Art University Library (Hachioji Campus, Japan), 'Minna no Mori' Gifu Media Cosmos (Japan), and National Taichung Theater (Taiwan ROC). He is the recipient of the Royal Gold Medal from the Royal Institute of British Architects, the 22nd Praemium Imperiale in Honor of Prince Takamatsu, the Pritzker Architecture Prize and the UIA Gold Medal, among others.

Jon Lang headed the joint M.Arch/MCP Program in Urban Design at the University of Pennsylvania, USA, where he taught for 20 years before settling in Australia in 1990. At the University of New South Wales, Australia, he headed the School of Architecture in the 1990s and early 2000s. His writings include *Urban Design: The American Experience* (Van Nostrand Reinhold, 1994), *Urban Design: A Typology of Procedures and Products* (Architectural Press, 2005; Routledge, 2017), and (with Nancy Marshall) *Urban Squares as Places Links, and Displays* (Routledge, 2016). His most recent book is

The Routledge Companion to Twentieth and Early Twenty-First Century Urban Design: A History of Shifting Manifestoes, Paradigms, Generic Solutions and Specific Designs (Routledge, 2020). In 2010, he received the Reed and Malik Medal from the Institution of Civil Engineers in London.

Casey Mack is an architect and the founder of Popular Architecture in Brooklyn, New York, USA, an office combining simplicity and innovation in design work across multiple scales. He graduated with a B.A. in Art History from Vassar College and an M.Arch from Columbia, afterwards working with the Office for Metropolitan Architecture and teaching urban design at the New York Institute of Technology and housing at the Parsons School of Design. His work has been published in *OASE*, *Harvard Design Magazine*, *Avery Review*, and *Inflection*. He is currently writing *Digesting Metabolism: Artificial Land in Japan 1954–2202* (Hatje Cantz, 2022).

Kiwa Matsushita, Ph.D., is an architect and Professor at the Shibaura Institute of Technology, Japan. She received a B.A. from the University of Pennsylvania, USA, majoring in art history, and an M.Arch from Harvard University, Graduate School of Design, where she was a member of Harvard Design School Project on the City, a research project led by Rem Koolhaas. After returning to Tokyo, she worked at Maki and Associates. She was one of the curation members of "METABOLISM: THE CITY OF THE FUTURE" exhibition at Mori Art Museum in 2011 and its catalogue includes her essay "Fumihiko Maki: City and Crowd" (Shinkenchiku, 2011).

Raffaele Pernice is an Italian architect and Senior Lecturer in Architecture and Urbanism at the University of New South Wales, Sydney, Australia. He holds a Ph.D. in Architecture from Waseda University in Tokyo and a M.Arch. from the University IUAV of Venice in Italy. He has extensive research and teaching experience in Australia, East Asia, and the Middle East, and his interests and activities lie at the nexus of architecture and urbanism, ranging from design practice through to the theory and history of architecture and city planning, with a focus on the evolution of the cities of Japan and the Asia-Pacific region. He has been the recipient of scholarships and grants from universities and national and international institutions, such as the Japanese Ministry of Education (MEXT), the Italian Ministry of Foreign Affairs, the Japan Foundation, the Australian Department of Foreign Affairs and Trade (DFAT), and the Japan Society for the Promotion of Science (JSPS).

Peter Šenk, Ph.D., is an architect and Associate Professor of Architecture and Spatial Planning at the Department of Architecture, Faculty of Civil Engineering, Transportation Engineering and Architecture, University of Maribor, Slovenia. He is a co-founder of the architecture office Studio Stratum, IPoP – Institute for Spatial Policies, the artistic research platform FWC (First World Camp), and the House of Architecture Maribor. His research interests include architectural theory, urban theory, and the theory of visual culture. He has lectured and published articles, books, and conference papers in these fields, and has shown his work at exhibitions internationally. He is the editor of *City-Edge* (Zalozba Pivec, 2014) and *Funkcija v arhitekturi* (*Function in Architecture*, Zalozba ZRC, 2020), and is the author of *Capsules: Typology of Other Architecture* (Zalozba ZRC, 2015; Routledge, 2018).

Ken Tadashi Oshima is Professor of Architecture at the University of Washington, Seattle, USA. He served as President of the Society of Architectural Historians from 2016 to 2018, and has been a visiting professor at the Harvard Graduate School of Design and taught at Columbia University. From 2003 to 2005, he was a Robert and Lisa Sainsbury Fellow at the Sainsbury Institute for the Study of Japanese Arts and Cultures in London, UK. His publications include *Kiyonori Kikutake: Between Land and Sea* (Lars Müller, 2016), *Architecturalized Asia* (Hong Kong University Press/ University of Hawaii Press, 2013), *Global Ends: Towards the Beginning* (Toto, 2012), *International Architecture in Interwar Japan: Constructing Kokusai Kenchiku* (University of Washington Press, 2009), and *Arata Isozaki* (Phaidon, 2009). He curated "Tectonic Visions between Land and Sea: Works of Kiyonori Kikutake" (Harvard GSD, 2012), "SANAA: Beyond Borders" (Henry Art Gallery 2007–2008), and was co-curator of "Frank Lloyd Wright: Unpacking the Archive" (MoMA, 2017) and "Crafting a Modern World: The Architecture and Design of Antonin and Noemi Raymond" (University of Pennsylvania, University of California, Santa Barbara, Kamakura Museum of Modern Art, 2006–2007).

Yasutaka Tsuji is Assistant Professor at the University of Tsukuba, Japan. He specializes in the history of art and architecture after 1945. He was a visiting scholar at Columbia University, USA, with a Japanese Government Fellowship from the Agency for Cultural Affairs in 2014–2015, and a research fellow of the Japan Society for the Promotion of Science at the University of Tokyo in 2014–2016. His publications include "Too Far East is West: The *Visionary Architecture* Exhibition as a Background to Metabolism", in *East Asian Architectural History Conference 2015 Proceedings*, October 2015. He has also written "Outdated Pavilions: Learning from Montreal at the Osaka Expo," in *Invisible Architecture: Italian and Japanese Movements in the 1960s* (Silvana Editoriale, 2017), and "Displaying the Phenomenal City: Installation of the 1975 Shinjuku Exhibition at the Museum of Modern Art in New York", in *East Asian Architecture in Globalization* (Springer, 2021).

Julian Worrall is Professor of Architecture and Head of the School of Architecture and Design at the University of Tasmania, Australia. An architect, critic and scholar with a Ph.D. in architectural history from the University of Tokyo (2005), he has worked with Klein Dytham Architecture and OMA, and has taught architecture and urban history at Waseda University, Sophia University, and the University of Adelaide. His research explores themes of publicness, displacement, neutrality, and temporality, particularly as manifest in the architecture and urbanism of Japan and East Asia. His publications include (with Erez Golani-Solomon) *21st Century Tokyo* (Kodansha International, 2010), and his critical writings have been widely published, including in *2G*, *Domus*, *Icon*, *Architecture Australia* and *The Japan Times*. He has contributed to numerous exhibitions, including A Japanese Constellation (MoMA New York, 2016) and The Far Game (Korean Pavilion, Venice Biennale, 2016). His most recent book, a collaboration with artist Aglaia Konrad, is *Japan Works* (Roma Publications, 2021).

Hajime Yatsuka is an architect and Emeritus Professor of Architecture at Shibaura Institute of Technology, Tokyo, Japan. His concern as a researcher and critic focuses on architecture and urbanism of twentieth-century Japan and the world. Among his book publications are: *Le Corbusier: Urbanism as Biopolitics* (Seidosha, 2013), *Metabolism Nexus* (Ohmsha, 2011), and *Shiso toshite no Nihon kindai kenchiku* (*Modern Japanese Architecture as Intellectual History*, Iwanami, 2005). A prolific and esteemed scholar, his translated texts have been published in many journals in Japan, the USA, East Asia and Europe.

ACKNOWLEDGMENTS

The genesis of the research project presented in this book coincided with the decision to move from China in 2018, where I served as a lecturer in urban planning and design for six years, to Australia upon my appointment as senior lecturer in the Architecture program at the University of New South Wales (UNSW). Under Sydney's blue skies, I could devote much more time to the rediscovery of Metabolism architecture and city planning theories, the focuses of my Ph.D. dissertation I submitted to complete my doctoral studies at Waseda University in Tokyo in 2007. With great enthusiasm, I finally had the opportunity to revert to my old studies and interests in Japanese postwar architecture and urbanism, which linked to my personal experiences and the beautiful memories of Japan, especially Tokyo. Here I lived and worked for several years, first as a Japanese Ministry of Education Scholarship recipient and then as a postdoctoral research fellow of the Japan Society for the Promotion of Science.

During my initial research in Japan, which commenced many years ago, the supportive and insightful guidance of my doctoral supervisors, Professor Shinichi Nishimoto and Professor Takeshi Nakagawa, helped me familiarize myself with the reality of Japanese academic culture. This made my transition from Europe smooth and successful. Later, as a postdoctoral researcher, I could expand my knowledge and interests in Japanese cities thanks to Professor Masahiko Takamura and Professor Hidenobu Jinnai of Hosei University. My sincere gratitude and appreciation go to all these individuals.

Several people made this research project possible. I am very grateful and express my respect to Hajime Yatsuka for his fundamental contribution and support in preparing the international symposium on Metabolism at UNSW in 2021, of which this book is a direct result. When I proposed the idea of an international conference to celebrate the 60th anniversary of the publication of the Metabolist manifesto to him, Professor Yatsuka responded with enthusiasm. Further, upon my request, he introduced me to many scholars who would contribute to the event.

I want to thank all the speakers/authors of the essays presented at the international symposium and then re-edited for this book's purpose, including Hajime Yatsuka,

xviii Acknowledgments

Botond Bognar, Jon Lang, Ken Tadashi Oshima, Julian Worrall, Kiwa Matsushita, Peter Šenk, Yuriko Furuhata, Hyunjung Cho, Philip Drew, Tsuji Yasutaka and Casey Mack. Their scholarships, expertise, and vast knowledge of the themes presented in the book are priceless, along with their commitment to this project's success.

I am much indebted to architect Toyo Ito and Professor Gevork Hartoonian, who kindly accepted my invitation to write the Foreword and the Afterword for this book. I want to thank Yuma Ota and Tetsuya Yaguchi, who curated the translation of Toyo Ito's Foreword in English, and Elicia O'Reilly and the Japan Foundation Sydney for their constant and active support at the various stages of preparing and executing the international symposium.

I wish to thank the Capstone Editing staff for the initial polishing and editing of the various essays presented at the international symposium on which this book is based.

I appreciate the effective support of the editors Francesca "Fran" Ford and Trudy Varcianna, as well as Adam Guppy and Jon Lloyd at Routledge. Many thanks for their patience and great work and assistance during the various stages of the book's production.

The preparation and completion of this manuscript would not be possible without the fundamental support from several institutions, which generously financed the research project and the international symposium on which it is built. The Japan Foundation Grant Program for Intellectual Change (Ref. No.: 10126897), the Japan Foundation for Japanese Studies Fellowship, and various UNSW Sydney Faculty Research Grant Schemes provided funds for my research travels, the preparation of the international symposium at UNSW, and the publication of this book.

FOREWORD

The Logic of Metabolism

Toyo Ito

I studied architecture in the 1960s, when the "Metabolism" movement was at its peak, as an architecture student at the university from 1961 to 1965, and as a staff member in Kiyonori Kikutake's office from 1965 to 1969.

Kenzō Tange was one of the professors at the University of Tokyo while I was an undergraduate student. He supervised Arata Isozaki and Kisho Kurokawa at his laboratory, who were still students on the doctoral course. Tange was already known as an internationally renowned architect, and I seldom saw him on campus because he was fully committed to the Yoyogi Gymnasium project for the Tokyo Olympics in 1964. However, the presence of Tange accelerated the emergence of the next generation of architects in Japan in the 1960s. These included Fumihiko Maki, Masato Otaka, Kiyonori Kikutake, Arata Isozaki, Kisho Kurokawa, and Hiroshi Hara. The group called the "Metabolists" consisted of Maki, Otaka, Kikutake, and Kurokawa, along with industrial designer Kenji Ekuan and graphic designer Kiyoshi Awazu. In addition, the architecture critic Noboru Kawazoe participated as the theoretical leader of the young Metabolists.

As an architectural student in the 1960s, I was devoted to the logic of Metabolism and wrote an undergraduate thesis on a study of the conception of time in Metabolism. I was particularly attracted to the design practice of Kiyonori Kikutake, and upon graduation, I worked in his office for four years. Kikutake was around 30 years old when he proposed urban design projects such as Tower City (1958) and Marine City (1959), and realized his own residence, Sky House (1958).

One of the most well-known ideas of Metabolism is the idea of making a clear distinction between what changes and what does not. In other words, like the life cycle of the leaves and trunk of a tree, there is a distinction between replicable equipment with a short life span (leaves) and unchangeable structures (a trunk) in architecture. From his early days in the field, Kikutake incorporated the concept of Metabolism into his practice, and his projects in the 1950s clearly reflect that philosophy.

In particular, the Sky House is notable for its composition; a one-room square living space raised into the air by four wall pillars and surrounded by covered-outdoor terraces. The roof comprises four HP shells that form a square with a strong sense of pure completeness. On the outside of the terrace is a *Maira-do* (a sliding door for storm protection that allows ventilation and lighting through a horizontal louver) used in traditional Japanese houses, and steel sash glass doors and *shoji* screens border the interior and exterior. The living space floor is covered with a white carpet instead of *tatami* mats, and the ceiling is kept relatively low. While the overall space has a Japanese feel, the kitchen and bath units are installed on the terrace, and a temporal children's room is suspended in the center of the interior, visualizing a clear conceptual composition of Metabolism. This Sky House was probably Kikutake's first practical application of the Metabolism logic.

Japanese architects such as Kiyoshi Ikebe, Makoto Masuzawa, Kenji Hirose, and Kiyoshi Seike created a series of low-cost but delicately designed houses during this period. While these houses were suggestive of Japanese tradition, Kikutake's Sky House was supported by bold structures and expressed an entirely different traditional Japanese space from those houses. While the other architects' houses reminded me of the *sukiya* style (*the wooden structure for a traditional tea ceremony*), Kikutake's reminded me of a *minka* (*vernacular wooden houses for farmers, artisans, and merchants*). This may have been because Kikutake was from a wealthy household in a village where his father was the headman in Kurume, Kyushu. It should be noted that the Sky House is a clear expression of the logic of Metabolism and, at the same time, it is a house whose legacy will persist in the history of postwar Japanese housing.

The works of Kiyonori Kikutake in the 1960s are overwhelming. In particular, the Izumo Taisha Shrine Office Building (1963), the Kyoto International Conference Hall Competition Proposal (1963), Hotel Tokoen (1964), Miyakonojo Civic Hall (1966), and Pacific Hotel Chigasaki (1967) reveal his talent as a visionary architect. While working in his office, I witnessed the completion of the Tokoen, Miyakonojo, and Pacific Hotel projects.

Of these, Pacific Hotel Chigasaki is the one that stands out the most for its Metabolic expression. This work can be said to be a realistic representation of Tower City in the 1950s. The sudden appearance of the hotel as driving along the coastal road was striking. The view of the bath unit protruding out of the spiraling main structure symbolized Metabolism. During the pre-opening period of the hotel, staff members were allowed to stay for a test. When we entered the bath unit, we felt as if we were floating in the air, and I still remember the overwhelming sensation I felt from the power of the space created by the transcending logic. I also experienced this floating sense at the top-floor guest room in Hotel Tokoen. The room, which was suspended from a large beam rather than supported from below by pillars, gave me a different sense of space. During my tenure at Kikutake's office, he repeatedly amazed me with his creativity and ideas that he physically thought out. This kind of physical sensation in architectural design is the greatest lesson I learned from him.

In the late 1960s, I worked on developing a prefabricated bath unit for a corporate client. At that time, Japanese society was moving towards industrialization after the Tokyo Olympics in 1964. It was a time when architects' interests shifted from visionary future cities to the economic development of real cities. There was a gap between the client's intentions and Kikutake's image of the prefabricated bath unit. The corporate client wanted to create a prefabricated bath unit for quick mass production for the rapidly growing urban hotel and condominium market. Therefore, their main concern was the standardizing/economic aspect of the production, not the quality of the design. They did not show any interest in the cantilevered expressive bath units protruding from the exterior walls of the Pacific Hotel, and the project ultimately never materialized.

The late 1960s is the age when the logic of architects was in the process of crumbling in the face of economic reality. The study of bath units is one example of this process. Expo '70 in Osaka became the final stage for the blossoming of architects' visions of the future city.

A team led by Kenzō Tange, Arata Isozaki, and other Metabolists designed the master plan and infrastructure facilities for Expo '70. Each of the team members was in charge of designing the central elements of the Expo, equivalent to designing the main plaza and monumental architecture of the actual city. As a staff member in Kikutake's office, I witnessed the designing process of Expo first-hand.

Tange was commissioned to design the vast festival plaza, Isozaki was in charge of designing the two robots in the festival plaza, and Kikutake was in charge of designing the Expo Tower near the plaza. I participated in their weekly meetings as a staff member, and my responsibility was to represent all the decisions during the discussions on drawings by the following weekly meeting. I was also involved in the design of the tower as a member of Kikutake's office.

Due to the enormous amount of construction activities, including the Expo's pavilions, construction costs skyrocketed during this period. The repeated design changes cruelly shattered the architects' vision for a better future. In comparison to Buckminster Fuller's domes, Frei Otto's tents, or Habitat '67, which were built as a model for housing complexes at the Montreal Expo in 1967, there was no architectural achievement from the Osaka Expo that made me think of the future.

It seems that the broken dream at Osaka Expo was an accurate indication of the collapse of Metabolism's vision of a future city. Except for Kisho Kurokawa's Nakagin Capsule Tower Building, there has been little in the Metabolists' architecture since the 1970s that expresses the logic of Metabolism.

Metabolists use plants as a metaphor, employing the constant and ephemeral elements during a plant's growth to describe the logic of Metabolism. However, I have always questioned this concept of time within Metabolism, as it is a notion that is mechanically driven. Even if machine parts are replaced when they stop working, the machine itself never changes or grows. However, a plant is a living organism, constantly shedding its leaves, creating new buds, growing, and changing in order to survive.

Similarly, what is required of architecture is to change and grow over time, like a plant. To achieve the concept of growing architecture, it is necessary to create architecture in the dynamic evolving time rather than the static mechanical time—in other words, to give life to architecture. It is not about the logic of replaceable parts, but about allowing architecture to transcend through various experiences (activities), in order to allow architecture and people to become one holistic body.

Note on the text

Translator's notes in italic are not in the original Japanese version. Translation by Tetsuya Yaguchi, AIA, AICP.

INTRODUCTION

Raffaele Pernice

The year 2020 will be remembered as the year of the global coronavirus (COVID-19) pandemic, which has transformed the world and abruptly changed our cities. From China to Europe to the Americas and other corners of the Earth, COVID-19 has posed an existential threat to entire societies and the economies upon which these were recently built. It has disrupted ways of life, enduring practices, and established institutions. At every level and everywhere, cities are in a state of crisis to contain the spread of the virus. A state of emergency has forced people to reduce or altogether stop their movements, halting their working and commercial activities, need for education, and legitimate quests for leisure and different social and cultural experiences. The current challenges posed by the pandemic, coupled with recent digital revolutions in work and study, will unquestionably and inevitably force planners, architects, and designers to reconsider how the city of the future should be built. This simultaneously forces rethinking large parts of urban spaces and their physical and functional characteristics to adapt to their inhabitants' economic, social and physical well-being needs. We are witnessing an unprecedented crisis in modern times, with relevant consequences in the near future. Still, the challenging times ahead provide us with a great occasion to control this important process of creative destruction and drive inevitable change for both cities and societies to come.

Coincidently, 2020 marked the sixtieth anniversary of the Metabolist manifesto publication: *Metabolism 1960: The Proposals for New Urbanism*. The Metabolism movement was an avant-garde group of young Japanese architects and urban, graphic, and industrial designers who promoted their manifesto at the World Design Conference in Tokyo in May 1960. Critic Robin Boyd[1] labeled the movement a declaration of the independence of modern Japanese architecture. The visionary nature of the Metabolist group's urban and architectural projects—an "academy of the utopian,"[2] according to Italian critic Manfredi Tafuri—along with their original, innovative approach to themes such as urban growth structuring or flexible architectural design garnered an enormous influence and instant favor from Western critics and architectural elites. This drastic transformation phase in architectural language and urban forms helped

DOI: 10.4324/9781003186540-1

promote Japan's image, especially that of Tokyo, as a land of technological innovation and futuristic cities. This transformation was also portrayed in Andrei Tarkovsky's movie *Solaris* (1972), and was expressed as an expanding and amorphous city made of tentacular highways superimposing a hyperdense and chaotic built landscape.

The main members of the movement were architects Kiyonori Kikutake, Noriaki "Kisho" Kurokawa, Masato Otaka, Fumihiko Maki, critic Noboru Kawazoe, industrial designer Kenji Ekuan, and graphic designer Awazu Kiyoshi. The architects of the original group presented their manifesto at the World Design Conference in 1960 as a collection of independent papers, proposing ideas and concepts regarding their vision of the city of the future. As a critic and original group member, Noboru Kawazoe[3] highlighted the manifesto references to the spatial form of the city of the future:

> What will be the final form? There is no fixed form in the ever-developing world. We hope to create something which, even in destruction will cause subsequent new creation. This "something" must be found in the form of the cities we are going to make, cities constantly undergoing the process of metabolism.[4]

The influence of Metabolist projects was extraordinary during a time of fast economic growth and a strong evolution of the language of architecture and urbanism. This period embodied the hope and anxiety of the progressive fading of modernist influence and the lessons of the International Congresses of Modern Architecture (CIAM) simultaneously. A Metabolist member first coined the term "Megastructure,"[5] while architect Reem Koolhaas described Metabolism as "the first non-Western avant-garde movement in architecture and the last moment that architecture was a public rather than a private affair."[6]

Metabolism's period of genuine creative elaboration has spanned Japan's strong economic growth and industrial development since the late 1950s. The urban development accelerated and transformed Japan into a huge industrial archipelago and Tokyo into an incubator of innovative ideas and ambitious projects. This greatly reflected the economic policy's direction of the central government. This fostered Japan's massive industrialization by reverting all the national resources, contraction of new production plants, and main infrastructures in limited areas to create clusters of heavy, petrochemical, and manufacturing industries, and to capitalize on this concentration of different productive activities. During this period, Japan was propelled into the center of the world's attention through a series of international events: the World Design Conference (Tokyo, 1960), the Olympic Games (Tokyo, 1964), and the World Expo (Osaka, 1970). The Osaka World Expo marked the apex of success in the group's ideas and schemes for historians and critics. The event would become an extraordinary international and public showcase for Metabolism's futuristic architectural projects.

In Tokyo, the 1960 World Design Conference had the main theme of "visual communication," joining graphic design and environmental design experts.[7] It was an occasion for the public presentation of Metabolism's manifesto, which was published at its authors' expense. It was also the final stage of a series of two-year-long informal meetings held by the group members since 1958 under the mentorship of Kenzo Tange.

From the beginning, projects by Metabolist architects caught the attention of the Western audience. Further, the success of their futuristic and highly technological visions was so strong that some of these projects were invited to the international exhibition at the Museum of Modern Art (MoMA) in New York, the first Japanese works to be displayed there.

Developing key themes for designing new architectural ideas ran simultaneously with intensive public works preparing Tokyo for the 1964 Olympic Games. New highways and streets were built on the network of the ancient water canals, which crisscrossed the city. Kenzo Tange introduced a proposal for the urban reorganization of Tokyo at the World Design Conference under the title "A Plan for Tokyo, 1960: Towards a Structural Reorganization." This was a project where he translated the basic structure of the modern city into a system of extensive mobility and communication infrastructures integrated by massive megastructure units. Tange's scheme, which proposed converting the city's core from a traditional "civic center" into an innovative "civic axis," was fundamentally intended to indicate a comprehensive and multiscale solution to the problems caused by the capital's rapid and uncontrolled growth.

In parallel, the Metabolism manifesto published on this occasion featured various projects with radical schemes unveiling an intellectual attack on and controversial response of young architects to the government's inefficient urban policy, which was unprepared to control the urban sprawl of the big cities, especially because of the city's inadequate city planning methodologies and tools.

Metabolism's name stressed the basic idea of an endless change that occurs within an organism and in its nearby environment. The Japanese architects that joined under this name promoted flexible architecture and dynamic cities that could develop and grow through eliminating their exhausted parts and regenerating new components according to the needs of the socioeconomic environment. The city is conceived as a metaphor of the human body and is observed as a structure composed of elements (cells) that are born, grow, and then die, whereas the entire body continues living and developing.

Linking their theories with the Japanese cultural tradition of impermanence derived from Buddhism thought, Metabolist architects believed architecture should not be static, but should be capable of undergoing "metabolic" changes. Further, instead of thinking of fixed forms and functions, they developed structures and projects composed of mobile and flexible elements.

High-technological devices became a key feature common to most projects by Metabolists. Thanks to the innovative mix of futuristic technology and appealing forms that fulfilled their drawings, two projects presented at the World Design Conference of Tokyo were invited to participate in the exhibition of "Visionary Architecture" held at MoMA in New York in 1961. Those projects were "Marine City" by Kikutake and "Agricultural City" by Kurokawa. This artist did not hesitate to deny the Rationalist hierarchical order in favor of a completely free relation among the urban elements, creating a new type of urban space, drawing inspiration from Japanese concepts such as *en* space, which translates as "intermediate space." According to Kurokawa, intermediate space links directly to the quality of the spatial tradition of ancient Japanese architectures and cities.[8]

Many Metabolist projects presented high-rise megastructures supporting clusters of prefabricated apartment capsules. These were modified and replaced according to their life cycles, social demands, and fashion. During the 1950s, many experts in the prefabrication of industrial components for housing were invited to Japan by the Japanese government and independent professional associations to join seminars and conferences. Among others, architects Konrad Wachsmann, Louis Kahn, and

4 Raffaele Pernice

Buckminster Fuller were invited. Their activity was stimulating for the subsequent development of big housing companies in the industrial design and production of architectural components.

Since the meetings in preparation for the World Design Conference and in all the writings published subsequently, all Metabolist members recalled the influence and inspiration suggested from the Japanese architectural tradition, specifically from the analysis of the ancient shrine of Ise and the imperial villa of Katsura. The concepts of endless reconstruction, taken from the former, and cyclical change, suggested from the latter, poured into the theory and general Metabolist methodology. Other elements of modern architecture, such as the concept of standard, use of modules, and industrial prefabrication, suddenly appeared as "modern" tools that had belonged to Japan's national architecture for centuries.

In the years culminating in the 1970 Osaka World Expo, the Metabolists' unconventional aesthetic language combined more conviction architecture with urbanism. Capsules were interlocked with enormous joint core systems and blended into huge infrastructural supporting systems to form fascinating megastructures suspended above ground. Massive buildings and imposing structures rousing in the air or floating on the sea became the most recognizable physical expression of modern Japanese architecture. Metabolism's aesthetic vocabulary in these years, which was intended to herald completely new urbanism envisioning complex, changeable, and monumental megascale cities, was inspired by the mechanical world's brutal force, industry's technological language, and alluring images of factories and plants. It was expressed via their urban projects as biological forms that attracted the attention of international audiences, prompting interest in modern Japanese architecture like never before.

The book

Recent years have witnessed a revitalized and growing interest in the city models and architectural ideas proposed by the Metabolists some 60 years ago, especially in the Asia-Pacific region. Without question, the close of the twentieth century saw the Metabolist group earn a special place on the stage of new architectural and urban theories. Links of some of their urban projects with key phenomena in current discourses on urbanism have attracted much attention in the early decades of the new millennium. Such attention includes studies on compact cities and high-density architectures, responses to rapid urbanization, and the quest to design flexible urban spaces and replaceable architectural elements inspired by the key themes of cycles of uses, nomadism, modular design, and recycling. Moreover, Metabolist architecture is being rediscovered for its presumed affinity with the adaptability of proposed urban forms to radical and sudden transformations of the natural environment. Its revival extends to exploring new urbanization forms in alternative habitats, such as the sea (marine cities and floating urban platforms), through innovative eco-urban design approaches that rely on more sustainable and energy-efficient constructions and design models.

This book presents a collection of chapters that draw from the presentations of scholars and academics from Japan, Australia, Europe, South Korea, and the USA at the international symposium of the University of New South Wales (UNSW) in Sydney on February 22–23, 2021. The event celebrated the sixtieth anniversary of the Metabolist manifesto's first publication. Invited speakers included scholars, academics, and researchers from various disciplines, such as architecture, urban studies, visual media, urban planning, history and theory, and art design. Symposium participants have extensive knowledge of modern architectural and urban design theories, conducting relevant research on Metabolism and modern Japanese architecture and urbanism throughout the year. They discussed the historical lessons of Metabolist ideas and schemes, focusing on aspects of the movement's urban and architectural works. Notably, the discussions involved interpreting themes related to the city destruction/regeneration dichotomy and its impact on urban forms, innovative urban landscapes, and mass housing models. The symposium aimed to elicit healthy reflections on Metabolism's legacy on enduring research into new ecologically responsive urban design strategies. These strategies are crucial for tackling the current climate crisis and progressive yet seemingly unstoppable environmental disruption. They reflect the need for more efficient, effective, and sustainable forms of large-scale urbanization and habitat design in the twenty-first century. The chapters are based on discussions that extend existing scholarly contributions on Metabolist architects, planners, and debates on the city of the future designs. They broaden the knowledge of and investigations into new urbanization forms suited to our current age of rapid and radical change.

The collection of chapters in this volume thus explore and promote (within the specific arguments of each author) various reflections and thoughts on how the lessons of Metabolism's experience can inform the current debate on creating cities and future practice in architectural design and urban planning. They aim to uncover and highlight the persistent yet subtle links between the present and past to help reimagine new urban futures and the design of innovative intraurban relationships and spaces. While each author has produced what can be considered a personal account and interpretation of Metabolism, together these chapters can help understand lesser-known aspects while contributing a more comprehensive outline of the movement's significance, like tiny pieces of stones of different colors and sizes creating a larger and more meaningful mosaic.

The framework in this book combines the two central themes authors were tasked with adhering to in their symposium contributions. The first theme touched on *Metabolism Lessons in the Age of Climate Change, Eco-urban Design, and City Regeneration*. Here, the authors tackled the connections between the current challenges posed by recent threats to urban society (e.g., global warming, the climate crisis, sustainable urban development notions, and overurbanization and livability, emphasizing recycling and regeneration practices in post-industrial cities). The authors also addressed the key ideas of Metabolist design schemes and models. The second theme was *Metabolism and the Future of the City*. Here, the authors presented their reflections on Metabolists' urban proposals and investigations into various aspects of urban futures (i.e., city form, economic structure, tradition and society, and cultural meaning) in the broad context of historical studies of the city and current evolution of city planning and urban design theories.

Various chapters discuss and comment on the legacy of Metabolist visions, ideas, and city schemes, and their potential impact on current challenges in contemporary cities concerning built forms, technological innovation, aesthetic language, urban theory, and sustainability. Meanwhile, their multifaceted and critical analysis of Metabolist vocabulary and paradigms in architecture and urban planning evaluate whether and how Metabolist visions can continue to stimulate new ideas for a more sustainable design process. More specifically, the chapters evaluate and comment on Metabolist visions as drivers of a healthier ecological responsible urbanization process aimed at redeveloping contemporary cities while functioning as blueprints to plan the city of the future.

Therefore, this book is both a statement and celebration of Metabolism's importance as an innovative architectural movement. It should be interpreted as contributing to delivering fresh insights into the theories, visions, and reasons for the ideal Metabolist city of the future. It aims to provide a broad understanding of the conditions and ambitions behind its innovative projects while proposing lessons on planning and designing the next city of the future following the challenging times of the early twenty-first century.

Among the visionary projects and grand avant-garde design concepts embraced by the charismatic group of young Japanese designers and architects who funded Metabolism are capsule architectures, marine cities, vertical cities, and resilient buildings responsive to the reality in which they were conceived. With a narrative that focused on the phenomena of replication and mutation, as observed in living organisms, the Metabolists responded to new challenges of urbanization and economic growth of 1950s Japan with energy and optimism. They saw these challenges as opportunities to think equally big and innovate. They embraced then-emerging technologies, including capsule architecture and prefabrication, and eschewed traditional timber for new concrete. They relied heavily on mechanical rather than manual power to produce structures that were bold in vision and execution, embodying the determination to re-create a new and better world.

While the retro-future aesthetic of the Metabolists' work is symbolic of their time, its value today is more than simply nostalgic. The Metabolists experimented with ideas seeing renewed relevance worldwide due to population growth, global heating, and other enviro-social challenges. Further, their work prefigures current trends toward living and poetic architecture. With some obvious adjustments, their bold ideas reflected concerns that are important to us now in the twenty-first century.

Some aspects of the Metabolist movement have maintained relevance over the decades, such as believing design was a tool for managing human populations and relationships. For example, they focused on disaster preparedness and the application of cutting-edge technologies to improve urban environments beyond the limitations posed by traditional conventions and old practices. The creative exploration of alternative technologies and proposition of human-made habitats that were unprecedented in scale in the twentieth century—like marine cities and vertical communities built on a gigantic scale and suitable for modern living—truly captured the spirit of innovation that characterized Metabolist projects during the 1960s.

Several of the Metabolists' projects still appear radical by today's standards, which is one of the reasons they continue to captivate designers. This book's production offers an invitation to reflect on the lessons that can be learned from the movement. Can the visions of this dynamic yet fleeting movement be adapted to address the needs of contemporary cities in this new millennium haunted by unprecedented global challenges (e.g., climate change and global warming, sea levels rising, the irresponsible depletion of natural resources, and the unstoppable trend toward aging societies) and the continuous alteration of natural habitats with the destruction of entire ecosystems, and the forthcoming new technological revolution? If so, how? These are questions only the future—or, indeed, the past—can answer.

Notes

1 Robin Boyd, *New Direction in Japanese Architecture* (New York: George Braziller, 1968).
2 Manfredo Tafuri and Francesco Dal Co, *Modern Architecture*, vol. 2, 2nd ed. (Milan and New York: Electa/Rizzoli, 1986).

3 Noburo Kawazoe et al., *Metabolism 1960: The Proposals for New Urbanism* (Tokyo: Bijutsu Shuppansha, 1960).
4 Kawazoe et al., *Metabolism 1960*, 49.
5 Reyner Banham, *Megastructures: Urban Future of the Recent Past* (London: Thames & Hudson, 1976).
6 Rem Koolhaas and Hans Ulrich Obrist, *Project Japan: Metabolism Talks* (Cologne: Taschen, 2011).
7 Kathryn B. Heiesinger and Felice Fisher, *Japanese Design: A Survey since 1900* (New York: Philadelphia Museum of Art, Harry Abrams Inc., 1995), 18.
8 Intermediate space or "En" space is a type of space, half-private and half-public, which indicates the edge and connection space in and outside the house, and around the buildings in the urban block of the ancient Japanese cities. On this topic, see Kisho Kurokawa, *Metabolism in Architecture* (Boulder: Westview Press, 1977), 171–187.

1

BACK FROM BEHIND THE CURTAIN OF OBLIVION

Metabolism and the Postwar Actuality of Japan

Hajime Yatsuka

Metabolism has been one of the benchmarks of modern Japanese architecture since the 1960s. However, the passage of time has brought the movement to the edge of oblivion. Due to its futuristic outlook, the Metabolists' projects now seem to belong in the past, a past which was never realized—mere fragments of dreams on paper. This fundamentally negative reflection of the movement partly reflects the enormous difference between Japan now and then; most Japanese people today tend to regard the issues of the 1960s as somehow wrong. To our regret, both the design and theories of Metabolists are of no concern to the present anti-intellectualism. Only stereotypical images of Metabolism, such as the megastructures and capsules, remain in ruins, deprived of historical significance. These images, without historical context, look simply utopian. This chapter will set them right against the reality of Japan in their time.

1

This chapter shall start with two projects: Kiyonori Kikutake's Tower-Shaped Community and Kisho Kurokawa's Agricultural City. Both projects were exhibited in the 1960 Visionary Architecture exhibition at the Museum of Modern Art (MoMA), New York, curated by Arthur Drexler, and displayed official images of the Metabolists' work to the West. In the same year, the World Design Conference in Tokyo provided the occasion for the group to launch their works to the global design community. Drexler must have been impressed by the brochure of their works, distributed at the conference as the first manifesto of the group.

These two architects, more than any other members of the group, represented the utopian aspect of the movement—if we are still to characterize their work as such. However, it should be noted that these projects were designed not for tabulae rasae, but for sites with specific conditions—for example, agricultural hinterlands that were often damaged by floods caused by typhoons, which had been ignored overseas. Unlike many utopian projects in the West, the locations of the projects presented the core issue that those projects faced. Disasters such as floods are outcomes of natural and

DOI: 10.4324/9781003186540-2

geopolitical conditions, and the damage is still a serious problem worldwide, which has now been accelerated by global warming.

2

Traditional agricultural districts were controlled by feudal landlords. Kikutake was from such a wealthy family. However, immediately after the war, his family lost their vast territory through the Occupation Army's 1947 Agricultural Land Reform Law, which aimed to liberate farmers from the feudal, prewar system. The future architect was 18 years old at the time and remembered this disgrace well. He never admitted that such ancient social systems were feudalistic and irrational. Later, he insisted that the officers from the postwar national government knew nothing of the reality of the Japanese agricultural community. However, in the milieu of postwar Japanese democracy, the young and promising architect was obliged to keep silent on the issue. It was only toward the end of his life that he began to express his criticism of postwar democracy. He mentioned it to me privately and in an interview with Rem Koolhaas, which was published in *Project Japan*. Koolhaas was greatly surprised by Kikutake's remark that his indignation underlay his projects—quite an unexpected comment from the ultra-modernist.[1]

When the architect built his 1958 home, the well-known Sky House, it contained only one room, raised above the ground on bulky concrete piers. He called its central area a symbolic "space for a couple's love." The candid label indicated his intentions to establish an archetypal home for a young couple in the new society. Accordingly, his house was hailed as a crystallization of the postwar democratic ideal. However, for Kikutake, in the depth of his mind, this space was a successor to an interior space of the farmhouses (*Minka*) in the countryside of his hometown—a large, central space open to every neighbor, the center of the community dominated by their godmother, his grandmother. In Sky House, areas for future children were to be added later, suspended from the main floor slab—as secondary, temporary living equipment, true to the idea of Metabolism (Figure 1.1). Dialectics between the raised floor acted as a supporting structure for the children's equipment. The planning of Sky House was provocative and coincided with a period when planners were trying to modernize traditional life and homes. Kikutake leaped from the prewar extended family to a minimum social unit of only one couple, bypassing postwar ideology that emphasized the importance of the nuclear family.

His transmodern avant-gardism was also incorporated in the 1959 Tower-Shaped Community project and its deviation, the Koto ward project (Figure 1.2). It was planned for the downtown area of Tokyo, most of which was lower than sea level and frequently flooded. Kikutake, who recently came to the capital city to attend the Waseda University, confronted the same situation there with his hometown. Kikutake's project restructured the mixed-use area consisting of townhouses and small factories as vertical, artificial land with a huge tower to which individual small units of dwellings were attached.

At ground level, vast square platforms measuring 200 m by 200 m were used as plinths for the tower, following the existing grid of the downtown area. They were designed as sunken plazas, which were planned as reservoirs in the event of a flood. These plinths scarcely attract the concern of the people in the design community.

FIGURE 1.1 Sketch of Kiyonori Kikutake's Sky House, 1958. Image: collection of the architect's family.

Their concern was exclusively directed toward the tower-shaped megastructure and the capsule units he called "move-nets." Yet, for Kikutake, the plinths were of primary significance.

The structures that are ultimately safe against floods are floating structures. Since the Tower-Shaped Community project, Kikutake became obsessed with floating cities. The Marine City project, proposed in the same year as the Tower-Shaped Community project, was designed as a floating platform with huge cylindrical structures underneath, though the feasibility of the idea was yet to be proven. The crucial factor

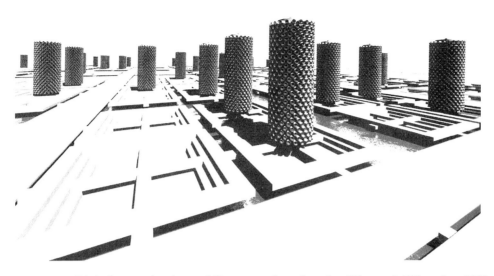

FIGURE 1.2 Digital reproduction of Koto ward project by Kiyonori Kikutake, 1959. Image: author's collection.

in overcoming this challenge was his contact with marine engineers from the United States (US) Navy. In 1964, Kikutake was invited to give a lecture at the American Institute of Architects in San Diego and observed first-hand the advances in US marine technology. This led him to reframe his approach. The revised 1968 version of Marine City sat on a platform connected by submerged cylindrical shafts (Figure 1.3). The project was further developed to commemorate the 200th anniversary of US independence. It was developed in collaboration with the University of Hawaii and the US Navy—which was ironic, considering his longtime private traumas generated by the Occupation Army. According to Kikutake, the project was agreed to by the US President Richard Nixon and the Prime Minister of Japan Kakuei Tanaka. However, despite initial optimism regarding the project, it was, to Kikutake's deep regret, eventually canceled in the economic crises that accompanied the 1973 oil embargoes.

In 1975, the Marine City was finally executed at the Marine Expo in Okinawa, called Aquapolis. The floating platform was 100 m by 100 m, a quarter of the size of the plinths of Tower-Shaped Community.

3

Kisho Kurokawa, the youngest of the Metabolism members, was the most brilliant, iconic maker of capsules. Through frequent and brilliant appearances in the mass media, Kurokawa looked like a typically *après-guerre* figure, totally free from the dark image of the agricultural district surrounding his hometown of Nagoya, which often suffered from typhoons. In 1959, for example, the Ise Bay typhoon killed more than 5,000 people. His Agricultural City project was a direct reaction to these recurring disasters. It was designed as a platform of artificial ground, a 100 m by 100 m grid that was superimposed on a rice field and raised four meters high to allow the settlement to be safe from floods (Figure 1.4). The grid system allowed the city to grow in

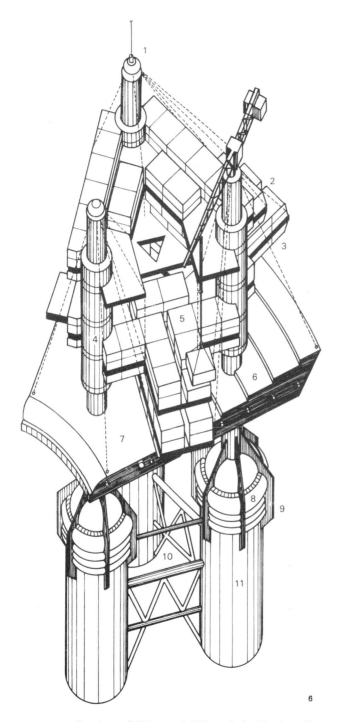

FIGURE 1.3 Section of Kiyonori Kikutake's Marine City, revised version 1968. Image: public domain.

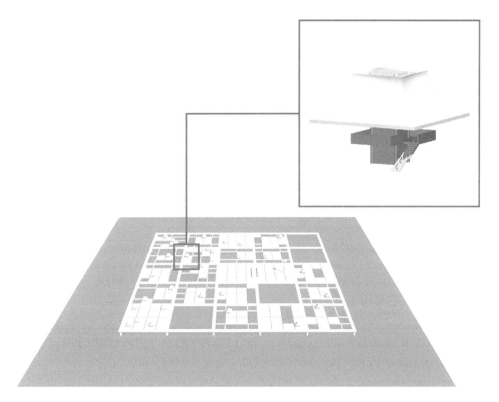

FIGURE 1.4 Digital reproduction of Kisho Kurokawa's Agricultural City, 1960. Image: author's collection.

every direction. Like the 1963 Freie Universität Berlin project of Candillis, Josic, and Woods, it was a growing project with no final form. However, whereas the Berlin project was introverted, the Agricultural City was extroverted.

The Agricultural City was based on Kurokawa's interest in the street culture that was unique to the old settlements in Japan. The raised platform served as a frame, carrying community infrastructure in a grid of roads, water service, electricity, and a commuter monorail. The concern for the street life was shared with other Metabolists, as well as his European colleagues, Team X, whose meetings he was invited to. The interesting thing to note is that his Agricultural City was planned around a shrine-like traditional community. Having learned in a Buddhist high school, Kurokawa was never insensitive toward the habitational tradition. The model house for the farmer in the Agricultural City was crowned by a unique form of the curved roof in concrete, called a Mushroom-Shaped House. The mushroom shape had often been claimed by the ethnological and agricultural researchers in Japan as a metaphor for the self-growing nature of the traditional farmers' houses, as well as their villages. The archetypal house was realized as the central lodge in the 1964 National Children's Kingdom project, which was a collective work by Metabolism members.

That these projects by Kikutake and Kurokawa were a reaction to the reality of Japanese regions provided the social background for establishing the national land development plans. The Metabolism group, as well as their mentor, Kenzo Tange, were very interested in the national land development plan, which was an attempt to rehabilitate the nations that had been damaged by the war. This distinguished them from most projects of contemporary European radical architects, such as Superstudio's The Continuous Monument of 1969, which was inspired by the scene of the flooded city of Florence three years before. However, Superstudio was concerned exclusively with the apocalyptic aspect of the disaster, not with the reality of life.

Among the Metabolism members, Kurokawa was the most inclined to design megastructures, the majority of which were biomorphic—the Agricultural City was an exception. An example of the biomorphic design is the Helix of 1961, whose shape was derived from DNA (deoxyribonucleic acid) structure, reflecting Kurokawa's strong concern for biology. It was a series of artificial land platforms on which residences were to be put, based on the choice of individual inhabitants. Like the residential megastructures on the sea by Kenzo Tange's Tokyo Bay Plan of 1960, the architects did not specify any design of the residences. Both are designs of artificial land megastructures, not architectural pieces. The Helix was one of Kurokawa's most futuristic designs. However, we can still find his concern for the provincial landscape of Japan. The projects had two variants, each based on the same principle. Each was designated a specific site—one in the Nihonbashi area in front of Tokyo Station in the center of the capital, and the other facing Kasumigaura Lake, located in the countryside 60 km north of Tokyo. One was in the very center of the capital, but the other was in the countryside surrounded by rice fields. In the perspective drawing, we can see the country boys chasing dragonflies—quite a nostalgic scene, which is almost impossible to find today, and far from being futuristic (Figure 1.5).

In the later period of his career, Kurokawa became obsessed with traditional ideas like Rikyu gray, the idea of ambiguous aesthetics by the great tea master of the sixteenth century. He also referred to the idea of conviviality, the mixture of Eastern and Western culture. He wrote an enormous number of texts on this idea. However, he failed to recall the integration of tradition and modernity convincingly. Rather, he achieved a superficial variation of postmodern eclecticism. The mixture of what he

FIGURE 1.5 Sketch of Kisho Kurokawa's Kasumigaura Lake Project. Image: public domain.

absorbed in the sensibility of youth, almost unconsciously illustrated in his earlier works, presented a much more convincing representation of Metabolism to me.

Metabolist megastructures were no more than proposals on paper and models, inviting criticism as simply utopian images. It is true that they worked on the rhetorical level of architectural discourses rather than in practice, and Kurokawa was the most eloquent rhetorician both in form and words. However, the narrow-minded criticism toward them makes the horizon of architectural language too limited. Even on a rhetorical level, these practices broaden the scope of our architectural projects, showing how we can confront the problem of urban density, for example. After the expansionist invasion of the Japanese Empire in neighboring countries proved to be a desperate failure, the ocean and air were the only remaining frontiers for the Japanese. They were forced to create megamachines for living instead of megamachines for killing. This seems to be the only positive way to interpret the adjective "visionary," as it was put by Arthur Drexler in the title of the MoMA show.

4

Masato Ōtaka, the eldest (and the least-known, especially abroad) member of the group, was from Fukushima, one of Japan's most underdeveloped provinces in prewar times and even today. He was 22 when the war ended and was far from being a "mechanomaniac," as is normally associated with the Metabolism group. When he was a small boy, he was deeply impressed by the drastic transformation of the agricultural area of his hometown through a series of infrastructure constructions, which appeared to him to be a breakdown in the new era of the Japanese countryside.[2] Subsequently, he became obsessed with the possibility of introducing new technology into a nation devastated by the war. However, his ideas on how to use technology were very down to earth and far from being utopian. Concrete structures became a sort of *idée fixe* for him. It was influenced by the late Brutalist works by Le Corbusier, derived via Kunio Maekawa, the ex-disciple of the French master and for whom Ōtaka worked as a chief associate before he became independent. In Maekawa's office, the team led by Ōtaka developed a series of experiments called the "technological approach" through multidisciplinary collaboration.

In 1958, Ōtaka oversaw the design of Harumi—an apartment building only ten floors high, yet still the tallest housing in Japan at the time. The team developed the concept of superimposing "major construction" and "substructures," conceiving a building as a series of layered artificial ground planes. The major construction component outlined areas that were three stories high and two units wide, within which floors and walls could be removed to accommodate future modifications. The designers predicted that the then-standard individual living unit would eventually be too small, and so, in the future, it would be combined into a larger unit. The project was apparently influenced by Unité d'Habitation by Le Corbusier. However, this idea of changeability was their original idea and is closer to the dialectic system of the megastructure and the minor structure that was the capsules. Anyone who believes that Harumi was not a Metabolist work, not utopian, and dissimilar to megastructures only needs to look at Kenzo Tange's 1959 megastructure project on Boston Bay. Tange's project was also designed as four to seven vertical layers of artificial grounds, each incorporating a street for car traffic in the air, with an additional three stories below for public transport and facilities. The dimensions were more exaggerated than those used in Harumi, yet Le

16 Hajime Yatsuka

Corbusier's Unité or Maekawa and Ōtaka's Harumi were still pieces of architecture that Tange conceptually extrapolated in the scale of a city by replacing their private corridors with public streets for automotive traffic. The megastructure on Boston Bay was then developed into an even huger residential megastructure in Tokyo Bay in 1960.

It was the critic Noboru Kawazoe who emphasized Ōtaka's early interest inspired by the transformation of his hometown. Being an ardent Marxist at that time, Kawazoe was determined to rehabilitate the devastated country. He was the theoretical leader of the Metabolist group. Earlier, in 1955, Kawazoe, then acting as the chief editor of *Shinkenchiku* (*Japan Architect*) magazine, organized a special issue of the magazine on the subject of "Architecture in the age of the Atomic Bomb." It was advocated initially by Takashi Asada, the former chief associate of Tange for the Peace Memorial Park Project and later a godfather of the Metabolists. They argued about how architects and scientists should confront society under the threat of nuclear war. When the Metabolism group was established in 1960 at the World Design Conference under the strong influence of Asada, Kawazoe wrote a short essay entitled "Material and Man," which began as follows: "Everything will come to an end if a nuclear war covers all the Earth with a shower of radioactivity."[3] The shadow of the atomic bomb, which culminated in the Cuban Missile Crisis two years later, was present at the inauguration of the Metabolism group.

After being independent of Maekawa's office, Ōtaka designed Motomachi housing in Hiroshima, beginning in 1968 and completed nearly ten years later. The historical context of the project is quite significant. It was located to the north, adjacent to Tange's Peace Memorial Park and the epicenter of the atomic bomb site. After the war, the devastated area had grown into a so-called "atomic bomb slum," which was home to more than 8,000 people. Hiroshima's city government felt obliged to provide them with housing. Asada was engaged for the preliminary study of the site and hired Ōtaka to help. When the bomb was dropped, Asada was working for the navy in Kure, the neighboring town of Hiroshima, and witnessed the effects of the bombing in person.

The Motomachi project, the largest public housing complex in Japan at the time, included more than 3,000 residential units in structures 20 stories high. Corridors, a variation of the street-in-the-air idea of the Golden Lane project by Alison and Peter Smithson (1952), the main structure was designed in two-story-high, two-unit-wide bays—the same idea observed in the Harumi apartment building (Figure 1.6).

During the lengthy construction, the goal was to attract other people who had suffered as a result of the war. According to the 1972 normalization of Japanese–Chinese diplomatic relations, many Japanese people who were born in Manchuria during the war, but were not allowed to return to Japan because of the difficult situation in the postwar years, were finally allowed to return, and Motomachi housing received many of them. However, most of them were unable to speak Japanese, despite being born of Japanese parents who had returned to the country much earlier. A recent film produced by a local TV station, made to commemorate the end of the war, featured a small boy from Osaka visiting his grandfather, who was living in Motomachi. The boy had difficulty communicating with the old man, who understood only Chinese. In the end, the community of the inhabitants, who had taken care of the ex-war victim for a long time and welcomed the boy from outside, was vividly depicted in the film, for which the street-in-the-air provides an impressive background. The scene must have been extremely rewarding for architects who decided to contribute to the rehabilitation of the wounded country.

FIGURE 1.6 Masato Otaka's Motomachi Apartments Project in Hiroshima, initiated in 1968. Image: courtesy Botond Bognar.

Ōtaka's obsession with the idea of the artificial ground was most clearly presented in his 1968 Saka'ide project in Shikoku Island. Saka'ide housing replaced the wooden slums that housed salt workers—one of the main local industries. Drastic changes lay ahead for the area, as it was rapidly industrializing. Ōtaka and Asada, who again provided architectural assistance, concluded that simply reconstructing the houses in concrete would not be enough. Instead of bringing the community together on a raised concrete platform four to seven meters above grade, like Kurokawa's Agricultural City, the plan introduced residences grouped around a shared open space in low-density conditions appropriate to the relatively rural community.

The original budget was exceptionally low—far from being enough for such a bold experiment. However, Ōtaka and Asada persuaded the prefectural government to contribute additional funds for the project and convinced the national government to pay for the costs of a raised platform. The platform's structural system was designed to allow relative freedom in terms of putting the smaller superstructures on the platform, modules of larger and smaller beams defining the height and width of housing built. The clusters of spare concrete boxes created a rich visual diversity on the platform, unified by their modular order (Figure 1.7). Openings in the platform varied in size and organization, and introduced light to the ground level, allowing plants to grow up through them. The spaces below were reserved for future shops, storage, and parking for visitors to the city center; at the time, private cars were only owned by wealthy people. However, the situation has changed since then. Today, small towns cannot function without automobiles. The parking area is now full of cars and other facilities, illustrating the validity of Ōtaka's typically Metabolist vision.

FIGURE 1.7 The residential complex of Sakaide in Shikoku Island, designed by Masato Otaka in 1968. Image: author's collection.

The initial phase of the project took four years to complete. In the successive phases, an auditorium, shops, and offices were added, which, together with additional housing, formed a new town center. Ōtaka's previous structural experiments gave him the courage to situate a grouping of tiered apartments on top of the 1,000-seat auditorium. However, the final phase allowed less design freedom, as it involved redevelopment along a street of private shops. The government did not purchase the site, nor did it use eminent domain (i.e., the power of the government to take private property and convert it for public use) to exert control. Therefore, Ōtaka proposed land re-adjustment; lines of shops were to be rebuilt following a setback caused by the platforms above, with the concrete frame accommodating both the housing above and shops below. Shops were not reduced in size, but his plan secured a broad walkway along their frontage. Regrettably, local architects, who were inferior and unsympathetic, were responsible for the design of the privately built shops infilling Ōtaka's framework. After this disappointing experiment, Ōtaka and his associate architect Masaya Fujimoto devoted much time to establishing the basic juristic conditions for the artificial ground plane, which were quite realistic and far from a futuristic dream, as if to prove the stereotype image of the group's works to be superficial.

5

Fumihiko Maki, the only living Metabolist, is also the only member from Tokyo. Maki is from a very wealthy family. Unlike Ōtaka, whose works—especially his written texts—were scarcely presented abroad, Maki had been studying and teaching in the US before he finally settled in his home country and established his own firm. He presented the project for Shinjuku at the World Design Conference in 1960, collaborating with his elder, Ōtaka. At that time, they seemed to be interested in establishing an urban design firm together, a goal that was never realized. The project was based on two hypothetical elements for urban design: artificial ground and group-form theory. These were investigated under the initiative of Ōtaka in the early years, and some say that he initially hypothesized group-form theory in his graduation thesis, which was written while he was studying at Tokyo University.

Maki appeared to be free from any private background. After moving to the US, he developed the theory while at Washington University in St. Louis, the outcome of which, *Investigations in Collective Form*, was published by the school's publishing office, crediting Ōtaka as a collaborator. However, from this point on, they went their separate ways—Maki on the international scene, renewing correspondence with the Team X members with whom he had become acquainted while in the US, and Ōtaka more inclined to the indigenous realities, refusing exposure to the outer world.

Investigations in Collective Form included many photos of the anonymous settlements, some of which were from the Near East journey Maki took before he finally returned to Japan, while others were from Japanese provincial agricultural villages. These showed the various morphologies of undesigned vernacular settlements. Maki's book was published in the same year as Bernard Rudovsky's exhibition "Architecture without Architects" at MoMA in New York.[4] The photos of Japanese villages in *Investigations in Collective Form* were not contemporary; they were taken to illustrate research by Japanese agrarian scholars on the agricultural villages in prewar years. Most of them were Marxist and were forced to avoid the investigation on the stern reality of Japanese laborers because of the difficult political situation at that time. There must have been complex unwritten feelings behind their geographical description of the seemingly unchanging lives of the farmers. Ōtaka, having grown up in the countryside, might have realized it, but Maki treated the photos only as illustrations of the morphological elements in the built environment.

Maki's actual designs based on the group-form theory were sophisticated, but the language was scarcely indigenous and typically modern. Unlike his mentor, Tange, and his Metabolist colleagues, he seems not to have been affected by the controversy on tradition in the Japanese architectural community in the 1950s. He did not design megastructural projects or capsules—the trademarks of Metabolism—either. For this, Maki was considered the least Metabolist of all the group's members. However, the problem is much more complicated than that because the issue relates not to the visible aspects of the city, but the hidden dimension within it.

The issue of Collective Form was a development of Maki's previous study on the medium spaces—spaces of linkage—completed in the early 1960s at Harvard. Maki's study discussed more complex modes of association with the elements of high-density use. The denser the mode of use becomes, the closer interrelations between inner spaces and external spaces. The duality of usable space and medium space can be taken as an application of Louis Kahn's dualism of served space and servant space. Through the extension of concept and scale in this application, the medium space of Maki assumed much more significance than Kahn's servant space. For Maki, in urban settings, medium space is even more important than usable space (floors in the buildings) because usable space is only for the users of the individual buildings, while the urban space involves the broader community.

These medium spaces included not only plazas and other kinds of exterior spaces but also what he called "interiorized spaces," such as atriums. The typical cases were the city room and city corridor that were planned as nodal spaces in Boston (1965). They were published as an outcome of the studio works at the graduate school of design at Harvard, "Movement System in the City," a short report of 40 pages. The plan for Boston was a study of the extension of the highway and subway, the design of the parking structures on the transfer spot, a proposal for the communal spaces of a higher order in the city center, and a plan for a network and its nodes. He depended upon the idioms of Kevin Lynch-like node, path, and linkage in his *The Image of the City*, which was also an analysis of the city of Boston. The transfer spot was a gate to the inner city, which was also influenced by Kahn's project for Philadelphia. The *Golgi* structures of 1968, the most esoteric of Maki's projects, present only the residual medium space in the densely built-up urban area without showing the surrounding buildings. Although seemingly a megastructure because of its scale, it was quite the opposite.

Relatively recently, Maki had been working on the spatial order of traditional Japanese quarters. Again, this was more like a morphological study of Japanese towns, preserved from premodern Edo to the present day. The object of his concern was the complex layering system of urban tissues, which he tried to incorporate in his urban design with extremely sophisticated modern architectural language. In this regard, the development from Maki's group-form theory in the 1960s to such later investigations appears almost seamless. Unlike other Metabolists' hypothetical theories, Maki's works were far from provocative. However, it would not be a distortion to mention that such coherence demonstrates that he was true to the cultural and historical environment of his country throughout his long career. His Metabolism lies not in the outlook, but in the hidden dimension of the works.

6

When asked on the lessons from Metabolism for this century, what can we make of the endurance visions of the group and what is their possible legacy? This is an extremely difficult task because of the drastic difference between the 1960s and the present. However, I would say that it should be a personal issue, reflecting the basic attitude toward the current situation. The reader should draw their own conclusions. For my part, I had been resisting the current Japanese tendency to ignore history. This makes everything superficial and devoid of a philosophical foundation. Even if the present works of Japanese architecture were fashionable throughout the world, I am convinced that they would fall into the bottomless darkness of amnesia soon. Architecture records the vision and feeling of the people of the day, generating the image of a city in perpetual mutation. You can understand it only through history. The lesson of Metabolism, if any, should be none other than the recall to such a foundation of architecture and city, the seriousness of our thinking.

Notes

1 I heard this from Kikutake in the preparatory research work for the 2011 Metabolism exhibition in the Mori Art Museum in Tokyo. For further information on Koolhaas' comment, see Rem Koolhaas and Hans Ulrich Obrist, *Project Japan: Metabolism Talks* (Cologne: Taschen, 2009), 133.

2 This was mentioned in Kawazoe's essay on Otaka. For details, see Noboru Kawazoe, *Architects: Person and Works* (Tokyo: Inoue-shoin, 1968), 12.

3 Noboru Kawazoe, "Material and Man," *Metabolism*, 1960. This brochure was distributed at the World Design Conference in 1960. The text was published both in Japanese and English (with the translation likely being performed by Maki). The brochure was also reproduced at the 2011 Metabolism Exhibition.

4 The analysis of Japanese traditional space was also achieved by a group of young scholars and designers around the laboratory of Kenzo Tange, guided by the historian Teiji Ito and rival architect of Metabolists of the same generation, Arata Isozaki, in an even more abstract manner. It is not by chance that the work and language of Maki and Isozaki were not absorbed into the indigenous social reality of postwar Japan, to which other Metabolists were heavily anchored, showing the scope of the movement that had been ignored so far.

2

THE AESTHETICS AND/OR FORMALISM OF CHANGE

Paradoxes and Contradictions in the Metabolist Movement

Botond Bognar

Japan in the 1960s was strongly defined by its rapid progress, often referred to as the "Japanese economic miracle." The government's top priorities were massive industrialization, robust gain in technology, and accelerated economic growth, all of which the country achieved beyond any expectations; indeed, it was unprecedented. Leaving behind the devastation of a lost war, Japan, with tremendous enthusiasm and growing self-confidence, was ready to define a new identity and shape its future.

However, these high-speed developments were not completely without major drawbacks. Despite the economic progress, uncontrolled industrialization and reckless urbanization were detrimental to Japan and Japanese society. Environmental pollution increased dramatically. Moreover, as many people flocked to the cities, congestion became a growing problem, exacerbated by the acute lack of public services, social infrastructure, and urban amenities. Thus, paradoxically, the more the economy advanced, the more the environmental and urban conditions worsened. Japan had to face the dark side of its progress. In the spirit of such recognition, the Metabolist movement was initiated in the late 1950s and, with a manifesto, it was launched officially at the 1960 Tokyo World Design Conference.[1]

In the complex circumstances of 1960s Japan, a multiplicity of contradictory forces played important roles in the new architectural development. Against this background, the Metabolist movement evolved following both idealistic and pragmatic impulses.[2] The idealistic impulses were underscored by Japanese architects' traditional love-and-hate relationship with the proverbial *Japanese City*, which began with Japan's modernization in the mid-nineteenth century. For these architects, the Japanese City (typically represented by Tokyo) was not merely the physical, built environment, but also a phenomenon that was often a proxy for the nation, acquiring almost mythical status. In line with their ideology and similar interpretation of the city, Metabolist architects, although diverse in their approach, proposed new types of urban formations and envisioned a new, open Japanese society—an undertaking Rem Koolhaas called *Project Japan*.[3]

DOI: 10.4324/9781003186540-3

The structure and form of Metabolist urban visions and architecture

Metabolist architects recognized the challenges of severe land shortages, growing land prices, and increasing congestion in Japanese cities, particularly in Tokyo. In support of urban expansion, Metabolist architects needed to find new ground for the future city. Kiyonori Kikutake, Kenzo Tange, and others initially found the place for the new city over the sea. The first visionary project was Kikutake's 1958 Marine City[4] (Figure 2.1). A couple of years later, Tange devised his famous Plan for Tokyo 1960, which was conceived as a linear system of bridge-like megastructures that stretched across Tokyo Bay[5] (Figure 2.2).

Other proposals envisioned new urban clusters "floating" above the existing urban fabric. Among these, Arata Isozaki's proposal was the most remarkable. In his 1961

FIGURE 2.1 Kiyonori Kikutake: Marine City project, 1958. Drawing courtesy of K. Kikutake.

FIGURE 2.2 Kenzo Tange: Plan for Tokyo 1960. Photo courtesy of K. Tange.

"City in the Air," also called the "Joint Core System," and his 1962 "Clusters in the Air," he promoted huge cylindrical service shafts as the only means of vertical support for the new "city," with enormous bridge structures spanning the shafts.[6] Here, as in all urban schemes by the Metabolists, the intent was to devise open models with the potential for orderly growth and renewal or change (Figure 2.3).

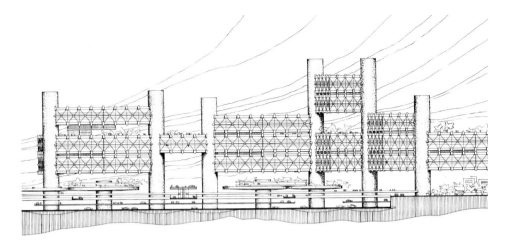

FIGURE 2.3 Arata Isozaki: Joint Core System. Drawing courtesy of A. Isozaki.

The Metabolists' conception of the urban environment of the future was also based on recognizing that some elements of the urban fabric, like cells in a living organism, deteriorate or become obsolete faster than others and need to be replaced more often. Therefore, the goal was to devise systems in which the constituent parts, particularly residential units and their sub-components, could be changed easily. Conversely, the supporting infrastructure had to be devised as a longer-lasting, independent, *generative* or *open system*, such as a massive frame or other structure capable of accommodating the architectural units. In most of the built and unbuilt schemes, this meant a megastructural solution.[7] With that, the age of *megastructures* in Japan was ushered in.

These visionary urban proposals manifested a curious ambiguous quality; they could be interpreted as either small cities or gigantic buildings. None of them had the chance to be realized, but many of their inherent qualities, including a hint of such ambiguity, were implanted in several subsequent Metabolist buildings—even in relatively small ones. In 1958, Kikutake completed his residence, the "Sky House," in Tokyo. This remarkable small house raised on four sturdy concrete wall-panels—a kind of "mini-megastructure"—displayed several new features with impressive clarity. Its unified central space was extended, like in traditional residences, by the surrounding verandah. Within this "add-on" zone, Kikutake designed the kitchen and bathroom as prefabricated *mobile* units. The house provided for largely unrestricted spatial rearrangement, great flexibility of use, and the easy replacement of the most important functional and technological components of the house[8] (Figure 2.4).

Subsequently, Kikutake began to apply quasi-megastructural systems, even in such projects as the one-story Shrine Office Building (1963) in Izumo and the Hotel Tokoen (1964) in Yonago, which, although eight stories high, was still small.[9] The application of dominant structural systems has, in both cases, resulted in paradoxical yet rather attractive solutions. The building in Izumo features as its main structure a pair of 50-metre, prestressed concrete girders, whereas the Hotel Tokoen applies a pair of story-high beams to *suspend* the fifth and sixth floors from it rather than supporting them

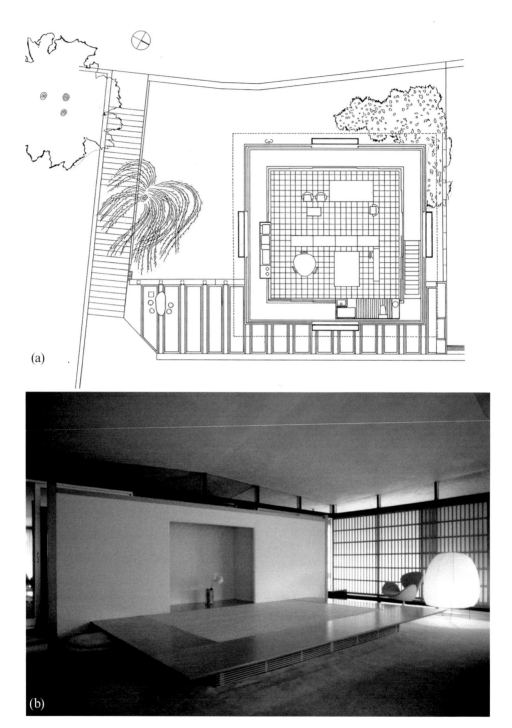

FIGURE 2.4 Kiyonori Kikutake: Sky House, Tokyo, 1958. a) Drawings. Courtesy of K. Kikutake; b) Interior. Photo by B. Bognar; c) Interior, on the left is Kikutake and on the right is Toyo Ito in August 1980. Photo by B. Bognar.

FIGURE 2.4 (Continued)

from below, which is achieved by the uniquely configured clusters of concrete posts.[10] The open space in the body of the building was meant to visually demonstrate that the two upper floors were suspended or "floating" in the air (Figures 2.5 and 2.6). Kikutake, like other Metabolists, produced architecture with expressive constructional technology and great structural virtuosity.

Metabolist buildings, intending to foster growth and change using highly industrialized methods, were prone to displaying an *unfinished* quality. They seemed to show a temporary state or impermanence in their planned process of change. As such, they were conducive to the emergence of a new, dynamic aesthetics of architecture. Such a genre of design characterized several examples of Metabolist architecture. Kisho Kurokawa referred to the unfinished quality of his Nakagin Capsule Tower (1972) as the "aesthetic of time."[11] Rem Koolhaas went further in saying that the Metabolists were able "to define the contours of a post-Western aesthetic …"[12]

With such structural and formal articulation, Metabolist buildings were bound to represent, by default, strong visual qualities. In Kikutake's Izumo and Yonago projects, followed by Masato Otaka's Tochigi Prefectural Conference Center (1969) in Utsunomiya, the articulation of the three-dimensional structural fabric with vibrant details and tactility evoked strength and unique spatial qualities, and produced fresh and convincing architectures (Figure 2.7). However, in numerous other examples, the *formal* expression of the inherent structural solution as a suggestion of growth or change was often exaggerated, even forced, where the solution was not logical, and nor its display was the logical result of the applied system.

FIGURE 2.5 Kiyonori Kikutake: Office Building of Izumo Shrine, Izumo, 1963. Photo by B. Bognar.

FIGURE 2.6 Kiyonori Kikutake: Hotel Tokoen, Yonago, 1964. Photo by B. Bognar.

FIGURE 2.7 Masato Otaka: Tochigi Prefectural Conference Center, Utsunomiya, 1969. Photo by B. Bognar.

The demonstration of the Metabolist theory of change was important for these architects. It could be argued that this need was rooted in their intention to display the novelty of the system visually, as an *image*, and in so doing perhaps to make a persuasive statement to "sell" the idea to the profession—domestic and foreign—and society at large. This was most obvious in the facilities the Metabolists contributed to the Osaka Expo in 1970. However, the argument here is not against the "aesthetics of the unfinished" or the "quality of the incomplete," and neither is it an objection to the structural systems contributing to such aesthetics; it is simply to point out the unnecessary, even trivial *simulation* of change where there was not any possibility for change.

One of the impressive features of Tange's Yamanashi Press and Broadcasting Headquarters (1966) in Kofu is the porous matrix of its architecture. It features 16 cylindrical service towers in a meticulous geometric arrangement as the only means of vertical support. The monumental, multi-story complex is not unlike Isozaki's visionary project, the Joint Core System. The cavernous open spaces that penetrate the building's body—a "three-dimensional space network"[13]—manifest an incomplete quality that exposes the complex's large-span, bridge-like structural matrix. Tange explained that the empty spaces were meant for the system's flexibility; that is, the further expansion of the building[14] (Figure 2.8).

The building was indeed one of the very few Metabolist structures that was extended or altered. However, Tange designed its 1974 extension only vertically, by adding several new floors over the existing ones. The much larger structure that resulted still retained many of its previous open cavities, although diminished in volume and modified in arrangement. Tange must have realized that without these interstitial spaces, his ideas regarding the *image* of incompleteness would not work well, and the quality of architecture would suffer. In this regard, the initial building—with its extensive gaps and more open spaces—better revealed the structure's seemingly unfinished, almost ruinous quality; it was vastly more dramatic and convincing than its more monolithic successor (Figure 2.9). The absence of interstitial spaces in the "three-dimensional space network"[15] is indeed bound to result in rather monotonous and less compelling architecture, as confirmed by Tange's 1982 Fiera District Redevelopment project in Bologna, Italy (Figure 2.10).

In his Hotel Tokoen, Kikutake exemplified the same issue. He too designed a building with an open space—the absence of an entire floor—to visually demonstrate the building's structural solution and unfinished quality, not because of any *real* functional role given to the space.[16] Unquestionably, here again, the permeability of the building makes its architecture work better. It is only unfortunate that neither Kikutake nor Tange turned these open spaces into inviting green terraces.

Although Tange's Yamanashi Press and Broadcasting Headquarters is, paradoxically, a monolithic, conventional, in situ-reinforced concrete building, it is still one of the quintessential examples of Metabolist architecture. It is the literal embodiment of a Metabolist/Structuralist architectural *diagram*. Conceived as an open system, the building was meant to have the capability of not only vertical but also horizontal growth, thus also extending into and over the city, which, though envisioned, could not and did not happen.

FIGURE 2.8   Kenzo Tange: Yamanashi Radio and TV Headquarters, Kofu, 1966 and 1974. a) Photo of the complex after its extension in 1974. Photo by B. Bognar; b) Section and 1F plan of the building. Courtesy of K. Tange.

The Aesthetics and/or Formalism of Change 31

(b)

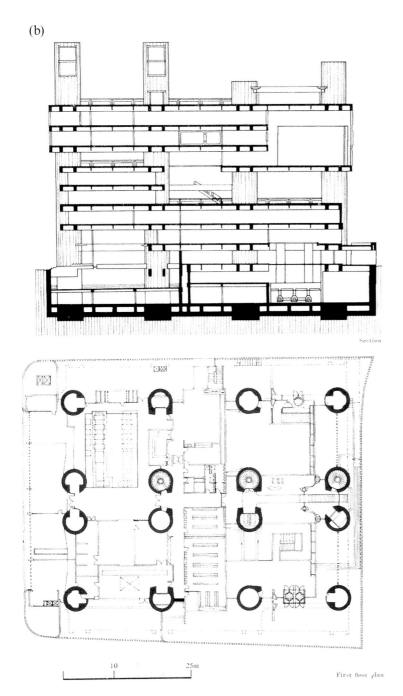

FIGURE 2.8 (Continued)

FIGURE 2.9 Kenzo Tange: Yamanashi Radio and TV Headquarters, Kofu, 1966, showing the original building before extension. Photo courtesy of K. Tange.

FIGURE 2.10 Kenzo Tange: Fiera District Redevelopment project, Bologna, Italy, 1982. Photo by B. Bognar.

Regarding the idea of the building's unlikely horizontal growth, another of the building's features deserves attention since such features appear in several works by Tange and many other Metabolist architects. The building has some quasi-structural details, especially in the joints, which demonstrate Tange's formalist or mannerist impulse. At strategic places on the monolithic reinforced concrete building, Tange added corbel blocks either as apparent extensions of existing beams or for the seeming support of additional structures for a future horizontal extension of the building. However, most of these add-on stubs were nothing more than mere visual suggestions: the image of flexibility or the continuation of the structural matrix (Figure 2.11). Tange's building in Kofu stands out for another reason: it became the built prototype of a vertical service shaft-based architecture, a type that Tange and many Metabolists, as well as other architects, began to produce in large numbers and for quite some time thereafter.

Many Metabolist buildings were indeed produced with only the appearance of replaceability or changeability of their constituent elements rather than with the real capability or need for it. Even when, in a very few cases, they had such capability, they remained frozen in time. Harsh criticism came as early as 1966, when Günter Nitschke, a scholar of Japanese architecture, wrote "as long as the actual buildings get heavier, harder, more monstrous in scale, as long as architecture is taken as a means of expression of power … the talk of greater flexibility and change-loving structures is just fuss."[17]

Much closer to the possibility of actual change or the replaceability of a building's components was the architecture of the increasingly active and ambitious Kurokawa, who became the champion of capsule architecture.[18] His efforts toward realizing the idea received a boost when Metabolist architects were assigned major roles preparing for the Osaka Expo in 1970, again under Tange's leadership. However, before completing what might have been the first examples of "real" capsule architecture within the Expo, Kurokawa ventured to build a small structure, the Odakyu Drive-in Restaurant in 1969. It was likely a test toward the one within the space frame of the Expo. This test did not turn out to be a success.

The building exemplified one of the least successful, inept examples of Metabolist architecture. The small, box-like unit of the restaurant was forced into an overwhelming tubular steel space frame, a cage of sorts, with a result that was structurally both illogical and overwhelming. The quasi-megastructure and the "capsule" in their combination were clearly incompatible. The supposedly changeable spatial unit of the restaurant was violated and imprisoned by the structural frame, which at the same time clearly emphasized the flexibility and "possible" continuity of the system. This was underscored by the ostentatious articulation of the joints, which, like in several of Kurokawas's and Tange's buildings, appeared merely as a masquerade of growth (Figure 2.12). Kurokawa's capsule architecture at the Expo 1970 was not much more convincing either.

The 1970 Expo in Osaka, like the 1964 Olympic Games in Tokyo, was again an opportunity for Japan to showcase its tremendous industrial might and advanced technical capability to a large international audience. To this end, as a clear representation of these accomplishments, architecture became one of the most important media. Thus, the numerous pavilions and capsules, designed especially by Japanese architects, offered an overwhelming parade of technology—what Hajime Yatsuka

FIGURE 2.11 Kenzo Tange: Yamanashi Radio and TV Headquarters, Kofu, 1966 and 1974, detail. Photo by B. Bognar.

FIGURE 2.12 Kisho Kurokawa, Odakyu Drive-in Restaurant, Hakone, 1969. Photo by B. Bognar.

called an "orgiastic celebration."[19] Kurokawa designed three pavilions: the first was the Capsule for Living in the space frame (the big roof over the festival plaza), which produced a somewhat better solution to that seen in his Drive-in Restaurant. The Capsule for Living was suspended mid-air in one of the open segments of the gigantic space frame, which acted as a "City in the Air" (Figure 2.13). In contrast, the Toshiba-IHI Pavilion manifested overindulgence in a "fuzzy" structural system made of over 1,400 small steel tetrahedral modular units, somewhat in the genre of structural kitsch. The most successful pavilion was the Takara Beautilion, where the capsules were well integrated into the cubical space frame. The addition of many open modules in the frame hinted at the potential (though here again unlikely) growth of the system.

After the Osaka Expo, a large variety of capsule architecture was designed by Japanese architects, though none with the same acuity and impact as that eventually realized by Kurokawa. Among the growing number of his works, the Nakagin Capsule Tower (1972) rightly attained a special reputation. This design came to epitomize those ideals that the Metabolists intended to advance both in theory and in practice: first of all, the *capability of change*.

The Nakagin Capsule Tower comprises 144 ready-made and fully outfitted capsules, each the size of a shipping container. Although the capsules were small, with Kurokawa's skillful design, they served as existential-minimalist studio residences. The capsules were attached to the supporting megastructure of two vertical service shafts merely by four high-strength bolts. Because all utilities hooked up through standardized connections, the capsules could be easily removed and transported to other locations with the availability of identical vertical docking structures. However, even though each capsule had a *real* capability for change, paradoxically, none of them was ever removed from, or added to, the building. Nevertheless, the Nakagin Capsule Tower best exemplifies the outcome of that Metabolist aspiration: the capability for change. Although it did not achieve the desired mobility of architecture—despite the applied advanced technology—it nevertheless succeeded in evoking the aesthetics of impermanence or the *image* of change[20] (Figure 2.14).

The vicissitudes of change and the changing of an era

However, optimism about capsule architecture, as much as the ideology of techno-utopia, proved to be premature. By the time of the Osaka Expo, there were already serious doubts about Japan's rapid and uncontrolled industrialization and technological enterprise; further, there were doubts that its architectural flag-bearer, the Metabolist movement, would be the panacea for all urban problems. As it turned out, the public remained largely indifferent to the promise of such a utopian world. Thus, while the Expo was meant to celebrate a bright technological future and its representation in the urban world, in effect, it revealed the bankruptcy of the ideology from which Metabolist architecture derived.

(a)

FIGURE 2.13   Kisho Kurokawa, Capsule for Living, Osaka Expo, 1970. a) The Capsule suspended in the Space Frame over the Festival Plaza by K. Tange. The Space Frame acted as a "City in the Air". Photo by B. Bognar; b) Close-up view of Kurokawa's Capsule in the Space Frame. Photo by B. Bognar; c) Kurokawa's Capsule for Living seen from below. Photo by B. Bognar; d) Floor plan of the Capsule. Courtesy of K. Kurokawa.

FIGURE 2.13 (Continued)

38 Botond Bognar

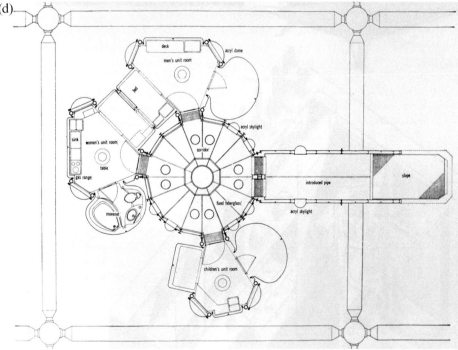

FIGURE 2.13 (Continued)

FIGURE 2.14 Kisho Kurokawa, Nakagin Capsule Tower, Tokyo, 1972. a) Exterior of the building suggestive of what Kurokawa characterized as "the aesthetic of time". Photo by B. Bognar; b) Interior of one capsule residence. Photo by B. Bognar; c) General floor plan of the Nakagin Capsule Tower. Courtesy of K. Kurokawa.

40 Botond Bognar

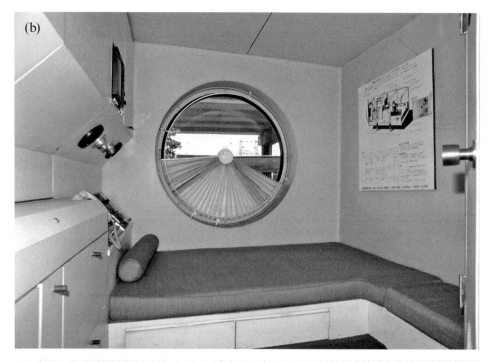

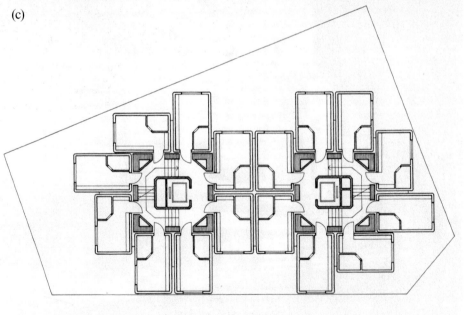

FIGURE 2.14 (Continued)

Hence, despite the architects and organizers' best intentions, the Osaka Expo, like a huge amusement park, ended up as entertainment rather than a genuine public place and a solution for the urban problems. It also proved that the belief of the modernists (including the Metabolist architects) in their capacity to singlehandedly create the public realm in the city and "design" society turned out to be an illusion. By 1970, the contradictions inherent not only between Metabolist theories and practice but also between Metabolist practice and the workings of society proved to be difficult to reconcile. The urban conditions continued to worsen and, just as much important, the public at large was by this time increasingly replaced by *consumers.*

Metabolist architecture, with its manifesto and practice, is considered to be an avant-garde movement.[21] However, when compared to other earlier movements in the West, a major difference becomes evident. Whereas the avant-garde in other countries emerged as protest movements working in opposition to power and rigid cultural norms, and was strongly anti-establishment, the Metabolists were closely tied to the authorities, government circles, and the industries with which they collaborated. Further, they were supported by these institutions, not the least by way of received commissions. Robin Boyd put it this way: "One thing that distinguishes Metabolism from most other avant-garde movements throughout the history of modern architecture is that it is so little ahead of the Japanese establishment."[22]

In 1961, Kikutake, Kurokawa, and Otaka became members of various government think-tanks and steering committees of numerous corporations and agencies. They also became consultants to the Nippon Prefabricated Housing Company, a consortium of leading construction firms, and worked in this capacity for several years.[23] However, it was Tange who, as the "architect of the nation," was perhaps the best connected to the political power of the country.[24] If so, this seems to present a case of the proverbial Catch-22 or indeed another paradox. The aggressive promotion of industrialization, industrial technology, and large construction projects was the government's privileged program, whose rampant advancement was one of the primary causes of the growing environmental and urban crises. Nevertheless, it was the close relationship between the visionaries of the Metabolist movement and their supporting authorities, including the National Planning Agency, which made the many remarkable achievements of these architects possible. In other words, the Metabolists, who relied heavily on industrialization, industrial materials, and technology in their architecture, not only benefited from but also contributed to (though indirectly) the same government program whose harmful consequences they wanted to remedy.[25]

The Expo also revealed that the "active metabolic development" and the possibility of those changes in architecture, and the city that the Metabolists envisioned and encouraged through their technological solutions, gradually gave way to some other, unintended kind of change.[26] These architects could not avoid or reconcile the fact that their promoted metabolic processes of the built environment, made recognizable by the spectacular image quality—especially of the pavilions at the Expo—also catered to the demands of the by-then increasingly consumer-oriented society and its laissez-faire economy. Projecting as much the idea of change as promoting the image of the represented corporations and their products, these pavilions shifted the role of architecture toward becoming another agent in consumerism.

It seems that the advancing free-market economy, globalization, and the increasingly profit-driven and volatile consumerist Japanese cities have effectively emulated the Metabolists' goals of change. In this process, buildings or components of buildings are replaced not merely for their functional deficiencies or obsolescence, but for their less than marketable image value, often long before their user value is up. This consumerist urban phenomenon was brought to its extreme in Japan during another period of accelerated and reckless economy in the bubble era of the 1980s and 1990s. It seems to continue even today. One might say that, ironically, "Metabolism" has won, but on a vastly different scale because of very different forces and with results unlike those the advocates of the movement had intended.

Legacies of Metabolism and the Japanese city today

Today the Japanese city and society operate under conditions very different from those that the Metabolists confronted, and upon which they were eager to improve some 60 years ago. In the post-industrial age, with a less-than-booming economy driven primarily by dominant information technologies, increased consumerism, globalization, and the much-changed world in the post-pandemic age, the Japanese architects face different challenges and have different responsibilities. Pollution in cities is less than it was, and many aspects of urban living have improved, yet architecture, the city, and the larger environment still face significant and even more pressing problems than in the 1960s. Several of these problems are common to other countries; some are unique to Japan.

Apart from its benefits, the workings of globalization have also resulted in dire consequences worldwide over the last half-century. Among these consequences, the foremost is global warming and the accelerated destruction of the environment. Halting and then reversing these trends demands urgent and significant *global* efforts with coordinated and effective policies to save energy while shifting to renewable energy sources, and to change societies' wasteful lifestyles. Architecture and cities as major energy users—and pollutants—are deeply implicated in this process and its resolution. Adding to the plight of the ecosystem and society is the recent catastrophic pandemic, another global phenomenon. It has already changed—in most respects permanently—contemporary urban life as we know it, and this change also necessitates the fundamental reconsideration of architectural and urban design, not just in Japan but also in other countries.

The elapsed time since the 1960s has also yielded numerous other challenges that are symptomatic mostly, or only, to Japan. Among the more recent challenges was the 2011 Tōhoku earthquake and tsunami that obliterated entire urban communities. In Fukushima, the lack of proper planning to mitigate against natural disasters subsequently led to one of the most disastrous nuclear accidents in human history. Moreover, unlike in the booming 1960s, today, Japan's population is aging fast, while the birth rate is decreasing at an alarming rate, leading to a shrinking population, including in urban areas.[27]

The question now is what legacies of the Metabolist movement could be harnessed to address these predicaments. In most respects, the Metabolists were correct in identifying the plight of their contemporary urban developments and then, with a broad vision, trying to address them. However, they were ultimately besieged by the dichotomy between their theories and practice. Although these architects understood the significant role that new types of structural systems and technology could play in the flexibility of architecture, their applied megastructures were often forced, overwhelming, and, for visual impact, excessive and unnecessary. So, instead of being genuinely adaptable, the buildings were heavy, monolithic complexes, even in the best examples.

Therefore, in most cases, the buildings were without the possibility of change and presented flexibility only as an image.

Nevertheless, the Metabolists pursued a vision that with some reorientation could directly address several of the challenges our cities face today. This reoriented vision could point to *real* flexibility, where change would not necessarily mean the eradication of entire structures and replacing them often with some flashy new ones for architectural or urban renewal. This flexibility should entail inherent *adaptability* to meet changing demands. Change and flexibility might also mean a capacity for regeneration, adaptive reuse or recycling, the use of recyclable materials and structures, renewable energy, and more eco-friendly technologies to give a second life to the built environment. Moreover, change might mean new types of "multi-purpose" architecture that could be reconfigured when needed, such as hotels remodeled to work as hospitals, office buildings remodeled to become residential buildings, or large public buildings rearranged to become temporary emergency shelters, for example. These multi-purpose buildings could also work well toward what is now called "pandemic urbanism," "disaster urbanism," and, ultimately, "sustainable urbanism."[28]

Notes

1 Under architect Kenzo Tange's leadership and patronage, the Metabolist group included the architects Kiyonori Kikutake, Kisho Kurokawa, Fumihiko Maki, and Masato Otaka; the previous editor of *Shinkenchiku*, Noboru Kawazoe; industrial designer Kenji Ekua; graphic designer Kiyoshi Awazu; and Takashi Asada, who organized the group and its participation in the Tokyo World Design Conference of 1960. Tange and Arata Isozaki were not members of the Metabolist group.

2 Recent scholars tracing the roots and development of Metabolist ideology put different emphases on the movement's influences, discussing either the pragmatic or the idealistic/psychological influences, depending on the context of their discussion. Zhongjie Lin underscored local and international events, or the Western traditions of utopian planning as influencing the movement, whereas Hyunjung Cho situated the emergence of the Metabolists mainly within the nation's "traumatic memories of wartime past and a persistent anxiety over [an impending] nuclear war." Zhongjie Lin. *Kenzo Tange and the Metabolist Movement: Urban Utopias of Modern Japan* (London: Routledge, 2010); and Hyunjung Cho, "Competing Futures: War Narratives in Postwar Japanese Architecture 1945–1970," PhD dissertation (University of Southern California, 2011), xi.

3 Rem Koolhaas and Hans Ulrich Obrist, *Project Japan: Metabolism Talks …* (Cologne: Taschen, 2009).

4 There were some proposals for marine developments in Japan that pre-dated Kikutake's Marine City, although these proposals were not made by architects. In 1957, the artist Taro Okamoto drew up his "Island of Leisure," the then housing developer Hisaakira Kano proposed "Yamato: A New Capital on Tokyo Bay." However, these proposals were land-reclamation projects. In this way, they merely continued a centuries-old practice in Japan, which started in Edo, Tokyo's predecessor, in the early seventeenth century. For details, see Rem Koolhaas and Hans Ulrich Obrist, *Project Japan: Metabolism Talks …*, 272 and 274–277.

5 Tange had an earlier (1959) project, "A Community for 25,000 over Boston Bay," which he assigned to his students when he was a visiting professor at Massachusetts Institute of Technology in Cambridge, Massachusetts. This project was the harbinger of his plan for Tokyo 1960.

6 The "City in the Air" or "Joint Core System" (1961) was proposed for Shinjuku, while the "Clusters in the Air" (1962) was proposed for Shibuya, both in Tokyo.

7 The first use of the terms "megastructure" and "megaform" is attributed to Fumihiko Maki in his *Investigations in Collective Form* (St. Louis: the School of Architecture, Washington University, 1964). Reyner Banham later wrote his book *Megastructure: Urban Futures of the Recent Past* (London: Thames & Hudson, 1976), in which he attributes the introduction of these terms to Maki.

8 These mobile units were relocated several times as the family changed and rearrangement of the house became necessary. This was stated by Kikutake in a discussion with the author in the Sky House on August 20, 1980.

9 The Izumo Shrine Office Building had a mezzanine level. The building was demolished in 2017. The Hotel Tokoen is still in use.

10 The vertical columns of the Hotel Tokoen replicate a type of traditional wooden structure, where the main post is supported by shorter ones using *nuki*, or small tie-beams. An example of this construction is seen at the *torii* gate of Istukushima Shrine on Miyajima Island in Hiroshima Prefecture.

11 Noriaki (Kisho) Kurokawa, "Challenge to the Capsule: Nakagin Capsule Tower Building," *The Japan Architect* (October 1972): 17.

12 Rem Koolhaas and Hans Ulrich Obrist. *Project Japan: Metabolism Talks …*, back cover.

13 Kenzo Tange, "Recollections, Architect Kenzo Tange, no. 7," *The Japan Architect* (October 1985): 8.

14 Kenzo Tange, "Recollections" in M. Bettinotti (ed.), *Kenzo Tange 1946–1996* (Milan: Electa, 1996), 45; and Kenzo Tange, "Yamanashi Press and Broadcasting Centre," *Works of Kenzo Tange and URTEC*. Special issue of *SD, Space Design* 1980/01: 42.

15 Kenzo Tange, "Recollections, Architect Kenzo Tange, no. 7".

16 Kikutake assigns this open space to "ventilation." *Kiyonori Kikutake: Works and Methods 1956–1970* (Tokyo: Bijutsu Shuppansha, 1973), 100 (in Japanese).

17 Günter Nitschke, "Akira Shibuya-City Center Project," *Architectural Design* (April 1967): 216.

18 It is important to remember that Kikutake was already envisioning such prefabricated units in many of his large "Marine City" and other early proposals. Eventually, he also used prefabricated units, though much smaller in size, in his own 1958 Sky House and also in his 1966 Pacific Hotel in Chigasaki, where the bathroom units were attached from the outside of each room. Yet, it was Kurokawa, not Kikutake, who first used the term "capsule" in relation to his architecture. Kikutake used the term "movenett" for his replaceable units. See Rem Koolhaas and Hans Ulrich Obrist. *Project Japan: Metabolism Talks*, 139.

19 Hajime Yatsuka, "Between West and East-Japan: The State of the Architecture," Part III, *Telescope* (Autumn, 1992): 87.

20 Kurokawa's own definition; Op. cit. 11.

21 Rem Koolhaas, "Singapore Songlines: Thirty Years of Tabula Rasa" in Rem Koolhaas and Bruce Mau (eds.), *S,M,L,XL* (Rotterdam: 010 Publishers, 1995), 1044.

22 Robin Boyd, *New Directions in Japanese Architecture* (New York: George Braziller, 1968), 22.

23 Wilhelm Klauser, "Introduction—Rules and Identities" in Christopher Knabe and Joerg Rainer Noennig (eds.), *Shaking the Foundations: Japanese Architects in Dialogue* (Munich: Prestel Verlag, 1999), 11.

24 Such close ties between architecture and authority have a long history in Japan, as the historian William H. Coaldrake pointed out in his book *Architecture and Authority in Japan* (London: Routledge, 1996).

25 The cause of Metabolism was greatly promoted by Atsushi Shimokobe, a previous graduate of Tange's laboratory at the University of Tokyo and later a high-ranking bureaucrat in the Ministry of Construction and the National Economic Planning Agency.

26 The quotation is from the Metabolist manifesto: Noboru Kawazoe et al., *Metabolism 1960: The Proposals for New Urbanism* (Tokyo: Bijutsu Shuppan-sha, 1960).

27 In 2019, people aged 65 or over made up over 28 percent of the country's total population, according to released government data: https://data.worldbank.org/indicator/SP.POP.65UP.TO.ZS?locations=JP (accessed January 20, 2021). Japan's fertility rate in 2020 was 1.369 births per woman: https://www.macrotrends.net/countries/JPN/japan/fertility-rate (accessed January 20, 2021).

28 Recently, several universities organized virtual symposiums on "pandemic urbanism," among them the University of Washington on 29 May 2020; pandemic urbanism is also the topic of a planned special issue of the journal *Sustainability* (Basel, Switzerland) entitled "'Pandemic Urbanism': Game Changer for Urban Resilience and Sustainability?"

3

ENGINEERING A POETIC TECHNO-URBANISM

The Metabolists' Visionary City in Postwar Japan

Raffaele Pernice

The Metabolist Manifesto was published in May 1960 when a group of young Japanese critics, designers, and architects vigorously announced their innovative proposals for a new urbanism. Since then, the fascinating concepts and bold forms in the images of their urban models have exerted an extraordinary power around the world. Metabolism developed in its architectural experimentation and urban design principles in response to the urban infrastructure developments and mass-housing problems of postwar Japan. This occurred in the context of unprecedented economic growth, massive urban expansion, and strong technological progress. The Metabolists' visionary urban forms and advanced technological architectures expressed the vitality and regenerative spirit of Japan's new impetus toward economic, social, and urban revival after the tragic recent past. They functioned as a catalyst and a magnifying glass for innovative concepts already circulating in Japan and elsewhere since the early 1950s from designers, planners, and engineers. Their urban architectures originated during a radical transformation in urban planning and design practice and theory, and they were inspired by the biological metaphor of organic growth. At the time, Modernist influence was fading. Instead, people envisioned a city built around new technological knowledge produced by the interbreeding of different scientific disciplines, which triggered the search for radical urban forms and new architectural concepts. This gave birth to peculiar and highly influential design models, collated around the fundamental notions of cycles of use, nomadism, modularity, compact urbanism, and replaceability.

The Metabolist aesthetic

Images of huge urban megastructures populated the various unbuilt design projects of the Metabolist city. These images were heavily rooted in the radical transformation of the urban landscape of postwar Japan, driven by industrial production on an exceptional scale since the early 1950s. Large industrial conglomerate corporations (*zaibatsu*) and construction companies led the rush toward national modernization

DOI: 10.4324/9781003186540-4

and economic growth to provide new infrastructure and vast urban development projects. This occurred with the open support of the government in one of the most efficient and notorious examples of state development.

Investigating the links between projects conducted by large construction companies and industrial firms can help improve the understanding of early Metabolist projects. This perspective may be more important than considering the influence of architectural theories and urban schemes proposed during the decade after World War II (WWII) in 1945.

The megastructural forms of many Metabolism schemes impressed Western laypeople and scholars alike during the 1960s.[1] The megastructures appeared like renewed polemical statements. They embodied a departure from the International Congresses of Modern Architecture (Congrès Internationaux d'Architecture Modern [CIAM]) and a theoretical reconsideration and criticism of the Functionalist discourse on architecture and urbanism, which was still mainstream in the profession and academia. From the beginning, the Metabolism design proposals for a new urbanism, as presented in the 1960 manifesto, appear to be built less on a comprehensive theory or methodological structure and more on direct observation and broad acceptance, further revaluation, and systemization of the typical design approach. The designs reflected many themes that builders, engineers, designers, and architects were already focusing on in Japan during the phase of progressive and aggressive reindustrialization led by the state.[2]

Metabolism images have influenced Western architectural culture and debates since the 1960s. While assimilating the most important aesthetic, theoretical, and technological lessons from European and American designers and planners, Metabolism was largely influenced by the construction industry, large-scale urban transformations, and numerous public works orchestrated by the government to reshape Japan from the ruins of defeat. Thus, the bold images and schemes of the early Metabolist projects had a freshness; they were derived from the drastic reshaping of the land and the transformation of the densely populated cities. This might explain the success of some of the most innovative and creative features of Metabolism.

Postwar Japan

For several years after WWII, many people constructed their own forms of shelter, which the government endorsed to rebuild from the ashes of the completely destroyed cities. However, a lack of building materials and basic supplies due to economic collapse meant that a significant part of the urban population lived in tiny houses, often very simple structures built from scraps. Several architects were engaged in designing low-cost houses for mass production using prefabricated industrial elements. Among the most representative models were the "Premos," designed by Kunio Maekawa. Then, in the first half of the 1950s, Kiyoshi Ikebe, Kiyoshi Seike, and Kenji Hirose designed several models of single-family houses destined for large-scale industrial production. Ikebe's projects were inspired by the modular and minimal houses of European Functionalism in the 1920s. They reflected his awareness of the exigencies of standardization, oriented to the mass production of low-cost housing based on industry. Hirose developed the first prototype of a house for mass production, the "SH-30," whose parts were made of standardized elements and used steel instead of traditional wood. This became a source of inspiration for other architects and industrial companies, who developed new and more advanced models of standard prefabricated houses.[3] New housing standards were set to face those changes.

One prominent housing transformation to reduce women's work and ensure a more functional arrangement of the living spaces was introducing the dining-kitchen (DK) unit. This open space arrangement was inspired by the 1920s German Frankfurt-kitchen, designed using scientific principles and functional articulation of the space.[4] This idea evolved during the 1950s and 1960s into the most common interior space for Japanese apartment and units, the "2DK," composed of two rooms and a DK space.[5]

The need to provide enough homes and limit the direct financial involvement of the government resulted in a push to foster house ownership, a trend that developed in Tokyo during the prewar years.[6] In 1950, the government established the Japan Loan Corporation (JLC) to provide financial support for housing construction. Low-interest loans helped people purchase land to build houses. In addition, the Japan Housing Corporation (JHC) was set up in 1955 to provide low-cost public housing to help alleviate the housing crisis plaguing Japanese cities. These new multi-story apartment blocks (*danchi*) were the first low-cost, mass-housing structures built after the war and inspired by Modernist principles. They were built to promote a modern

FIGURE 3.1 Bomb damage in Tokyo in 1945. Japanese photo depicting the aftermath of American air raids near Hisamatsu, part of what is now the Tokyo Metropolis. The Sumida River can be seen in the right portion of the photograph. Image credit: Wikimedia Commons/Public domain.

48 Raffaele Pernice

lifestyle and purportedly designed to integrate Japanese elements with Western typological and structural features inspired by Modernist European and Soviet architectural theories.[7] The flats were organized around an open space concept that connected the living, dining, and kitchen areas (LDK) to foster collective living and accommodate small apartments. These blocks were mostly built on large empty plots on the outskirts of large cities, where the land was relatively affordable and space was still available. However, these areas were far from factories and other productive zones, and lacked public services and basic infrastructure.

One consequence of this condition was a fragmented urban fabric in the suburban zones of Japan's highly populated industrial cities. This formed large conurbations covered by extensive blankets of fine-grained and dispersed residential areas, often unplanned, which would complicate large-scale urban restructuring in the following years. The proliferation of tram lines and railway networks was another important element that characterized urban development. These networks were mostly private, interwoven between large sections of the cities and their suburbia. They were effective mobility networks in a period of very low car ownership, and new stations had a strong influence on the morphology and spatial configurations of the urban zones where they were built. Many new stations, which were built on cheaper land far from the traditional commercial cores of the cities, quickly became pivotal in the life of commuters and citizens. They were nodal points in the expanding transportation system of these large conurbations.

Railway stations were frequented by workers commuting toward factories in central areas and quickly became powerful magnets for services and shops. This transformed the urban zones around the stations into new shopping streets and commercial centers, often in direct competition with the older business cores of the cities.[8] This new and highly dispersed suburban landscape was an expression of railway urbanism, where new urban development is often planned along existing railway lines. The neighborhoods are structured like a vast patchwork of small and dense low-rise, single-family houses revolving around commercial nodes (shopping arcades and department stores). These areas are focused on railway stations connecting to other local centers and the larger business districts of the main cities. Yasuo Masai, referring to Tokyo, expressed this landscape as of the megapolitan condition of the urban life.[9]

A fast process of urbanization in Japan peaked in the early 1960s and built on the unprecedented levels of immigration into large cities, with workers flocking to the large industrial areas following the progressive economic growth that started and was consolidated after the outbreak of the Korean War (1950–1953).[10]

The Korean War prompted the United States (US) to reconsider the role of Japan, which became an ally in the war against communism and whose strategic position was indispensable. Technological transfer and financial aid helped the various Japanese governments rebuild and modernize a new industrial apparatus. The archipelago quickly transformed into an industrial powerhouse designated for exportation. In the first year of the Hatoyama government (1954–1955), the Prime Minister heralded a national plan to gain economic independence and full employment in Japan. This was achieved in just two years. Subsequently, the Ikeda government (1960–1964) launched an ambitious plan to double the income and size of the Japanese economy in just ten years.[11] The economic growth dictated the agenda for the next several years, resulting in large budgets for constructing basic infrastructure and even larger industrial complexes, developed with the support of large business conglomerates.[12] Strong internal

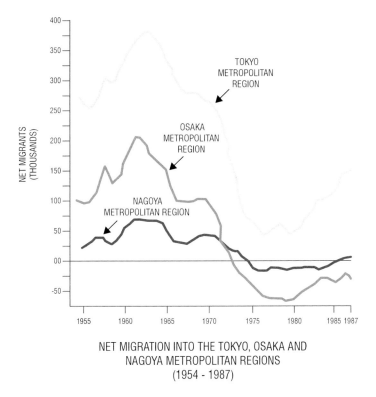

FIGURE 3.2 Chart depicting the share of immigration into the three main urbanized areas of Japan (Tokyo, Osaka, and Nagoya) in 1954–1987. Urban immigration peaked by early 1960s. Source: Fujita Kuniko and Richard C. Hill (eds), *Japanese Cities in the World Economy* (Philadelphia: Temple University Press, 1993).

immigration, enacted by the political decision to concentrate most of the productive plants in the major waterfront urban conurbations, led to overcrowding. The need for new urban spaces and residential areas prompted new bold planning developments which were often located at the extreme outskirts of large industrial cities, like in the case of 1966 Tama New Town west of Tokyo. Indeed, the extraordinary development of the Japanese economy and unprecedented industrial outputs occurred at the expense of citizens' quality of life in the cities, drastic alteration of the environment, and widespread contamination.

In particular, the frantic process of land reclamation and infrastructure developments in the major coastal cities (Tokyo, Osaka, and Nagoya) was justified to sustain the government's ambitious visions for increased industrial production. New imponent land reclamation projects altered the natural coastline of major industrial and commercial port cities like Tokyo, Yokohama, Osaka, Nagoya, and Fukuoka. Construction included new oil refinery and chemical plants, piers, and large port facilities and terminals. The ports were crowded with large container vessels and tankers following the rapid economic growth. In Tokyo Bay, a long strip of mostly artificial (reclaimed) land stretched from Kawasaki, through Yokohama and Tokyo, to Chiba, and transformed the natural waterfront landscape into a continuous series of heavy industrial plants; shipbuilding, steel and manufacturing factories; and various maritime facilities. This infrastructure had the strategic advantage of being located near metropolitan areas, with large consumption, and the main railway networks terminals connecting the inland with the sea.

The immigration-fueled developing suburbs, close to production facilities in the large cities, were mainly structured as compact, productive settlements of integrated factories, plants, and housing complexes (*kombinato*). These were inspired by the Soviet model of working units (*kombinat*). Many of these settlements were built close to the waterfront, which offered access to the export routes for finished goods and the import of raw materials for production. For example, the now-abandoned coal-mining facility on Hashima Island, in Nagasaki Prefecture, hosted a community of 5,000 people at its peak. It is a good example of the dense and multi-functional working unit, planned and built as a form of highly complex engineering work, whose mines and industrial factories were perfectly integrated with the residential buildings, communal services, and other basic public infrastructures serving a small community in a limited physical space.

Urban discourse in the 1950s

The postwar CIAM 7 (1949) and CIAM 8 (1951) set important directions for the development of architectural and urban theory, highlighting several contradictions that eventually caused the dissolution of the CIAMs at the conclusive meeting at Otterloo in 1959. Focusing on the GRID as a "thinking tool for organizing information" and on the theme of the "Heart of the City" (as the physical and symbolic core of the urban community), these congresses promoted, with little success, the idea of moving beyond the more formalistic and extremely technical approach in designing the built environment.[13] They were searching for alternatives to the very elementary vision of the cities, which were to be largely shaped according to the four basic urban functions indicated in the Athens Charter. Subsequently, the reconstruction and redesign of postwar cities in Europe were driven by economic recovery and inspired by a common language that relied on the structural studies, design aesthetics, social ambitions, and spatial organizations suggested by the Modernists 20 years earlier. This resulted in an unprecedented social engineering experiment that transformed the new European cities into clearly separated, functional areas. They were rebuilt with large-scale projects, featuring series of standardized multilevel apartment blocks with shared facilities, often separated by the street and disjointed by the street life, and confined around vast green and empty areas.[14]

Mass housing was imperative owing to the enormous scale of the housing crisis and further justified by the need to contain costs while integrating large parts of the population into the vital functions of the city. Therefore, experimentation and substantial state intervention in construction costs and intensive research were fundamental tools for urban development. In France, the CIAM formula for these mass-housing estates took the form of modern collective housing (*grands ensembles*). Meanwhile, in the Netherlands, sophisticated studies on the reality of public housing estates as social condensers led pioneer architects like John Habraken to search for alternatives to these standardized models of urban living. This is illustrated in his theory of "Supports and Infills" (1963), which bears a direct connection to the compositional principles of Structuralism in terms of potential growth, functional adaptability, and overall flexibility of the final architectural form.

The sense of general dissatisfaction and sociological problems for the residents of these urban enclaves triggered a rapid and profound change in the work and studies of some architects, who progressively shifted their attention from the large-scale design of functional separated spaces to more contained and tailored socially responsive places. This change of attitude was announced by the proposition of a new vocabulary used by the members of the group Team X, which relied on innovative key words like "cluster," "web," and "stem." They cast doubts on the effectiveness of the traditional Modernist language to effectively translate and satisfy the needs of a more complex ad various urban environment.

The "Greenbelt Towns" in the US and *microraion* superblock in Soviet Russia became the fundamental urban models that forged the organization of the community, socially and physically, in cities since the late 1940s. Each concept tried to spatially reproduce their ideological vision of the society of industry, as shaped by capitalist and socialist values.

From the 1920s to the 1950s, the fermentation of ideas and an orientation toward experimentation challenged orthodoxy in architecture and city design on a large scale. They were a mirror of a progressive cultural and economic shift toward large and more consumerist societies. Postwar urban growth, technological progress, and economic prosperity cemented the sense of collective belonging and fostered ambitions to achieve common goals.

The prospect of new technology was felt in the US after the war. This was heralded with the Futurama exhibition at the New York World's Fair, held in 1939, which portrayed the possibilities for the next 20 years. This technological promise was fueled by the dangers, anxieties, and possibilities caused by the Cold War and the Space Race, culminating in the moon landing in 1969, a year ahead of the Osaka Expo in 1970. Building on the Nazi Germany rocket program, which heralded a new age of space travel and interplanetary mobility since the 1930s, the US devoted much of the immediate postwar years to building a new global vision of the future. Compact capsule houses had an obvious connection with space and ocean exploration, and also related to the new reality of endless mobility in the city. Growing traffic and the individual liberty of circulation and leisure time expressed the power of the new capitalist order.

Highways began to shape the urban form of US cities. They represented pivotal mobility infrastructure with strong visual appeal, symbolic of the new age of transportation technology and pre-eminently American urban landmark. Mobile cabins, trailer homes, and automobile production increased exponentially with increasing federal investment in new highways and roads. These vehicles became a source of architectural inspiration like the space capsules.

The urban renewal projects that were proposed in the obsolete but lively cores of the US cities, displacing many residents and bringing a drastic transformation of the traditional American urban landscape, were opposed by new suburban developments like Levittown. These became the typical residential community and were attractive for the growing middle class. These suburban houses were also built for the returning veterans and their families as a symbol of the American Dream. The catalogs promoting these constructions featured a huge variety of prefabricated house types, with a multiplicity of interiors and prices, advertised as true forms of consumerist architecture. Yet the diffusion of these commercial, residential architectures, which were so popular in the American magazines, developed in parallel to the Case Study Houses program. The Case Study Houses were distinctive research projects for houses with high design quality and new formal concepts. They were supported from 1945 to 1962 to foster simple plans, structural modularity, and the aesthetic innovation of the new American home.[15]

Several old masters of European Modernism had fled to the US before WW II. For example, Ludwig Mies van der Rohe and Walter Gropius were headmasters in US universities, and Ludwig Hilberseimer and Luis Sert became new guides in the design and planning school in American academia. While in Europe, their main interest in city design revolved around the issues of density and compactness typical of industrial cities like Paris and Berlin. In the US, they examined the American experience, shaped by the extensive horizons separating the city from the country and the mobility infrastructure, which had large centers like Chicago, Boston, and New York as the core of vast interconnected regional territories.

As Dean of the Graduate Design School at Harvard University, Sert organized the first Urban Design Conference at Harvard University in 1956. Urban design was a new discipline encompassing knowledge and tools from architecture, landscape architecture, and city planning. It was viewed as embodying the civic vision and cultural importance of the city and the built environment that was somehow neglected by the programmatic points of the Athens Charter.[16] Sert's book *Can Our Cities Survive?* (1942) echoed the concern for the enormous urban expansion of the industrial city.

This sentiment was to increase after WWII because new factories in large cities and a more interconnected urban network of inter-regional roads and highways favored the intake of rural immigrants as workers in the large industrial complexes. In the

FIGURE 3.3 Cover of Luis J. Sert's *Can Our Cities Survive?* (1942). Image credit: Public domain.

middle of the twentieth century, the new urban dimension resulted from an abrupt urban paradigm shift, with the large city transformed into the megalopolis, as observed and described by Jean Gottmann in his 1961 book.

The Metabolist Group, 1960

The biological metaphor and organic reference used to represent cities were already circulating early in the twentieth century with Peter Geddes's famous *Cities in Evolution*, and more so in the years before and after WWII. CIAM 8 (1951) was titled "The Heart of the City," and Le Corbusier recurrently saw the streets working like multi-scale, intricate blood pipes. Between 1902 and 1909, the French architect Eugène Hénard had already compared Paris to a gigantic mechanic organism with parks as lungs, streets as its complex circulation apparatus, and the central business district as the pulsing heart of the entire system.[17] However, it was Metabolism that reaffirmed the biological analogy with new strong architectural images, especially in the early projects of the group.

Mentored by iconic architect Kenzo Tange, Metabolism was formalized in 1960 with the publication of a manifesto, *Metabolism 1960: The Proposals for New Urbanism*, which was launched at the Tokyo World Design Conference in May 1960. Instantaneously, the Metabolists were linked to the surging megastructure trend in the 1960s.[18] Indeed, they were a product of, and responded to, an extraordinary time. They emerged as postwar Japan entered a new age of prosperity and opened up to the world for the first time since the war. Cities were growing rapidly, and the need for housing and infrastructure spiked on an unprecedented scale. Seeking to transcend a conventional approach to development, Metabolists predicated on innovative solutions to urban planning problems.

Modern Japanese urban planning started in 1919 with the City Planning Law and the Urban Building Law, which introduced building codes, zoning, and general indications for planning vast urban areas. From 1945, a land reform was introduced, and a progressive decentralization of planning activities occurred, but was still supervised by the central government. However, key changes to the planning laws were not introduced until the 1960s. These included the 1963 Height Building Law, which allowed buildings to be more than 30 m tall; the 1968 New City Planning Law; and the 1970 Amendments to Building Standards Law, which delegated planning power to local governments, dealt with development permissions and processes, and allowed citizen participation in planning.[19]

The problem of mobility within the dense and congested Japanese cities, expanding as a sea of intricate urban fabrics of tiny dwellings and narrow alleys, was resolved by moving the circulation system in vertical structural cores or helicoidal frames, each with the potential for further extension and growth. The complete integration of urban infrastructures and architectural spaces, permeating the megastructures and condensing essential functions to create a complete organism, marked the blending of engineering processes and architectural aesthetics. The Metabolist urban prototypes responded to mass-housing shortages, limited urban circulation, and poor or non-existent collective services in the city with gigantic expressionist forms of miniature compact and self-regulating cities. These were designed according to the logic of technological replaceability and industrial prefabrication. The architects indicated the spirit of a heroic and new Promethean vision of humankind's expansion into the natural and newly built landscape. This is observed in Kiyonori Kikutake's various marine cities, and Kisho Kurokawa's grids and helicoidal cities. Many of these ideas then featured in Tange's much-acclaimed 1960 Tokyo Bay Plan.

Among the group, there was a progressive polarization of themes and aesthetic language. Kikutake and Kurokawa mainly promoted the technological and expressionist aspects of their projects. They devoted most of the years between the publication of the Metabolist Manifesto and the Tokyo Olympic Games in 1964 to the aesthetics of the vertical urban expansion. They shared architectural vocabulary based on the use of capsules and vertical shafts, designed according to the principles of modularity and replaceability, following the assumption of different cycles of use and the existence of the various elements composing the whole. Some of the most iconic Metabolist projects they proposed shared the idea of vertical expansion and functional separation of urban spaces, built as artificial support above their contextual natural environment, like the sea, rural settings, or on a pre-existing city. These pragmatic approaches were combined to design structures to rescue communities hit by natural disasters and propose alternative urban settlements integrating residential and productive facilities.

Industrially produced capsule architectures with minimalist designs rejected the idea of pretentious luxury homes, but alluded to working-class dwellings, a legacy to the 1920s social architecture of early Modernism. They linked directly to the growing interest for research about modular coordination in the construction industry that was so popular in 1950s Japan. The search for a social dimension in experimental proposals, planned as clusters of communities or small villages, demonstrated interest in the basic needs of the common people living in defined neighborhoods. The poor quality of the growing suburban zones on the outskirts of the contemporary Japanese cities, increasingly overcrowded and visually anonymous, prompted efforts to create urban spaces that could convey a sense of identity and belonging to the residents while providing enough collective services to enhance their daily life. These efforts included trying to reduce the inhabitants' feelings of estrangement, echoing an awareness of the dire conditions experienced by most rural immigrants in the industrial cities at the time. As progressive architects, they actively aimed to appreciate the vast repertoire of traditional Japanese architecture and the use of new technologies, which fostered the genesis of bold urban images. These designs often originated from contingent needs and pragmatic solutions to real problems, but were still reminiscent of traditional forms and collective symbols.

In 1959, Typhoon Vera hit the Japanese archipelago, causing catastrophic flooding and loss of life.

Kurokawa's Agricultural City, featured in the 1960 Manifesto, was a prototype of a rural settlement designed as a structural grid above the ground as a solution to flooding. It also had a form that could deviate from its original geometric purity and adapt, grow, and expand organically. This was similar to the plan of Katsura Villa and the scheme of Kyoto city. For Kikutake, a large series of marine city projects was inspired by real problems, such as the flooding of the Koto District in Tokyo in 1959 in a time when planners and architects focused on the restructuring of Tokyo Bay.[20]

Kurokawa's Helix City embodied early Metabolism affinity for architectural language inspired by expressionist forms. The spiraling city is structured as a gigantic volumetric vertical exoskeleton containing the general circulation and urban services supporting residential units. Reminiscent of Tange's central spine scheme (civic axis)

FIGURE 3.4 Destruction and floods in South Japan caused by Typhon Vera, September 1959. Image credit: Wikimedia Commons/Public domain.

for the 1960 Tokyo Plan, the project alluded to the biological world and conceptual analogies to blood circulation that nurtures the flesh. Its strong poetic architectural form responds to the housing crisis of urban immigrants proposing minimal residential units designed as detachable prefabricated capsules for mass production made of assembled industrialized elements, a concept which was then celebrated in several architectural proposals presented at the 1970 Osaka Expo.

In opposition to the tabula rasa and the rejection of the urban context, Fumihiko Maki and Masato Otaka proposed a contextual approach, paying attention to the surrounding landscape and mobility issues. In their Shinjuku Redevelopment project (1960), the integration of multiple urban functions was achieved by the extensive use of pedestrian decks forming a podium above the ground and by combining circulation and architectural spaces into distinct but unitarian forms capable of organic growth.

In 1969, Kikutake, Kurokawa, and Maki's entry proposal for PREVI experimental housing project competition in Lima, Peru, was among the three winning projects from 13 international architects. They used a precast concrete system with different loadings, which also included foundations. It was considered thoughtfully designed and likely to save costs while ensuring coherent urban growth. Housing plans grouped areas by considering the possibility of local industries producing equipment and units for kitchens, toilets, and storage in the future. The external spaces in their master scheme separated cars and pedestrian routes, while the layout of houses allowed for the growth of the unit to additional floors. This design would follow growing families and thus reflected a fundamental Metabolism concept.

56 Raffaele Pernice

FIGURE 3.5 Expo Tower, Osaka, Japan. Designed by Kiyonori Kikutake for the World Expo 1970 in Osaka. Image credit: Kirakirameister via Wikimedia Commons.

Engineering a Poetic Techno-urbanism 57

FIGURE 3.6 The Takara Group, Beautilian Pavilion, designed by Kisho Kurokawa, at the World Expo 1970 in Osaka. Image credit: m-louis/Wikimedia Commons.

Looking to the future

The rapid economic expansion and parallel population growth in postwar Japanese cities initially coincided with an undersupply in housing. This affected most of the incoming workers immigrating from rural areas. As a result, the government stepped in to drive the progressive urban development, but without imposing, at least for a while, strict regulatory measures to avoid curbing the economic growth. In this context, many of the initial innovative Metabolist urban proposals can be interpreted as pragmatic solutions to the government's call for controlled and functional urban development. This development was to be based on large-scale public works, infrastructure, and construction activities within a sustained and prioritized national industrial program orchestrated by the centralized Japanese developmental state.

Some of the most experimental designs sought to overcome the reliance on one of Japan's scarcest resources: land. For example, Kikutake's Marine City was conceived in 1958 as artificial land for residential and industrial uses, and underwent several revisions in scale and forms, but was never built; however, his Aquapolis, another floating structure he designed on a smaller scale, was built as the Japanese pavilion at the 1975 World Expo in Okinawa.

Like any movement, Metabolism had its merits and limitations. For example, little attention was devoted to waste production and management (with most of the urban garbage going to landfill), despite it being an issue in urban Japan at the time. Industrial waste contaminated the ground and the sea, causing deadly disease among the population and environmental upheaval. The Metabolists' projects used schematic designs based on somewhat simplistic notions of the functioning of cities, which are highly complex entities. They also made simplistic assumptions about how people use

FIGURE 3.7 3D rendering based on Kiyonori Kikutakes's Marine City, which was originally conceived in 1958. Images created by Antxon Canovas (image published with permission of the author).

urban spaces. Although these are weaknesses, they also lend the projects a fascinating utopian element that is open to further elaborations.

There is currently a global shift toward a social culture focused on the notions of re-use, recycle, and re-adapt, and climatic changes and global warming are bringing new threats like rising sea levels. Despite some limitations and a design language heavily embedded in the reality of Japanese industrialization during the 1960s, the current global situation can only bring renewed attention to the Metabolists' repertoire of imaginative urban forms and dynamic architectural prototypes.

Notes

1 Manfredo Tafuri, *Architettura Moderna in Giappone* (Bologna: Cappelli Editore, 1964); Robin Boyd, *New Directions in Japanese Architecture* (New York: George Braziller, 1968); Reyner Banham, *Urban Futures of the Recent Past* (London: Thames & Hudson, 1976).
2 William H. Coaldrake, *Architecture and Authority in Japan* (London: Routledge, 1996).
3 Noboru Kawazoe, *Contemporary Japanese Architecture*, rev. ed. (Tokyo: Kokusai Koryu Ki-kin, 1973). Further, Kawazoe noted that "it is an interesting fact that, in Japanese postwar houses, one can see repeated the historical development of Japanese architecture from Heian residential house to the tea house and tradesman's house of Tokugawa period" (at p. 49).
4 Kazuya Inaba and Shigenobu Nakayama, *Japanese Homes and Lifestyles: An Illustrated Journey through the History* (Tokyo: Kodansha International, 2000), p. 116.
5 Hiroshi Watanabe, *The Architecture of Tokyo* (Stuttgart and London: Edition Axel Menges, 2001), 118.
6 Special Issue: *The Japanese House. Architecture and Life after 1945* (Tokyo: Shinkenchiku-Sha Co. Ltd., 2017); Azby Brown and Joseph Cali, *The Japanese Dream House: How Technology and Tradition are Shaping New Home Design* (New York and Tokyo: Kodansha International, 2001).
7 Ann Waswo, *Housing in Postwar Japan: A Social History* (London: Curzon Press, 2002).
8 David Kornhauser, *Urban Japan: Its Foundation and Growth* (London and New York: Longman Group Ltd., 1976), 77–78; Andre Sorensen, *The Making of Urban Japan: Cities and Planning from Edo to the Twenty-First Century* (London and New York: Routledge, 2002), 195.
9 Yasuo Masai, "Metropolitization in Densely Populated Asia: The Case of Tokyo," in Ashok Dutt, Frank Costa, and Allen Noble, *The Asian City: Processes of Development, Character-istics, and Planning* (London: Kluwer Academic Publishers, 1994), 121–124.
10 Kuniko Fujita and Richard C. Hill (eds), *Japanese Cities in the World Economy* (Philadel-phia: Temple University Press, 1993).
11 Norman Glickman, *The Management of the Japanese Urban System: Regional Development and Regional Planning in Postwar Japan* (New York: Academic Press, 1979).
12 Cf. Fujita and Hill, *Japanese Cities in the World Economy*; Sorensen, *The Making of Urban Japan*.
13 Pierre Alain Croset and Andrea Canclini, "On the CIAM 7 Grid: From an Ideological to a Critical Tool," *The Plan Journal* 5(1) (2020): 1–29; Leonardo Marchi, *The Heart of the City: Legacy and Complexity of a Modern Design Idea* (London and New York: Routledge, 2017).
14 Vittorio Magnago Lampugnani, *Architecture and Planning in the Twentieth Century* (New York: Van Nostrand Reinhold Company, 1985); Leonardo Benevolo, *History of Modern Architecture* (Cambridge, MA: MIT Press, 1971).
15 Esther McCoy, *Case Study Houses 1945–1962*, 2nd ed. (Santa Monica: Hennessey+Ingalls, 1977).
16 Jonathan Barnett, "The Way We Were, the Way We Are: The Theory and Practice of Designing Cities since 1956," *Harvard Design Magazine* 24 (2006) (available at: http://www.harvarddesignmagazine.org/issues/24/the-way-we-were-the-way-we-are-the-theory-and-practice-of-designing-cities-since-1956, accessed October 12, 2021).
17 Benedetto Gravagnuolo, *La Progettazione Urbana in Europa* (Milan: Edizioni Laterza, 1991), 278.

18 Justus Dahinden, *Urban Structures for the Future* (New York: Praeger, 1972); Banham, *Urban Futures of the Recent Past*.
19 Sorensen, *The Making of Urban Japan*.
20 Cf. Raffaele Pernice, "The Transformation of Tokyo during the 1950s and the Early 1960s: Projects between City Planning and Urban Utopia," *JAABE—Journal of Asian Architecture and Building Engineering* 5(2) (2006): 253–260.

4

THE METABOLISTS IN CONTEXT

Jon Lang

The rapid technological advances of the early twentieth century sparked the imagination of many science-fiction writers. Popular science magazines portrayed cities full of skyscrapers and multi-level movement channels. Architects, too, were enthralled by the possibilities presented by the new machinery.[1] Some of the images they produced were based on projections of what their authors saw as current developments in transportation and building systems; others were based on imagined new technologies that could be employed to form the geometries of future cities. The former group might be regarded as realists, although their images were often fanciful, while the latter was composed of dreamers.

The realists included architects such as Francisco Mujica (1884–1954) in Mexico and Hugh Ferriss (1884–1954) from New York. They saw themselves as anticipatory design scientists. Their drawings show multi-layered cities full of skyscrapers and automobiles, transit, and pedestrians moving vertically, segregated in their own channels. Frank Lloyd Wright (1867–1959) thought similarly. His 1926 drawings of the skyscraper city show a city of tunnels, bridges, and skyscrapers standing on landscaped podiums.[2] In Russia, the constructivists had more dramatic dreams of what cities should be.[3]

The 1928 Wolkenbugel (sky hanger) proposal for Moscow by El Lissitzky (1890–1941) attempted to meet the (narrowly defined) functional requirements of a city using radical geometric forms that touched the ground lightly. The constructivists' goal was to lift buildings off the ground, but with a horizontal layout. They were opposed to skyscrapers. The Hammer and Sickle of Iakov Chernikov (1889–1951) illustrates the intention of freeing-up the ground plane. The Derzhprom complex of buildings (1925–1928) in Kharkiv, Ukraine, is the structure that came closest to meeting the constructivists' aspirations, but it is a more pragmatic total urban design than the constructivists sought. It consists of three buildings with towers linked by skyways, wrapped around a cul-de-sac. El Lissitzky felt that it was too closely tied to the ground. Meanwhile, the rationalists among modernists were promulgating their views of the city through the manifestos and generic ideas of Le Corbusier (1887–1965), the Congrès

DOI: 10.4324/9781003186540-5

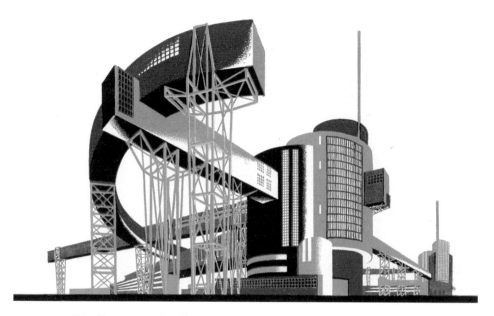

FIGURE 4.1 The Constructivist City: Hammer and Sickle, 1933 by Iakov Chernikov. Digital image 2021, Museum of Modern Art, New York/Scala, Florence.

Internationaux d'Architecture Moderne (CIAM, 1928–1959), and the Bauhaus. Their ideas saw their major implementation after World War II.

The post-World War II years

The postwar years, extending from the establishment of peace accords in 1945 until the end of the 1970s, were imbued with a great sense of optimism after the physical and spiritual devastation of the war in Europe and the Pacific. The problems of urban and city life were perceived to be overwhelming. Entrenched social stratification seemed to present barriers for the transformation of society; poverty and overcrowding were still rife, and the freedom of movement provided by the automobile appeared to be heralding the death of existing cities. They had to be re-invented. What people loved about urban life was forgotten; only its ills could be seen. Architects generally hated the city and wanted to reform it in their own image of a good world.[4]

All kinds of futures were possible with a little imagination. It was in this spirit that many ideas about the morphology of the future city were developed. It was the 1920s updated. Architects and engineers produced many exciting ideas about the geometric, spatial form of the future city. The rationalists led the way.

The mainstream of rationalist thinking about cities can be exemplified by José Luis Sert (1902–1983) and CIAM's view of what form the future Barcelona should take, and the plans for St-Dié, Antwerp, and Algiers proposed by Le Corbusier.[5] The qualities of streets that make a city a vibrant place for life and differentiate one city from another were regarded as antiquated. Much was built, but many schemes based on the Le Corbusian image have now been demolished, being replaced by more traditional, multi-functional schemes. It is an image that, nevertheless, still holds sway in East

FIGURE 4.2 José Luis Sert and CIAM's view of the future city: a design for Barcelona set against Ildefons Cerda's *Eixample*. Source: Sert and CIAM (1944) and Lang (2021). Courtesy of the Frances Loeb Library Fine Arts Library, GSD, Harvard University.

Asian countries. It is also the generic design type that Chinese architects are exporting around the world today. Architecturally bold, the designs have in common a paucity of behavior settings that enrich the daily lives of the people that inhabit them and visitors to them. They lack the vitality of existing urban environments.

Outside the mainstream of CIAM thought and the empiricist response to it, rationalist architects explored many other options for the city.[6] They included groups such as Team X, whose members were disenchanted by the ideology of CIAM and by individual architects in North America, Europe, and Asia. Some advanced the plug-in, clip-on concept.[7] To them, the mobile home was the prototypical, twentieth-century building block. Such units could be plugged into a substantial structure designed to accommodate them. Other architects worked in different directions, but were unified by their advocacy for multi-layered cities. Many were megastructures, a term coined by the Japanese architect Fumiko Maki (b. 1928) and later publicized by Reyner Banham (1922–1988) in his book *Megastructure: Urban Futures of the Recent Past*.[8]

Megastructures

A megastructure is a city or a precinct of a city in a single structure. The subset of interest here consists of a durable frame to which infrastructure elements and units serving a range of instrumental functions can be attached and detached. They have elements that, when their utility passes, can be removed and replaced with new components.[9] The building of such designs was promoted by individual architects and engineers such as Yona Friedman (1923–2020), Paolo Soleri (1919–2013), and Buckminster Fuller (1895–1983), and by groups such as Archigram in Britain. Arguably the collection of architects with the most thoroughly considered ideas was the short-lived Metabolists group in Japan.

In the early 1950s, Friedman presented his Ville Spatiale (a city on stilts/piles) as a way of solving the problems of the existing city. His model city consisted of three-dimensional layers. Each layer would have units developed by individuals to satisfy their own needs. Half of each layer would be left open to allow sunlight to reach the ground. Community facilities would be located, and vehicular circulation would take place on the lowest floor. Pedestrians would reach the upper levels via elevators in the piles. The whole structure, Friedman suggested, could be erected over an existing city, agricultural land, or a water body.[10]

Of all the megastructure proponents, Paolo Soleri most clearly articulated a vision of the future based on a well-developed ideology—arcology, a view of architecture and ecology.[11] He thought the settings that make a city should be clustered together to save resources and that they should be easily renewable. He produced many images of such worlds. Arcosanti, his best-known proposal, is being built, piece-by-piece, in Arizona. It is the only megastructure being implemented and at a much-reduced scale. It is a sculptural masterpiece rather than a lived-in, plug-in city.

Archigram was a contemporary 1960s group whose ideas were presented in their manifesto Archigram I (1961). Its members observed that wealthy people in economically advanced societies led highly mobile lives, and the products that they used were discarded when they were no longer needed. Archigram sought a high-tech, lightweight, modular built environment in which parts could be added and withdrawn as necessary.[12] It was a clip-on architecture. The ideas were presented in beautifully drawn, colorful, hypothetical schemes displaying a futuristic science-fiction aesthetic. One of the illustrative designs that captured the imagination was Walking City (1964), designed by Ron Herron (1930–1996). It was for a massive, mobile structure that could move under its own power to wherever a population of workers was needed. Several such structures could be joined into a unit to form a movable metropolis. Little was said about the qualities of life that they would offer their inhabitants.

Other contemporary rationalist design directions

Several designers saw specific problems that required solving. The vagaries of climates were one. The covering of large areas of the Earth's surface to provide a sheltered,

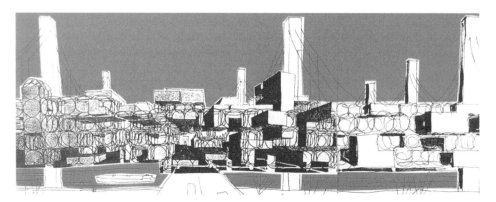

FIGURE 4.3 Yona Friedman's 'Spatial City' concept. Source: Friedman (1959) and Lang (2021). Courtesy of Le Fonds des Dotation Denise y Yona Friedman.

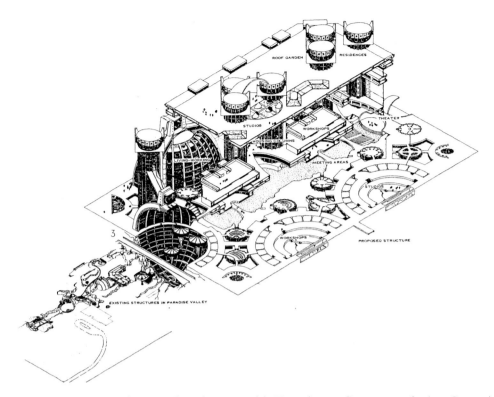

FIGURE 4.4 Arcosanti. Drawing by Tomaki Tanmiura. Courtesy of the Cosanti Foundation.

climate-controlled environment for everyday life was one innovative idea presented to the world. The German architect and structural engineer Frei Otto (1925–2015) proposed a 1.5 square-mile tensile envelope stretching across the frigid arctic environment to accommodate a human settlement. Arctic City (1970) would provide a hospitable environment for the daily lives of 40,000 people living in the far north. Crops and vegetables necessary for their lives could be grown in temperate conditions. Buckminster Fuller offered an alternative climate-controlling structural device in his proposal for New York. He had been experimenting with geodesic dome designs for several years before designing the American Pavilion at Expo 67 in Montreal. The Pavilion consisted of a space frame formed of aluminum tubes forming hexagonal panels. The panels were fitted with plexiglass elements. The whole structure was extremely strong. The idea, he suggested, could be extended to a two-mile-in-diameter (3.2 kilometers) dome over Manhattan.[13] Laissez-faire urban development responding to the demands of the marketplace could take place within it, but there would be neither slipping on ice in winter nor sweating in the summer.

Equally dramatic and large in scale was his vastly different design created with Jamaican American poet and feminist activist June Jordan (1936–2002) to solve social problems.[14] They sought to provide more salubrious and better living accommodation for the residents and businesses of Harlem without displacing them from the areas, although relocating them from their homes and establishments.

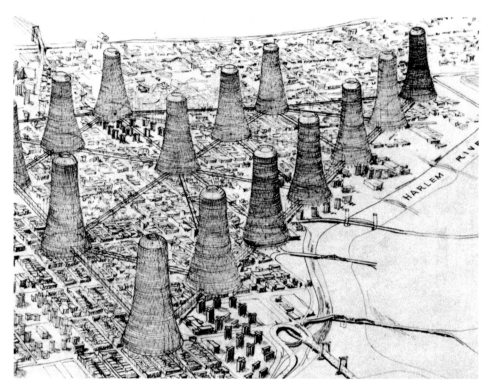

FIGURE 4.5 Skyrise for Harlem. Drawing by Shoji Sadao. Courtesy of the Estate of Buckminster Fuller.

Fuller and Jordan proposed 15 tapering towers for Harlem. Each would be encircled by ramps to enable cars to park at the front door of spacious apartments. Each tower would have shops, recreation facilities, and workshops, and would be linked to other towers by lengthy walkways. Once the towers were in place, the existing built environment would be demolished and replaced by parkland. The whole development would be Le Corbusier's City in a Park. Why Jordan considered, in the face of contemporary evidence, that such an environment would be good for low-income African American families is unclear. Nevertheless, such adventurous thinking and the advanced technology underpinning it captured the imagination of many people.

A disproportionate number of new, geometrically innovative urban structures were proposed by Japanese architects. Perhaps it was in response to the destruction of Hiroshima and Nagasaki. Certainly, many architects in the 1920s, and again in the 1950s, were shaken by the world wars. The group that most thoroughly worked out its ideas was the Metabolists. Yet, how sound were their ideas? What functions of city life did they afford?

The Metabolists

Japanese architects, even more than their European counterparts, had to deal with the havoc of World War II and the profound mental anguish resulting from the destruction of atom- and fire-bombed cities. The city had to possess a new form for assumed new ways of life of people. As such, it was in the mainstream of architectural thought; it is easier to design for imagined ways of life and imagined people than for the diversity of experiences that make life enjoyable.[15] Sociologists, in contrast, have striven to understand cities as they are lived. Some have sought analogies to explain the dynamics of urban growth.

The Chicago School of Sociology of the interwar years, under the direction of Robert E. Park (1864–1944), saw the city as a living organism. Cities, comprising individuals, communities, and the artificial environment, are born, grow, mature, decline, die, and then regenerate. The new replaces the old. Several architects have also found using analogies to be a powerful way to describe and explain their designs. Sometimes the analogy drives the design. Of all the people producing megastructures, the Metabolists both drew their name and their approach to design from analogies to the natural world, but also from allied Buddhist concepts of regeneration. Contemporary images coming from nuclear physics were another source of inspiration.

The Metabolists produced a series of exploratory visions of large, flexible—expandable and subtractable—structures of cities and/or their precincts that were an explicit analogy of organic growth in plants in a way that was largely implicit in the thinking of other clip-on megastructure proponents.[16] In a brief period, they produced an astonishing array of schemes consisting of towering structures with plug-in capsules.[17] Both infrastructure and, more easily, capsules could be replaced when, like decaying elements of plants, they were no longer of use. Several of the proposals were for cities to be built in ocean bays. The best known is the Plan for Tokyo from 1960 to 2025, prepared by Kenzo Tange (1913–2005) and illustrated in Chapter 2 of this volume.

The designs sparked the imagination of other architects around the world. Günther Freuerstein (b. 1925), a Viennese architect, was one. He produced several such explorations along similar lines to those of the Metabolists and of also of Archigram. They included an Urban Utopia for Salzburg.[18] It, too, remained on the drawing board.

The Metabolists were never presented with the opportunity to test their ideas in full. The little that was built, while visually representative of the plug-in idea, was hard architecture. It consisted of fixed feature elements from walls to interior layouts.

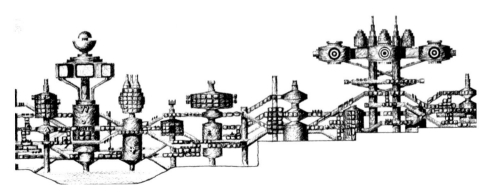

FIGURE 4.6 Salzburg Superpolis, 1965–1967. Source: Justus Dahinden, *Urban Structures for the Future*, trans. Gerald Ohm (New York: Praeger, 1972, 22). Collection of Jon Lang.

68 Jon Lang

Short-lived, as a group, the individual members soon went their own ways, producing more conventional structures in Japan and several other countries that were no doubt influenced by what they learned from their explorations. What, then, was their contribution?

An examination of the functions served (and not served) by the Metabolists' explorations, along with those of other megastructure proponents, enables their contributions to normative architectural theory to be put into perspective. This task is important because the imagery of designs that they produced and the way they submit their proposals to the public gaze continue to seduce architects.

The functions served (and not served) by the range of designs considered here

All the proposals presented here sought to reduce air and water pollution, energy consumption, and waste generation. However, the primary concern was with how their structures functioned: how they would fit together and the mechanisms (often poorly defined) for plugging in their parts. It was an architecture of structural dexterity. As such, much is thoughtful, but, in common, all the designs have little to say about life as lived or about enhancing for everybody the enjoyment of living in cities experienced by those with means. The designs were insensitive to the positive qualities of existing cities.

The megastructure proposals are based on a definition of "function" no broader than that of CIAM. Functionalism was reduced to dealing with the provision of the necessities of a mechanized reality, not a human reality.[19] It was more an *anthropozemic* architecture catering to the need of a mechanized world than an *anthropophilic* one responding to the richness of people's lives.[20] The former is important, but should not dictate the latter.

Architects such as Robert Venturi (1925–2018) and Denise Scott Brown (b. 1931) want a reluctant profession to adopt a broad definition of function as the basis for their work.[21] To understand what urban designs do afford and what they might afford, I, along with others, have argued that the work on the nature of human motivations of the humanist psychologist Abraham Maslow (1908–1970) provides the basis for such a model.[22] The built environment can function to meet people's needs, from survival and safety to the need for belonging, or to higher cognitive needs in addition to the intellectual, aesthetic demands of the cognoscenti. The model must be adapted when considering other animate species, such as songbirds that enrich the sonic landscape of cities and, in some places, creatures such as monkeys, squirrels, and even sloths.

The human needs of comfortable shelter, safety, and efficient movement are basic. The Archigram and Metabolists' designs were supposed to make cities healthier for people by reducing water and air pollution. Their members strove to develop designs that would conserve the natural environment by reducing their footprints on the Earth. They recognized that cities are constantly being changed in a piecemeal manner and sought to enhance the process. All these goals are important. The question is: what did the proponents of all these ideas propose to be the mechanisms or patterns of form to do so? How do they provide for the display of personal identity? The pods of the Metabolists' and Friedman's proposals were designed to afford people the opportunity to shape their living accommodations as they desired. This idea is laudable, but how exactly was this to be done? Once set in place, its components of the megastructures are not easy to change compared to most traditional building types.

How do the large-scale proposals foster or afford the development of a sense of locally based communities? True, for many upper- and middle-class urban populations today in a world of instantaneous communication, neighborhood qualities are largely unimportant other than placing individuals and families in a social status classification and, perhaps, serving them as a local service area. Children roam considerably less independently today than before, and in most rationalist proposals, the environments provide little for them to explore. As Aldo van Eyck noted, around the corner is an endless hygienic boring world. Much the same can be said of the megastructure proposals as they have been presented.

Many megastructure proponents said they were solving social problems. Schemes such as the Fuller-Jordan proposal for Harlem were viewed as a solution to the social inequities and their consequences for poverty-trapped African Americans in a district of Manhattan. As such, its authors fell into the trap of deterministic thinking. The assumption that by changing the built environment, social problems could be eliminated had already been shown to be fallacious.[23] Urban renewal was destroying existing social networks that sustained people. It was also assumed that the residents of Harlem would like to live in environments well-removed from the ground plane of cities and away from street life.

The economic bases of the megastructure towns such as Soleri's Arcosanti were idealistic. Arcosanti was to be an agrarian, crafts-making community. Its future as a self-sustaining entity is uncertain other than as an attraction for tourists interested in its architectural qualities and the creative spirit of its founder. Like most of the other idealized urban structures, it was proposed as a mechanism for reducing urban sprawl by housing a large population on a small unit of land. The compact city is an alternative way of addressing this concern, although civil libertarians are bitterly opposed to the planning policies required to create it.

All these schemes were explorations of ideas, so methods of implementation were poorly considered. It was the dissemination of ideas that was important. However, Buckminster Fuller did argue that his design for doming Manhattan would pay for itself in a decade by reducing the cost of maintaining the public realm.

Lessons for today

Space exploration, which was already being imagined in the late nineteenth century, resulted in the successful landing of human feet on the moon in 1969. It sparked a new generation of images of future habitats for humans. Future cities could be located on other planets or swirl as detached elements in space. Now we are living in an era of changes brought about by the development of information technology. It is easy to be seduced by them in the way that planners in the 1950s embraced the needs of automobile drivers.

We live in a changing world. Making predictions about the future is fraught with difficulties. How far can we look ahead with any certainty? What will cities have to accommodate even one generation ahead in 2045? Will the size of the world's population be stabilizing by then? What will be automated? Will autonomous vehicles be ubiquitous in a decade? Will deliveries be made to specific sites by drones? The city of today is essentially that of 25 years or even 50 years ago. Will the city of 2045 be very different? Changes have occurred much more slowly than our contemporary conceit allows.

FIGURE 4.7   Urban designs for 2045: the mile-tall Sky Mile for Tokyo (left) and the proposal for the smart city of Rublyovo-Arkangelskoye, near Moscow (right). Image courtesy of Kohn Pedersen Fox, architects (left) and a rendering courtesy of Flying-Architecture (right).

The laissez-faire city of taller and taller buildings of diverse geometric forms will continue to dominate urban growth. All cities, of any consequence, will have several urban design projects within them. Some will be dramatic. In vying for attention, they will follow different design paradigms with many hyper-modernist schemes competing for attention. All cities are likely to be smarter both in terms of integrating information and management systems, and as places that creative people want to live. Meanwhile, hyper-modernist urban designs are being produced at varying scales around the world, but particularly in nations aspiring to be seen to be up to date and where cities vie to attract financial investment in a competitive, neoliberal world. The proposal for Arkangelskoye, near Moscow, a work of Zaha Hadid Architects, is an example of this. Proposals for specific projects such as the mile-tall Sky Mile for Tokyo Bay may seem to owe an intellectual debt to the work of the Metabolists, but it does not possess the plug-in, organic characteristics of the Metabolists antecedents.

Ultimately, the architectural aesthetic is largely unimportant to anyone other than the cognoscenti. Buildings can take various forms provided the quality of the urban realm and the behavior settings that enrich life are developed. The health of the biogenic environment is equally crucial for the future of people, other species, and the planet itself. The nature of streets, squares, and other elements of the public realm becomes crucial in defining the quality of a city. In looking ahead, what is more important is to establish a rich behavioral program before the urban design and architectural programs are established.

Looking ahead

Today, like a century ago after World War I, we are gripped by the possibilities of new technologies. Although the effect of the emerging communications technology was yet to be felt, 60 years ago, observers such as Marshal McLuhan (1911–1980) were predicting that it would result in a world where the territorially based community would be replaced by audio-visual contacts among people. "We shape our tools and, thereafter, the tools shape us" was McLuhan's message, echoing Winston Churchill's observation on the internal layout of the Houses of Parliament in London.[24] Change has been slower in coming than expected. The city in 2045 is likely to be much as it is today.

Despite all the predictions that neighborhoods no longer make sense when propinquity is unimportant, in an era where adults live metropolitan lives and children no longer roam, a close examination of cities everywhere shows that the local neighborhood remains important as a living environment and as a mechanism for establishing a sense of place and identity for its residents. Cities and their precincts need to be considered a nested, often overlapping set of behavior settings that serves a multiplicity of functions for a range of people and not as simplified versions that fit the images (and program) of architects seeking geometric novelty in their design ideas. Urban designs, whether at the city or block level, need to be based as much on maintaining what people enjoy about their lives as on resolving malfunctions in the existing environment. The latter seems to be overwhelming, so, in attempting to resolve them, we forget about the former. The megastructure proposals were simply not functional enough.

Conclusion

The dividing line between utopian and dystopian thinking is often blurred. During the twentieth century, architects presented the world with a host of manifestos on the design of cities.[25] Each addressed specific functions of the built environment. Buckminster Fuller, Yona Friedman, the Archigram Group, and the Metabolists produced a rich set of generic designs and specific proposals for the city employing advanced versions of existing technologies. Many of their proposals continue to receive accolades and design awards for the bold innovativeness of their designs.

In looking at the ideas presented in this chapter, several unaddressed questions arise: what is the model of men, women, and children of different physical and social competencies living in different cultural and terrestrial zones implicit in the proposals? What are their imagined ways of life? What happens to all the qualities of existing cities that people, including the proponents of the concepts presented here themselves, enjoy—and that people have enjoyed for centuries? Do we really live in "Kleenex" societies in which everything has a short life and is disposable? Are the Metabolists' designs more adaptable than those afforded by the patterns of the laissez-faire-built city? What are the multiplier and side effects of the designs? How much embodied energy would they possess? And the list goes on. The mainstream architectural thinkers consider these questions to be irrelevant; it is the boldness of the architectural idea that counts.

However, it would be "a poor world," as the Welsh poet W. H. Davies (1871–1940) noted, "if we have no time to stand and stare."[26] The same is true if we do not have time to examine possibilities for future living environments for all animate and inanimate species. According to the theoretical physicist Stephen Hawking (1942–2018), we have only between 1,000 and 10,000 years of possible life left on our planet. If the world continues to warm up and we fail to find an alternative planet to inhabit, maybe we will have to re-examine the ideas of, at least, Buckminster Fuller and the Metabolists.

Notes

1 Reyner Banham, *Theory and Design during the First Machine Age* (Cambridge, MA: MIT Press, 1960).
2 Frank Lloyd Wright, *Skyscraper Regulation, 1926* (Scottsdale: Frank Lloyd Wright Foundation, 1969).
3 Moisei Ginzburg, *Style and Epoch*, trans. Anatole Senkevitch (Cambridge, MA: MIT Press, 1982), https://monoskop.org/images/e/eb/Ginzburg_Moisei_Style_and_Epoch.pdf.

4 Morton White and Lucia White, *The Intellectual versus the City: From Thomas Jefferson to Frank Lloyd Wright* (New York: New American Library, 1964).
5 Jon Lang, *The Routledge Companion to Twentieth and Early Twenty-First Century Urban Design* (Oxford: Routledge, 2020).
6 Lang, *The Routledge Companion to Twentieth and Early Twenty-First Century Urban Design.*
7 Reyner Banham, *A Clip-on Architecture* (Minneapolis: Walker Arts Centre, 1965).
8 Reyner Banham, *Megastructure: Urban Futures of the Recent Past* (London: Thames & Hudson, 1976).
9 Banham, *A Clip-on Architecture.*
10 Yona Friedman, *Prodomo*, English edn (Barcelona: Aktar Publishing, 2006), https://issuu.com/actar/docs/prodomo.
11 Paolo Soleri, *Arcology: The City in the Image of Man* (Cambridge, MA: MIT Press, 1969).
12 Justus Dahinden, *Urban Structures for the Future*, trans. Gerald Ohm (New York: Praeger, 1972).
13 Richard Buckminster Fuller, "Domed Cities: Design Science-Engineering, an Economic Success of All Humanity," in *Urban Structures for the Future* (New York: Praeger, 1972), 202–203.
14 Claire Schwartz, "June Jordan and Buckminster Fuller Tried to Redesign Harlem," *New Yorker*, August 22, 2020, https://www.newyorker.com/culture/culture-desk/when-june-jordan-and-buckminster-fuller-tried-to-redesign-harlem.
15 Russell Ellis and Dana Cuff (eds), *Architects' People* (New York: Oxford University Press, 1989).
16 Noboru Kawazoe (ed.), *Metabolism 1960: The Proposals for New Urbanism* (Tokyo: Bijutsu Shuppansha, 1960).
17 Dahinden, *Urban Structures for the Future.*
18 Günther Freuerstein, *Urban Fiction: Strolling through Ideal Cities from Antiquity to the Present Day* (Fellbach: Edition Ariel Menges, 2006).
19 Mónica Arellano, "Archigram and the Dystopia of Small-Scale Living Spaces," *Arch-Daily*, trans. Maggie Johnson, https://www.archdaily.com/948954/archigram-and-the-dystopia-of-small-scale-living-spaces.
20 Kiyo Izumi, "Some Psycho-social Considerations of Environmental Design," mimeograph.
21 Denise Scott Brown, "The Redefinition of Function," in *Architecture as Signs and Systems for a Mannerist Time* (Cambridge, MA: MIT Press, 2004), 142–174.
22 Jon Lang and Walter Moleski, *Functionalism Revisited: Architectural Theory and Practice and the Behavioral Sciences* (Farnham: Ashgate, 2010).
23 Herbert Gans, *The Urban Villagers: Group and Class Structure in the Life of Italian Americans* (New York: The Free Press, 1962).
24 Marshall McLuhan, *Understanding Media: The Extensions of Man* (New York: McGraw-Hill, 1964).
25 Lang, *The Routledge Companion to Twentieth and Early Twenty-First Century Urban Design.*
26 William Henry Davies, "Leisure," in *Songs of Joy and Others* (London: A. C. Fifield, 1911), 15.

5

THE INFRASTRUCTURE OF CARE

Metabolist Architecture as a Social Catalyst

Peter Šenk

At the World Design Conference in Tokyo in 1960, the Metabolist group emphasized mobility, growth, and change. Although these themes had been discussed in architectural circles before, they were given strong organic imagery and connotations by the Metabolists, who compared them to biological processes.

This chapter discusses a selection of contemporary urban regeneration themes illuminated through the lens of Metabolist ideas, particularly when understood as enabling, directing, and caring infrastructural interventions. The organic analogies present in the writings and projects of the Metabolists form a background to the perception of the interconnectedness of concepts and proposals on the urban environment that addresses contemporary urban sustainability issues. In addition, two specific concepts used by the Metabolists are exposed, namely, those of *artificial ground* or *artificial land* and the *capsule*. These relate to the social and personal spheres, respectively. Organic analogies inform material practice at both the urban and architectural levels, and, consequently, act at the political level.

While the space of flows may be abstracted in the analysis of the contemporary city shaped by flows of materials, energy, people, and information, these are embedded in the material world in the form of infrastructure. In our contemporary era, infrastructure is the most visible trace of human enterprise in the Anthropocene. It results from our technological development, critically affecting our ecosystem. In response to our activities, new environmental conditions determine the scope and directions of future development. The term "infrastructure" refers to a wide range of programs or community services and includes public utilities, transportation, and energy. It further denotes other (public) programs such as education, healthcare, science, sports, social care, culture, and housing.[1] As we will further elaborate, the term is used in its broader sense—as a physical substratum enabling other programs to thrive. Realizing public space through infrastructure may still be a reasonable, generally accepted path. However, using it in response to housing scarcity as a city infrastructure problem may be more challenging still.

The Metabolists' concepts of the interconnectedness of common (public or semipublic) *artificial ground* infrastructure and private prefabricated housing infrastructure as

DOI: 10.4324/9781003186540-6

74 Peter Šenk

capsules in relation to civic space can be reflected in contemporary cities. In the latter, open public space, together with affordable housing, is becoming an important social and governance agenda issue and is seen as a key component of complex infrastructure. Simultaneously, housing can itself be viewed as an "infrastructure of care."[2]

The infrastructure of care—three layers in Metabolist thought that consider the contemporary city: the urban environment, the social and the personal

Organic analogy: toward the sustainability paradigm

In *Metabolism 1960: The Proposals for New Urbanism* manifesto,[3] presented at the 1960 World Design Conference in Tokyo by the architects Kiyonori Kikutake, Fumihiko Maki, Masato Ōtaka, and Noriaki (Kisho) Kurokawa, the critic Noboru Kawazoe, and the designer Kiyoshi Awazu, issues of mobility, growth, and change resonated with their contemporaries, who emphasized the meaning of transport infrastructure and its influence on societal changes in general, and community changes in particular.[4]

Metabolist organic analogies in specific architectural propositions were diverse, informative, suggestive, instrumental, and poetic. They were reflected in architectural projects through concepts and drawings and their communication, explanations, and graphics, with several given evocative names. These include Kurokawa's Helix City (1961), Plant-Type Community and Bamboo-Type Community (1960), and Mushroom-Shaped House (1960); Kikutake's Tree-Shaped House (1966); Maki's Golgi Structures (1968); Ekuan's Pumpkin House and Tortoise House (1964); and Kawazoe's enigmatic writings, such as "I Want to Be a Seashell," published in *Metabolism 1960*.

Nature has been an inherent reference in human thought throughout history; however, the Metabolists' ideals were brought to the fore at the crucial moment of "reinvented nature," forming part of the general discourse of the 1960s. With his response to the growing concerns of urban ecology, from 1965, Abel Wolman was attributed as the founder of *urban metabolism*.[5] He defined the metabolic requirements of the city as "all the materials and commodities needed to sustain the city's inhabitants at home, at work and at play," with water supply, waste disposal, and air pollution control as central issues.[6] In this context, the legacy of the Japanese Metabolists' proposals and writings is occasionally acknowledged and highlighted in the ecological sciences in general and industrial ecology in particular. Kurokawa is credited with the notion of a continuously changing urban system as an ecosystem,[7] which relates to contemporary studies of biomimicry and flows.[8] According to Kurokawa, an understanding of the continuity and harmony of technology, humanity, and nature in modern society provided Japanese design with universal validity.[9] Simultaneously, cultural resilience as a notion of a national identity system was achieved. For Meike Schalk,[10] the Metabolists approached this less in an ecosystemic fashion than as an adaptation urgency in times of crisis in technical, socio-ecological, and cultural terms. Moreover, their approach can be seen as a step toward contemporary sustainability thinking.

However, alongside the philosophy, analogies, technical solutions, and project names, a level of branding appears extremely effective in presenting the Metabolists' concepts. Recognizable projects were also supported by graphic design. The cyclical processes embedded in Metabolist projects can be related to contemporary sustainability issues. The branded *sustainism* of Michiel Schwarz and Joost Elffers,[11] with its expressive graphic symbols, could be seen as interpretations of Taoist *yin* and *yang* varieties, traditional Japanese crests, and the derived Metabolism symbol designed by Awazu—all of which were placed on international display by Günther Nitschke[12] in *Architectural Design* in May 1967.

Metabolist infrastructure: capsules and the artificial ground

The concept of "duality-in-unity" can be seen as transposing the Japanese tradition into modern times by technical means. It is manifested in the established relationship between the parts of architectural or urban infrastructures according to their intended durability. The stable, durable, or "permanent" megastructural cores or frameworks, referred to as "formal vertical artificial ground" or "a-formal in-between spaces," serve and support the metabolic transitivity of unit spaces. These spaces are primarily capsular living units with shorter lifespans, which are connected to the "permanent" structure. While the concept of artificial ground may not be regarded as new, we can at least trace the development of modern infrastructural-megastructural platforms to Le Corbusier's 1930s Plan Obus for Algiers. Takamasa Yoshizaka coined the phrase "artificial ground" in the mid-1950s;[13] it was utilized by group members and those associated with Metabolism in a Metabolic spirit that orchestrates architecture as second nature. However, the differentiation of its elements is not an end in itself. On the one hand, this enables the establishment of a relationship between buildings and the inhabiting organism. On the other hand, it extends to accepting the transitivity of

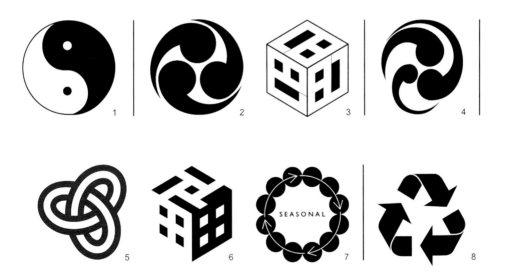

FIGURE 5.1   1) Taoist yin and yang; 2) and 3) traditional Japanese crests (featured on the cover of *Architectural Design* magazine in May 1967); 4) Metabolism symbol designed by Kyoshi Awazu; 5), 6), and 7) *sustainism* symbols, designed by Joost Elffers (Source: Michiel Schwarz and Joost Elffers, *Sustainism is the New Modernism: A Cultural Manifesto for the Sustainist Era* (New York: Distributed Art Publishers, 2010)); 8) recycling symbol.

76 Peter Šenk

individual life and understanding the public platform as a permanent structure that transcends it. The flexibility and adaptability in these propositions are also related to social and political demand for individual power and autonomy in Japan's emerging modern society.[14]

The concept of the "living or functional unit"—the *capsule*—is defined as a minimal, compact, mobile, fully equipped, and ergonomically shaped living or functional unit with prescribed durability. Its development can be traced through modernist discourses on subsistence minimum, functionalism, technology, utopian, extreme, mobile, self-sufficient, expendable, and pop designs for housing and residential equipment.[15] In direct response to changing social conditions, the problems of urban life and housing raised by Kawazoe,[16] or demands to accommodate new lifestyles enabling post-World War II personal and social transformations, the concept's global legacy can be found in numerous domains: the universalist technocracy of Buckminster Fuller; the ad hoc expression of counterculture movements; the avant-garde directions of the second machine age through ethics and aesthetics, existentialism, and pop; New Brutalism and the *une architecture autre* of Reyner Banham, Alison and Peter Smithson, Archigram, and Cedric Price; and the Japanese Metabolists, with Kiyonori Kikutake, Kisho Kurokawa, and Kenji Ekuan's GK Design as the most visible pioneers in Japan.[17] Justus Dahinden[18] recognized the novelty and importance of radical technological, self-contained microenvironments while highlighting the importance of the public sphere and community. These latter were supposedly projected and under an undefined threat in the proposed urban structures of the future. While offering liberation from existing social structures through architecture, they relied heavily on the constraints of accepted technology of the time. Arata Isozaki, who, with Kenzo Tange, was very much associated with but was a non-member of the Metabolist group, reacted to the uncritical technological approach of some Metabolist projects through his dystopian views of "the city as ruin." He rejected the idea of the possibility of social revolution through technology.[19] In a different vein, Kurokawa, too, disbelieved in a social environment created by urbanists and architects relying on technology alone. Knowing that a system is a necessity in spatial planning, he advocated a non-repressive participatory system emphasizing the individual and his or her empowerment: a space divided into independent shelters, where each inhabitant "can fully develop his [sic] individuality."[20]

Kisho Kurokawa, as the most visible capsule theorist in Japan, related the capsule's development to the concepts of "unit space" and "cell" already present in the late 1950s. Besides Kurokawa's most recognizable built examples of capsules in the early 1970s (classified as *connective cells*) at the 1970 Osaka World Expo—Takara Beautillion and the Capsule House in the Theme Pavilion, followed by Nakagin Capsule Tower, Capsule House "K," and Leisure Capsule for Usami Capsule Village—GK Industrial Design Associates' *autonomous* capsules, the Komatsu Ski Lodge (1965), and "YADOKARI" Hermit Crab Capsule Lodge (1969), deserve special mention. Kurokawa's theoretical proposal *Capsule Declaration* was a reaction to the conditions of Japan's emerging modern society and a manifesto for its transformation—it was also intended to be facilitated by architecture.[21] Although Kurokawa seemed primarily focused on capsules, their spatial locations in communal space were anticipated as a "spiritual haven": the *social space* that also provides for the individual's identity. Kurokawa describes these spaces as information centers, multifunctional spaces of "spiritual fulfillment," meeting points or in-between spaces, and self-organized spaces that form changing and changeable "temporal communities." Despite the potential misfortune of such spaces becoming contemporary, controlled *non-places*,[22] the Metabolist approach is highly affirmative for the discipline of architecture. Unlike classical urbanism, which used a geometric approach to establish order and place-related communities, the Metabolist approach had the ambition to create a dynamic, open structure of cities and buildings, and a multifunctional layout in which temporal communities and events can take place. Architecture, according to Kurokawa, is "nothing more nor less than an aggregate of countless functions (therefore, capsules) and may be defined as a group which comes into being when a number of capsules encounter each other."[23] With such an approach, contemporary public participation becomes apparent and moves beyond the notion of architecture as a mechanism of societal control. Architecture is no longer treated as a defining agent, but as an enabling agent: "architecture is no longer a device to control men: It is a means whereby men control technology and machinery."[24] This is a noble affirmative proposition for an architecture of freedom with utopian zeal. However, skepticism about the technological environment was also shared by Fumihiko Maki. In his description of megastructure or megaform, he expresses the warning: "Technology must not dictate choices to us in our cities. We must learn to select modes of action from among the possibilities technology presents in physical planning."[25]

In the megastructures tradition, Kiyonori Kikutake established a duality between the artificial land and prefabricated "plug-in" or "clip-on" living units in his urban and architectural projects in the late 1950s, albeit from a different position. In his 1958 project, Tower-Shaped Community, Kikutake shows that the capsular living cells, for which he used a different name *move-net*, were not his main focus. Already in his early work, he positioned architecture and urbanism as agents of social change. While the capsular living units are transient and steel-made with plastic interior finishes, the artificial land (megastructure or infrastructural core) is intended to be concrete-built. The 157-meter-high cylindrical tower was planned to operate as a production plant for 1,250 living units and attached to its perimeter. To conceptually close the cycle, after the living unit had completed its duty, it would be "remanufactured for the new housing unit for [sic] new family."[26] Since a clear division exists between "the served" and "servant" spaces in many Metabolists' proposals, aided by the terminology of Louis Kahn, Kiyonori Kikutake nurtured the supporting servant spaces as crucial agents in the Metabolic transformation of the city. While Kahn explained his concept of "master space" or "served space" in schools, using the classroom as an example in contrast to the corridor, which he treated as servant space, Kikutake opposed this assessment. Indeed, unlike the classroom, with its mainly one-way communication, the corridor was more important to Kikutake: it contained more information about many people and different generations, and formed and provided a network system; it should have been called the master space.[27]

Kikutake's position should also be understood in its biographical context.[28] Following his landowner family's social role of selflessly helping people in times of disaster, famine, and war, Kikutake sought to re-introduce this tradition of *care* in postwar Japan's social and spatial contexts. His proposals were a response to the scarcity of free land for construction due to the proliferation of low-rise private housing, the limited possibilities for providing public infrastructure, and even the "state of confusion and paralysis in metropolitan cities," as stated in *Metabolism 1960*.[29]

Such a proposal of vertical infrastructure was intended as one of housing infrastructure. It was meant to free up space for necessary *horizontal civic infrastructure* while establishing the identification point for inhabitants. Similarly, Kurokawa called for the architecture of the street and the architecture of the plaza as a "means of regaining the organic function of the cities by designing streets integrated with architecture and architecture containing streets."[30] In this context, Kikutake and Kurokawa both emphasize the importance of the civic infrastructure, the street, as a traditional and modern social as well as structural space of the city.

The expressed longing for a democratic society is similarly observed in Fumihiko Maki's conceptualization of urban spatial formations. When Maki proposed a taxonomy of *collective forms*—namely, the classical-architectural *compositional form*, the structural-technological *megastructural form*, and the sequential *group form*—he offered a contemporary adaptation of traditional contextualism with the latter. His proposal for the group form transcends the top-down logic of megastructural infrastructures, since the former is developed from the bottom up from within society. It reflects his idealistic yet explicit concern that "the biggest issue in contemporary politics and economics is the organization of an orderly society without sacrificing the fundamental freedom of the individuals who make up the society."[31] A group's coherence depends on creating exterior spaces and architectural forms. At the same time, its total image relies on the group's continuity, even if some of its elements are added in, taken out, or changed.[32] These elements of group form, even interchangeable ones, "are often the essence of collectivity, a unifying force, functionally, socially, and spatially," and the form should derive from the needs of the environment.[33]

While megastructures provided a technological platform for the capsules, the free configurations on the fringes of anti-bureaucracy, uniformity, systematic thinking, or even anarchy, were likewise interpreted by Kurokawa[34] and Ekuan.[35] These could be understood as an ad hoc free logic of a group form. Kurokawa even described capsule architecture as a "group form which expresses the individuum."[36] In the case of megastructural capsular formation, this may contradict Maki's definition, since, in his view, the "group" significantly does not depend on megastructure. Nevertheless, the in-between social spaces formed on the artificial ground between buildings or capsules, either in a megastructural formation or in a group form, can be considered as the civic space of the *infrastructural system*.

Since the infrastructure approach is traditionally concerned with constructing the site itself, with preparing the ground, services, networks, and conditions for future buildings, and with programs, movement, communication, and events,[37] open Metabolists' proposals can be seen as twofold propositions. The *artificial ground* as both megastructure and an in-between space of the group form is an infrastructural architecture par excellence. On the one hand, it establishes a public or semi-public, in-between, vertical or horizontal infrastructure on which further development can occur. It provides identity, establishes a locality with a sense of place in the space of flows, and becomes an "urban organnector"—an organic urban connector or media space, to use Kurokawa's terms[38]—by locating a concentrated and compacted program while freeing up space for horizontal civic infrastructure.

The plug-in capsule—an artificial ground relationship—utopianly hinted at social transformation based on freedom, individualization, and mobility with the promise of participatory urban development, is considered (on a metaphorical level at least) to be a model in contemporary urbanism.[39] The plug-in can be defined as a kind of procedural type of urban design that refers to designing and implementing an infrastructure project to achieve a catalytic effect.[40] As a mode of thinking, it can be regarded a continuation of the Metabolism discourse with either a megastructure or group form analogy.

Further, it can be understood as analogous to enclosures in various scales of contemporary urban agglomerations. In Capsule Declaration, Kurokawa explains that instead of the unity of the whole, groups or clusters within the segmented city or architecture can be referred to as infrastructure that stimulates diversity and its Metabolic character.[41] It is an idea of open compositions of different programs with self-contained production processes, but which share the in-between social space. However, since Kurokawa believed in the total fusion of the architectural capsule with

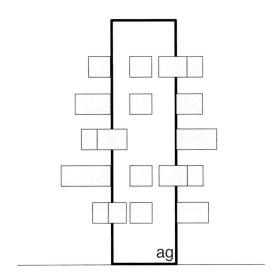

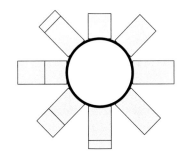

FIGURE 5.2 Metabolic infrastructure: vertical megastructural form. Artificial ground (ag) with program (capsule) units. Plan and elevation. Adapted from Šenk, 2013.

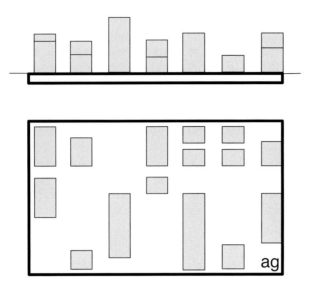

FIGURE 5.3 Metabolic infrastructure: horizontal megastructural/group form. Artificial ground (ag) with program (capsule) units. Plan and elevation. Adapted from Šenk, 2013.

an organism and cyborg architecture can be understood as a liberating proposition, this brings doubts and the risk of failure at different scales. Just as technology allows the individual to adapt to the small-scale capsule beyond one's desires, a similar threat can be expected with contemporary technological *smart city* solutions.

The form that these concepts enable provides the legibility of infrastructural formations crucial to understanding one's individual position in the territory and their relation to the collective.[42] Coupled with Kikutake's ambition to achieve a truly Metabolist architecture that holds symbolic potential for connecting an individual to the community and architecture to the city,[43] the infrastructural logic of interference with the existing city demands distinct architectural operativity and expression—in this case, directed by an organic metaphor as guiding principle.

Infrastructure is about care

In the infrastructural approach, the duality of architectural and urbanistic is overcome, melted beyond specialization. When the basic function of architecture is considered protection from the atmospheric impacts and maintenance of the body's vital functions, the notion of the architect as a specialist working within the professional bubble of the discipline appears contradictory. Nevertheless, the value of architecture, which exceeds simply furnishing the above requirements, goes beyond the technical or the technocratic. It can inspire, provide a cultural framework in which social relations flourish, support transformational processes of social habits and personal fulfillment, and stimulate the imagination. In this respect, the Metabolists' supporting or framing artificial ground with embedded living units can be seen as a care-based concept in which infrastructure is treated architecturally. It is a sound solution to emergent problems in the city and provides them a much-needed imaginative aspect. Fisher and Tronto's[44] definition of "care" is broad, but is applicable to environmental and urban issues. It suggests that "caring be viewed as a species activity that includes everything that we do to maintain, continue, and repair our 'world' so that we can live in it as well as possible. That world includes our bodies, ourselves, and our environment, all of which we seek to interweave in a complex, life-sustaining web."

Deeply immersed in the sustainability paradigm with economic, environmental, and social aspects, though not traditionally considered as such, Elke Krasny[45] views architecture as a form of *care*. A similar argument can be made for infrastructure. The environmental and social aspects are particularly emphasized in this concept. From an architectural viewpoint (as with other activities), this is understood as the reciprocal process of caregiving and caretaking. It means enabling multiple caring activities, especially when we enter the city environment. An agenda of care reveals the operativity of infrastructural architecture as an urban Metabolic agent.

Conclusion

In emphasizing themes of mobility, growth, and change, Metabolist critical revisionism derived from the uniquely Japanese tradition. It drew on engineering, modern technology, and economics in an attempt to create the conditions for Japan's emerging modern society. The organic analogy has been observed on three levels: the urban environment, the social, and the personal. Moreover, the relationship between the social, the individual, community building, and providing a personal retreat was traced in the Metabolists' architectural concepts of artificial ground and compact, prefabricated, mobile housing units (i.e., capsules). This relationship can be reflected in contemporary cities, with their trends of micro-apartments and new collective living.

With the prescribed various durability of architectural and urban elements, the cyclical "organic" process of creation, decay, and perpetual re-creation was envisaged. In this sense, elements of contemporary concepts of urban metabolism, circular economy, and the ecosystemic metaphor of cities represented resource efficiency and closed loops. All outputs are potential inputs[46] that can be recognized. Metabolism and its Japanese name stand for renewal and regeneration, and encompass meanings related to the material and cultural, including spiritual domains. In this respect, the Metabolists' comprehensive approach, which calls for interdisciplinarity, research, and an understanding of the complex economic, societal, energetic, and ecological functioning of urban systems, can be seen as a valid and valuable precursor to contemporary sustainability thinking.

Beyond utopianism, the Metabolists responded to spatial and social needs, and were eager to implement proposals that were also technically supported. In contemporary times, the infrastructural plug-in concept enables participatory planning with the principle of "forming conditions" and not "conditioning forms." In the infrastructure approach, the duality of architectural and urban planning is overcome and committed to interdisciplinarity. As support to unfolding life, infrastructure enables programs, activities, and events, while setting up locations and places, which adhere to a public character. Infrastructural architecture is connective, participatory, and caring.

On the other hand, Metabolist proposals were the product of the technological and scientific revolution, and an awareness of the urban environment as an artificial formation. As with many contemporary Western examples, the confrontation of demands for open opportunities for all was accompanied by concerns about the future and potential threats posed by still-unfathomable technological progress. In this regard, the artificial environments in Metabolist projects can be read as an illustration of settings with potential threats to idealized ecological, humanistic, democratic principles. Structures conceptually based on openness, freedom, and participation could be turned into their opposite by management and control mechanisms supported by the same "liberating" technology. Designed as technological habitats that meet the psycho-physical needs of the modern individual, capsules and artificial grounds can also be interpreted as acontextual and controlled (and controllable) instruments for conditioning, with individual and societal adaptation in transcending democratic principles. While the Metabolist projects may inspire the search for eco-urban regeneration possibilities of the future, they also provide a platform to reflect on technological solutions for the contemporary *smart city*.

In this sense, Metabolist proposals for changeable, growing, responsive, and responsible building typologies and infrastructures offer tools to reflect on our contemporary conditions and can be regarded as an optimistic affirmation of architecture as a social catalyst.

Notes

1 Peter Šenk, "Arhitektura infrastruktura," *Architect's Bulletin* 223 (2020): 20–23.
2 Emma R. Power and Kathleen J. Mee, "Housing: An Infrastructure of Care," *Housing Studies* 35(3) (2020): 484–505.
3 Noburo Kawazoe et al., *Metabolism 1960: The Proposals for New Urbanism* (Tokyo: Bijutsu Shuppansha, 1960).
4 Alison M. Smithson (ed.), *Team 10 Primer* (Cambridge, MA: MIT Press, 1974).
5 Sabine Barles, "Society, Energy and Materials: The Contribution of Urban Metabolism Studies to Sustainable Urban Development Issues," *Journal of Environmental Planning and Management* 5(4) (2010): 439–455; Christopher Kennedy, John Cuddihy, and Joshua Engel-Yan, "The Changing Metabolism of Cities," *Journal of Industrial Ecology* 11(2) (2007): 43–59.
6 Abel Wolman, "The Metabolism of Cities," *Scientific American* 213(3) (1965): 178–193.
7 Kisho Kurokawa, *Metabolism in Architecture* (London: Studio Vista, 1977).
8 Vanesa Castán Broto, Adriana Allen, and Elizabeth Rapoport, "Interdisciplinary Perspectives on Urban Metabolism," *Journal of Industrial Ecology* 16(6) (2012): 851–861; Martin Dijst et al., "Exploring Urban Metabolism—Towards an Interdisciplinary Perspective," *Resources, Conservation, and Recycling* 132 (2018): 190–203.
9 Kurokawa, *Metabolism in Architecture.*
10 Meike Schalk, "The Architecture of Metabolism. Inventing a Culture of Resilience," *Arts (Basel)* 3(2) (2014): 279–297.
11 Michiel Schwarz and Joost Elffers, *Sustainism is the New Modernism: A Cultural Manifesto for the Sustainist Era* (New York: Distributed Art Publishers, 2010).
12 Günther Nitschke, "The Metabolists," *Architectural Design* (May 1967): 207.
13 Rem Koolhaas and Hans Ulrich Obrist, *Project Japan: Metabolism Talks* (Cologne: Taschen, 2011).
14 Cherie Wendelken, "Putting Metabolism Back in Place," in *Anxious Modernisms: Experimentation in Postwar Architecture Culture*, ed. Sarah Williams Goldhagen and Réjean Lagault (Cambridge, MA: MIT Press, 2000), pp. 279–299.
15 Peter Šenk, *Capsules: Typology of Other Architecture* (New York: Routledge, 2018).
16 Noboru Kawazoe, *Contemporary Japanese Architecture* (Tokyo: Kokusai Bunka Shinkokai, 1968).
17 Šenk, *Capsules.*

18 Justus Dahinden, *Urban Structures for the Future* (New York: Praeger, 1972).
19 Zhongjie Lin, *Kenzo Tange and the Metabolist Movement: Urban Utopias of Modern Japan* (Abingdon: Routledge, 2010); Günther Nitschke, *Architectural Design* (October 1964): 496–520; Hajime Yatsuka, "Architecture in the Urban Desert: A Critical Introduction to Japanese Architecture after Modernism," in *Oppositions Reader: Selected Readings from a Journal for Ideas and Criticism in Architecture, 1973–1984*, ed. K. Michael Hays (New York: Princeton Architectural Press, 1981), 253–287. The article was published in *Oppositions* 23 (1981).
20 Kurokawa, *Metabolism in Architecture*, 79.
21 Kisho Kurokawa, "Oh! Saibogu no Okite [Oh! The Code of the Cyborg]," *SD: Space Design* 3 (1969): 50–53; Kurokawa, *Metabolism in Architecture*, 75–85.
22 Marc Augé, *Non-places: Introduction to an Anthropology of Supermodernity* (London: Verso, 1995).
23 Kurokawa, *Metabolism in Architecture*, 85.
24 Ibid.
25 Fumihiko Maki and Mark Mulligan, *Nurturing Dreams: Collected Essays on Architecture and the City* (Cambridge, MA: MIT Press, 2008), 48.
26 Kikutake, in Kawazoe et al., *Metabolism 1960*, 19.
27 Kiyonori Kikutake, interview by Peter Šenk, *unpublished interview*, Tokyo, June 18, 2009, trans. Hiroshi Kohno), audio transcription and authorized text, author's archive.
28 Kikutake, *unpublished interview*; Kiyonori Kikutake and Maurizio Vitta, *Kiyonori Kikutake: From Tradition to Utopia* (Milano: l'Arca Edizioni, 1997); Koolhaas and Obrist, *Project Japan*.
29 Kikutake, in Kawazoe et al., *Metabolism 1960*, 10.
30 Kurokawa, *Metabolism in Architecture*, 180.
31 Maki, in Kawazoe et al., *Metabolism 1960*, 58.
32 Maki and Mulligan, *Nurturing Dreams*.
33 Fumihiko Maki, "Notes on Collective Form," *Japan Architect* 4 (1994): 247–98. First published as *Investigations in Collective Form* (Washington University: School of Architecture, 1964).
34 Kurokawa, "Oh! Saibogu no Okite"; Kurokawa, *Metabolism in Architecture*.
35 "GK: Kono Ten-i-muhou na Kotai no Sahou" [GK: The Proprieties of This Flawlessly Composed Organism]," *SD – Space Design* 3 (1969): 54–55.
36 Kurokawa, *Metabolism in Architecture*, 105.
37 Stan Allen, "Infrastructural Urbanism," in *Points+Lines: Diagrams and Projects for the City* (New York: Princeton Architectural Press, 1999), 46–57.
38 Kawazoe et al., *Metabolism 1960*; Kurokawa, *Metabolism in Architecture*.
39 Peter Šenk, "The Plug-in Concept: Technology and Aesthetics of Change," *Arhitektura Raziskave* 1 (2013): 42–51.
40 Jon T. Lang, *Urban Design: A Typology of Procedures and Products* (Oxford/Burlington, MA: Elsevier/Architectural Press, 2005).
41 Kurokawa, *Metabolism in Architecture*.
42 Neeraj Bhatia, "Collective Form: Forming a Collective," *Log* (Summer 2020): 41–50.
43 Kikutake, in Kawazoe et al., *Metabolism 1960*.
44 Berenice Fisher and Joan C. Tronto, "Toward a Feminist Theory of Caring," in *Circles of Care: Work and Identity in Women's Lives*, ed. Emily K. Abel and Margaret K. Nelson (New York: State University of New York Press, 1990), 35–62, at 40.
45 Elke Krasny, "Architecture and Care," in *Critical Care: Architecture and Urbanism for a Broken Planet*, ed. Angelika Fitz and Elke Krasny (Cambridge, MA: MIT Press, 2019), 33–41.
46 Josephine Kaviti Musango, Paul Currie, and Blake Robinson, *Urban Metabolism for Resource-Efficient Cities: From Theory to Implementation* (Paris: UN Environment, 2017).

6

"SUNDAY CARPENTER" METABOLISM

Artificial-Land Housing and Resident Decision-Making

Casey Mack

In 1961, the Metabolist Noboru Kawazoe, the group's operative critic, envisioned that an increase in free time for Japanese people would allow a cultural flourishing in domestic life, leading to the expansion beyond the weekend of what he calls the "'Sunday carpenter' of the Do-it-yourself persuasion."[1] Sunday carpenter, a term that can be both literal and metaphorical, is indeed a term in Japan for DIY. Recalling the vernacular and self-built housing that had inspired Kawazoe's Waseda University Professors Wajiro Kon and Takamasa Yosizaka, Sunday carpenter-type people would have "their own freedom of expression" in building their dwellings, a freedom to be enabled, Kawazoe thought, by stacked plots of "artificial land." Introduced by Yosizaka in 1954 as a solution to Japan's postwar housing crisis, the concept of artificial land is arguably the core concept of Metabolism, with its pairing of a durable infrastructural frame infilled with variable homes provoking the movement's focus on a time-based architecture.

Housing driven by diverse residents' desires was a situation also sought at times by Kenzo Tange and the Metabolists Kiyonori Kikutake and Kisho Kurokawa. Yet it is quite absent from the built record of the movement, despite it appearing as a key objective in Metabolist folklore. The built record's image is more associated with official expressions of national prestige, such as Expo '70, and large prefabricated components. Kurokawa's Nakagin Capsule Tower is the movement's icon.

This chapter aims at a small repair to this disconnection through examining a more participatory housing tradition that can be found in and interwoven with Metabolism, through architects who, if not Metabolists, could be called para-Metabolists. Instead of a technocratic salaryman briefly occupying a capsule, for whom Kurokawa himself provided the image, what may be the value of an alternative avatar for the movement in the form of a Sunday carpenter, representative of a person or people willing and able (with the help of architects) to make and change their environments for living? Analyzed through several housing initiatives spanning from 1954 to 1993, resident decision-making in collective housing is put forward as a vital condition for housing's democratic rationalization and a culture of collaboration, at a time when the corporate monopolization of housing as a product threatens with a renewed aggression

DOI: 10.4324/9781003186540-7

FIGURE 6.1 Takamasa Yosizaka, artificial land sketch, 1954.

to overwhelm housing as a process.[2] A culture of resident participation speaks to Metabolism's original intentions, which were quickly lost in the consumerism of the late 1960s and beyond.

Maximum dwelling: Yosizaka House

> As luck would have it, the sky space above Tokyo is very little occupied.
> Takamasa Yosizaka, 1954[3]

An architect little acknowledged as an influence on Metabolism is Takamasa Yosizaka. A member of "Team Tokyo," the vague and short-lived group planned as a sequel to the Metabolists who debuted in 1960, Yosizaka had an influence through his Ura House (1956) on Kikutake's far-better known Sky House (1958), a design that launched Kikutake to fame.[4] Another early Yosizaka project was his own house from 1955 that stood in Shinjuku. It was a seminal if tiny articulation of the idea of resident participation via artificial land.

Having graduated in 1941 from Waseda, where he had participated in Wajiro Kon's surveys of variations in *minka* (vernacular "houses of the people"), in 1950 Yosizaka went to Paris to work with Le Corbusier. He spent three weeks on the Unité d'Habitation Marseilles construction site as a supervisor. Spending days with the massive structure, he felt that such an impressive system did not need to be so repetitive.[5] Indeed, he saw an alternative in Le Corbusier's unbuilt 1931 design for Fort l'Empereur in Algiers, designated as "artificial land" through offering a giant skeleton frame in which people could purchase plots of indeterminate size and, with the help of their

FIGURE 6.2 Kisho Kurokawa in the Nakagin Capsule Tower, Tokyo, circa 1972. Image credit: Tomio Ohashi.

own architects, construct housing however they pleased and could afford. This critique of modern housing's typical obsession with standardization and the minimum dwelling seems to anticipate Le Corbusier's later comment that "it is always life that is right and the architect who is wrong."[6] Architecture needed to leave room for decisions by others. Yosizaka returned to Tokyo in 1952 with artificial land in mind as a solution for his nation's enormous housing shortage, the result of American bombings, vast firebreak construction, and massive influxes to urban areas.

A Japanese pro-democracy slogan of the early 1950s was "Architecture of the People, for the People," and Yosizaka perhaps saw artificial land as the slogan's instantiation.[7] In 1954 he debuted his new thinking on the housing crisis using the concept. In the essay "The Home is the Boundary between the Individual and Group's Profit: One Proposal to Solve Housing Shortage," published in the journal *Kokusai kenchiku*, he addressed the topic through a critique of the Congrès internationaux d'architecture modern (CIAM). The organization was a main inspiration for the public housing ideology then emerging in Japan, which Yosizaka felt was overly infatuated with mass production. While CIAM's principles of "sun, space, and greenery" were important, he felt its faith in standardization had caused an imbalance between group profit and individual freedom. His essay proposed instead that:

> It is not necessary to make all the fine details of the home with our current budget for public housing. What we need to do is to make land. This land, however,

FIGURE 6.3 Le Corbusier visiting Yosizaka at his artificial land house in Shinjuku, Tokyo, 1955.

does not need to be earth. A land that can provide the electricity, gas, water supply, and sewage required for modern technology could be a land made of concrete. We should make land that is suitable for housing, and that can make effective use of what little city space we have by being able to be layered. We do not need any more than this. If we think of this instead of providing all the small amenities in the homes, it does not seem impossible. All we need to do is loan the land. The people can then rent a piece of this land, set with all its facilities, and build their own homes as they want, wherever they want.[8]

While derivative of Le Corbusier's declaration of artificial land made in *The Radiant City* (1933), Yosizaka's call addresses specific Japanese realities, to which the concept promised to be uniquely responsive.[9] Most immediately, like many left homeless by the war, he was living in a "barrack" shack he'd built, in his case on the site of his parents' burned-down house. Tokyo offered the example of a vast city partly remade from the bottom up. Indeed, Kawazoe has called this early postwar period "an era of self-construction."[10] Why not expand this self-build process vertically through layered land?

The resourcefulness and self-reliance of the barracks and Kon's survey work were inspirations, but Yosizaka was not proposing a vertical slum. Instead, he took the responsiveness of the barracks and formalized it—that is, made it legal and safe—through a creative approach to the Government Housing Loan Corporation (GHLC).[11] Founded in 1950, the GHLC was established to provide low-interest loans of public money to individuals for the private construction of single-family homes. Within the cramped, horizontal density of Japanese cities, terrestrial land was increasingly expensive and difficult to acquire, and the search for affordable sites contributed to urban sprawl. The GHLC required loan applicants to have a site in order to be approved, and so Yosizaka's idea of layered land could provide new sites in the heart of the city, thereby helping more people to receive GHLC assistance.

Put simply, people would own a home on a rented aerial site. Through homeownership, Yosizaka proposed an alternative to rental public housing by suggesting an idea of the "maximum" dwelling. This is not maximum in the sense of biggest or fanciest, but rather the dwelling maximally suited to a given household within the limits of its members' needs, tastes, and budget, in an attempt to escape the minimum dwelling's constriction of lifestyle to a statistical average. In a 1955 article in *Shinkenchiku*, Yosizaka imagined the progressive completion of the home "alongside the progression of the lifestyle in the home."[12]

At the time he was writing, right next to his barrack, Yosizaka was building his new home that would be a practical test of his theory. He first erected a concrete frame, with formwork made from salvaged US Army lumber, and indeed financed by a loan from the GHLC. Then he waited. Over the following year, his two layers of concrete ground were fit only for parties and sleeping on summer nights. After a period of saving, he made his experiment habitable by infilling it with concrete block walls, and then inserting windows and doors, done with the help of his students from Waseda, one of whom was Shokan Endo, later the vice president of Kikutake's office.[13] Years later, when Yosizaka's wife complained bitterly about the roof leaking, he solved the problem with perfect artificial-land logic by adding an attic.

FIGURE 6.4 Wajiro Kon, sketches of barracks after the Great Kanto earthquake, 1923.

FIGURE 6.5 Takamasa Yosizaka, artificial land house frame (left) and enclosed with infill (right), circa 1955.

Major-structure and Metabolism

Another veteran of Le Corbusier's, Kunio Maekawa, completed another seminal project for Metabolism in 1958: the Harumi Apartments in Tokyo. Employing a massive concrete frame with typical bays containing two apartments in width and three in height, this composition was referred to by Maekawa's staff engineer, Toshihiko Kimura, as "major-structure" and "minor-structure." With the minor-structure conceived as changeable over time, this terminology put artificial land's spatial flexibility into structural terms that went on to become the Metabolist Fumihiko Maki's term "megastructure." Harumi's project architect, the soon-to-be Metabolist Masato Otaka, described the minor-structure of apartments as inspired by wooden *minka* that were open to ongoing modification.

It should be noted that in Tange's keynote speech at the 1960 World Design Conference (WoDeCo) in Tokyo, where Metabolism debuted, he presented the Harumi-inspired work of his recent studio at the Massachusetts Institute of Technology (MIT) as having a major-structural frame for accommodating dwellings that could be "left up to individual tastes." He would later use this same description for the housing in his A Plan for Tokyo, 1960.[14] This promise of residential freedom within a major-structure is one of the generic impressions of Metabolism, a promise given more abstract expression by Tange's call at WoDeCo for an architecture accommodating "shorter" and "longer cycles" of change. The strategic combination of longer and more short-lived architectural components is the de facto central concept of Metabolism, an idea whose

90 Casey Mack

FIGURE 6.6 Kunio Maekawa, Harumi Apartments, Tokyo, 1958. Image credit: Chuji Hirayama.

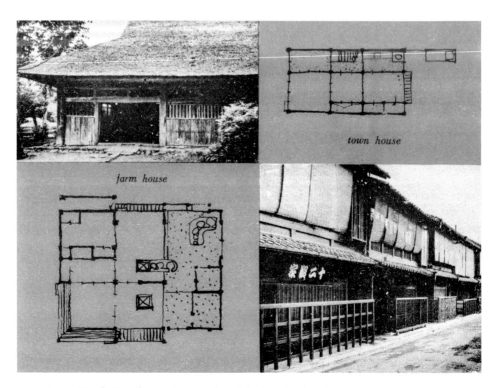

FIGURE 6.7 Kunio Maekawa, Harumi's *minka* inspiration, 1957.

"mind-numbing simplicity" Reyner Banham saw as fundamental to the movement's success.[15] And this concept has an origin in artificial land, that is, a participatory idea of mass housing.

Despite Tange's proclamations, an interest in dweller decision-making, along with an interest in housing in general, would soon cease to be a concern for him. In trying to build the stature of the Japanese architect, a profession that struggled for respect in postwar Japan, perhaps it was too risky to leave oneself open to taking the opinions and design directions of laypeople, and to therefore not be an absolute expert. It was perhaps too risky to want to be a serious architect and take housing seriously. Arata Isozaki said as much.[16]

However, some approximations of dwellers exercising their freedoms do exist within Metabolism. There is the PREVI housing in Lima, Peru, designed in 1969 by the team of Kikutake, Kurokawa, and Maki, and intended to enable residents' modifications. Yet this project, despite the compelling adaptations that have indeed been performed over the years, does not draw on the artificial land concept that Kawazoe saw as enabling the Sunday carpenter within the context of a vertical urbanism.

Looking to the Nakagin Capsule Tower, we find a hegemonic concept of dweller choice. Sold like cars, its capsules offered only circumscribed options, and were entirely constructed within the control of the factory.[17] While Nakagin has been adapted to multiple uses since its completion in 1972, it is notable that these changes have happened in totally different ways than the architect wanted, and they have been enabled (or provoked) by the building's physical deterioration.

Another example is Kikutake's Stratiform Structure Module, a lengthy research and design project initiated in 1973, and lasting into the late 1980s. The project never progressed beyond two prototypes. Its A-frame structure of artificial land is notable for its reliance on Japan's prefabricated house industry, as seen in the work of companies such as Misawa and Sekisui, whose designs by the early 1970s had a high level of commercial success far greater than that of any capsule-type housing ever designed by a Metabolist. The brilliance of the Stratiform team was to piggyback on this existing

FIGURE 6.8 Kenzo Tange/MIT proposal, community for 25,000 people over Boston Bay, 1959.

industry, appropriating it as a ready-made design-build system with a sophisticated showroom network poised to supply residential infill for the A-frames. According to Shizuo Harada, a project architect for Stratiform in Kikutake's office, the design team spent little time thinking about housing in any detail, since they took it for granted that prefab houses would "complete" their infrastructure.[18]

However, while the prefab industry did (and does) allow for a high level of customization in its products, if we turn to Kawazoe's essay "The City of the Future," where he introduced the figure of the Sunday carpenter, we see that he is after something beyond merely buying variation: he wants people to develop their own creative powers.

Noboru Kawazoe's city

As emphasized in Metabolist scholarship in the past decade, the outlook and agendas of the Metabolists were hardly uniform.[19] The *Metabolism/1960* book released at WoDeCo was not a homogenous manifesto. Indicative of this diversity, soon after WoDeCo, Kawazoe began to articulate a more defined Metabolism, at least for himself. We know from Rem Koolhaas and Hans Ulrich Obrist's *Project Japan* that Kawazoe was a lifelong re-reader of Volume Three of Karl Marx's *Capital*, a habit Koolhaas and Obrist do not explore. In a passage of Volume Three discussing Marx's idea of metabolism, we find him insisting that shortening the work day is essential for a true blossoming of human freedom, a freedom also requiring humankind's enlightened metabolism with nature, where metabolism is understood as the ways in which humans work or process nature.[20] The call for the reduction of the work day to allow

FIGURE 6.9 Kiyonori Kikutake et al., Stratiform Structure Module, 1977.

new forms of culture—through voluntary work—is also a call made by Kawazoe and is expressed by the Sunday carpenter.

Kawazoe's essay, published in English in *Zodiac*, stresses the need to resist a "total image" of the city.[21] Instead, the city should be developed in a way open to suggestions and revisions. Such development, he writes, calls for a positive introduction "of the time factor into city planning." Further, this development of the city must be in unison "with the metabolism of civilization and nature."[22] It is important to clarify here that Marx, in parts of *Capital* Kawazoe certainly knew, saw that metabolic processes can be healthy or damaging—metabolism unto itself is not good or bad abstracted from specific bodies and environments.[23] In postwar Japan, civilization and nature were both metabolizing rapidly, but often through destruction, often due to pollution.

"Artificial land-sites" are seen by Kawazoe as a method able to resolve this conflict between humans and nature, as well as humans and humans—conflict shorthanded from Marx by sociologist John Bellamy Foster as the "metabolic rift."[24] Discussed throughout the essay, artificial land is seen by Kawazoe as able to integrate new mass transit, free the terrestrial ground to be rewilded with flora and fauna, and as a technique for "unleashing" the "potential energy" of people to "build their own dwellings."[25] The "Sunday carpenter," the hobbyist *bricoleur*, is introduced as a character type primed to take up such self-building activity. "Sunday carpenter" as a term seems at least in part to have been popularized by Wakisangyo, a maker of home-improvement tools, who used the phrase in its advertising latest as of 1963, but perhaps earlier, at the time of Kawazoe's writing in 1961.[26]

Returning to Marx's influence, Kawazoe is interested in a shortening of the work day to allow people to graduate from "simple consumption" to "more constructive pastimes." The Sunday carpenter is seen as the "embryo" of this transition to "freedom of expression," with constructive possibilities enabled by "factory-produced parts … capable of endless combinations and change by means of standardized systems and joints." Kawazoe is quick to admit that this situation will not by itself be sufficient "for ushering in an earthly paradise."[27] The pursuit of "freedom of expression" could easily feed disposability. Interpreted I think most optimistically, Kawazoe's freedom of expression is about education and creative control, in a way reminiscent of John Habraken's mass-housing question that entwines architects and residents: "*who* decides *when* about *what*?"[28] As Kawazoe writes: "The idea that only an architect can make a house must be discarded."[29]

The Two-Step Housing System

Kawazoe's description of components with "standardized systems and joints" wielded by resident-builders suggests methods of construction more to hand—literally—than is typically associated with Metabolism. This contrasts with Nakagin or Stratiform's reliance on the unitized products of prefabrication, which, like cars—the inevitable model for prefab housing—have embodied costs from vast marketing, dictate choices, and rely on the planned obsolescence that comes with such large, capital-intensive industry.

But an example of a dynamic and standardized system that was available to the amateur space-maker exists. It is likely that Kawazoe had in mind the *kyo-ma* system from the Edo period. In fact, he mentions this system of modular coordination in his book *Ise: Prototype of Japanese Architecture* (1961), written with Tange.[30] In brief, *kyo-ma* was an interpost measurement system that established construction modules measured to the inner faces of columns. This was a rejection of the *inaka-ma* system that was based on a module set to column centerlines. The significance of this change, apparently stemming from the needs of commoners instead of the upper classes, was that dimensions for *tatami*, *fusuma*, and other interior space-defining elements could be standardized. With *inaka-ma*, custom fabrication of tatami and other elements was required to accommodate the varying interpost distances due to the thickness of columns, an expense fewer people could easily afford.

One outcome of the popular diffusion of this rationalization was the appearance in Kansai in the late Edo period of *hadaka-gashi*, or "bare rental," in which landlords would rent *kyo-ma* dimensioned apartments without any interior elements.[31] As these had all become coordinated by the 6.3 *shaku* module of the system, Kansai residents could move and modify dwellings with ease, confident that the space-defining components in which they had invested would fit other regional housing. The popularity of *hadaka-gashi* was such that an active market emerged for the sale, repair, and recycling of *kyo-ma* products, which lasted up until World War II. Composed of organic materials from renewable sources, the system is an example of an intelligent metabolism that was once alive in vernacular reality.

Kawazoe was not alone in being inspired by this system. In the late 1970s, Kazuo Tatsumi and Mitsuo Takada, academics at Kyoto University's Department of Architecture, developed the Two-Step Housing System (TSHS), a method for making housing in a way sympathetic to Yosizaka's model of artificial land, as well as the vernacular metabolism of *hadaka-gashi*. Indeed, Tatsumi and Takada called TSHS a *hadaka-gashi* system for "modern times," similarly promoting modular elements for indeterminate private infill, but now within durable skeletons that they saw ideally constructed by public agencies. They envisioned such infill coming from small regional construction companies, as was the case with *kyo-ma* components during the Edo period, with dimensional standardization and local manufacture helping to

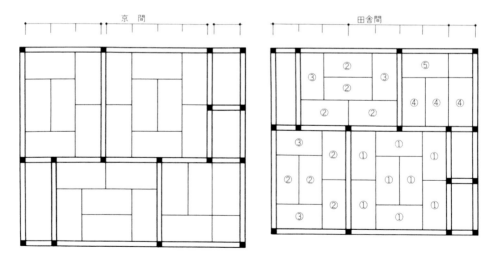

FIGURE 6.10 Yositika Utida, comparison of *kyo-ma* (left) and *inaka-ma* (right) measurement systems, 1977.

a remake a culture of sustainable housing where non-professionals could significantly modify their living spaces.[32]

While TSHS residents would have control over the design of their apartments, they would not be abandoned in a DIY situation that might be overwhelming. Consultation with an architect was a key part of the TSHS process for the creation of each apartment. Through this engagement, it is important to recognize that the Sunday carpenter-type was not necessarily creating architecture without architects. TSHS instead proposed that architects could work directly with multiple households to help form a community.

NEXT21

In the early 1990s, Rem Koolhaas remarked that, in bubble-era Japan, one finds "*incredible buildings that are about nothing.* They have no program, no social ambition."[33] True as this may have been at the time, the concept of artificial land suggests that the absence of any fixed program could in fact be a social ambition. The architect Yositika Utida recommends that we "think of a given building not as a residence … but as space for living that can serve society's shifting needs by transforming into a hospital, a nursing home, a seminar room or an office."[34] Such responsiveness drives Utida's NEXT21 Experimental Housing, built in Osaka for the Osaka Gas Corporation and first occupied in 1994 by staff of the company. Conceived as a laboratory for studying lifestyles and energy systems for the twenty-first century, the project is a time machine for simulating changes that might otherwise not have happened for decades.

Utida gathered trusted collaborators for the project, which started in 1989. These included TSHS inventors Tatsumi and Takada, as well as the structural engineer Toshiko Kimura. Kimura had engineered past Utida projects and had been a member with Utida—as well as with Maki and Otaka—on the 1962 Artificial Land Committee convened by the Architectural Institute of Japan. The skeleton Kimura engineered for NEXT21 allowed the boundaries of apartments to be conceived independently of each other, a freedom assisted by a raised floor system enabling considerable flexibility in locations for bathrooms and kitchens.

While taking inspiration from Dutch experiments in resident participation, NEXT21 also drew on artificial land's Japanese legacy, harkening back to the kind apartment variation "left to individual taste" that Metabolism advocated but hardly delivered.[35] The project's 2007 brochure from Osaka Gas in fact describes the design as "artificial ground."[36] To perform an initial variability test at NEXT21, Utida invited 13 architects to make designs for a range of lifestyle scenarios concocted for 18 "parcels" in the project.[37] Seen together, the scenarios testify to the end of the "housing miracle" that had flooded the country with so many identical apartments from the 1950s into the 1970s. The nuclear family, for which the typical postwar unit was intended, was in decline by the time of the bubble economy context of NEXT21, with Japan's demographics trending toward lower birthrates, fewer marriages, a more elderly population, and greater affluence. Indicative of these changing conditions and the notion of Japan as a "lifestyle superpower" are the names of the scenarios: Warm, Comfortable House; Young Family House; Independent Family House; Extended Family House; Active Oldsters' House; Garden House; House with Office; House of Harmony; Woody House; Next Generation House; House for Home Party; House with

96 Casey Mack

FIGURE 6.11   Yositika Utida et al., NEXT21 Experimental Housing, Osaka, 1993. Photo taken in 2010.

"Sunday Carpenter" Metabolism **97**

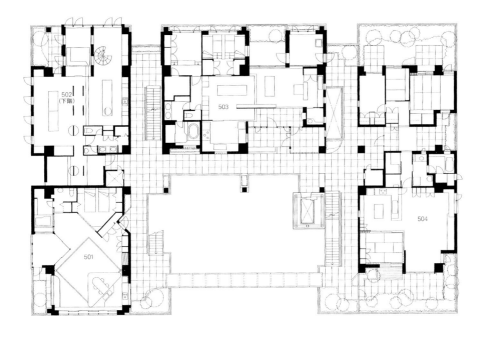

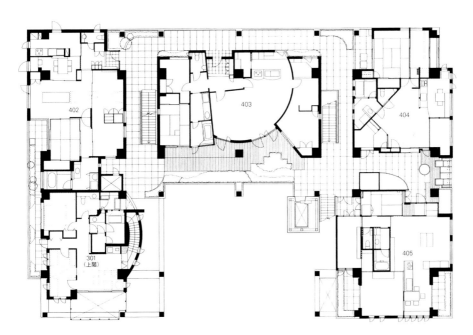

FIGURE 6.12 Shu-Koh-Sha Architecture and Urban Design Studio, NEXT21 floor plans, circa 1993.

Handicraft Studio; House for Relaxation; House with Fitness Room; House for Time Creation; Changeable House; House for Unmarried City Dweller; and DINKS Apartment.[38] Thanks to the involvement of Tatsumi and Takada, all of the units imagined for these imaginary residents needed to be built using an infill system attempting the spatial flexibility of *kyo-ma* components.

Though most of NEXT21's units were designed around these fictive programs, some were designed in consultation with the residents-to-be. In this way, and in the team's description of the project as "collective housing," NEXT21 also seems to take inspiration from a local phenomenon: since the early 1970s, the Osaka architecture office HEXA had been helping people (including its own staff) form co-ops for designing, building, and managing their own housing, finding the freedom to avoid the expensive and predetermined apartments of the speculative marketplace. This is not to say that this freedom was easily achieved—forming a co-op is a lot of work. It is a kind of work more palatable to people of a do-it-yourself persuasion. Indeed, the organization that HEXA formed for leading co-op initiatives was dubbed the Association of People Who Wish to Create Their Own Urban Apartment Buildings with Their Own Hands, abbreviated to "Tojuso." By 1987, 13 Tojuso co-ops had been built in a neighborhood just northwest of NEXT21. As HEXA architect Osamu Nakasuji noted, while a co-op process could result in an "ideal" apartment building both socially and architecturally, designing was an ordeal of trial and error to fit the puzzle pieces of non-standard units within a single volume.[39] NEXT21's artificial land approach can be read as one for easing the assembly of such a puzzle.

Conclusion

The architect Osamu Ishiyama has said "there is no more that we can learn from Tange, while there is much more that we can learn from Yosizaka."[40] While this is a questionable position as an absolute truth, the juxtaposition is suggestive. We can compare the versions of artificial land at Yosizaka's house with Tange's, sprawled over Tokyo Bay. Tange's proposal required waiting for the machinery of the developmental state to roll into motion, while Yosizaka's needed only a bit of property, a little money saved up, and some eager students willing to get their hands dirty. In this way, Yosizaka's approach to a communal infrastructure enabling difference and change offers a model of individual agency missing from what Tange offers us. Yosizaka offers a hypothesis you can live in and test yourself, or with some friends. You can work on it in your spare time on the weekend.

Notes

1 Noboru Kawazoe, "The City of the Future," *Zodiac* 9 (1961): 107. It should be noted that in order to indicate Kawazoe's status as "operative critic," this phenomenon of partisan criticism was identified and attacked by the architectural historian Manfredo Tafuri, who considered a key culprit to be the historian and editor Bruno Zevi, *Zodiac*'s founder.

2 For an example of this pursuit of monopoly, seen in the renewed quest for factory-built buildings that are to the detriment of local builders, see McKinsey & Company, *The Next Normal in Construction: How Disruption is Reshaping the World's Largest Ecosystem* (June 2020), https://www.mckinsey.com/~/media/McKinsey/Industries/Capital%20Projects%20 and%20Infrastructure/Our%20Insights/The%20next%20normal%20in%20construction/ executive-summary_the-next-normal-in-construction.pdf.

3 Takamasa Yosizaka, "Jukyo wa Ko to Shudan no Rieki no Kyokaisen [The Home is the Boundary between the Individual and Group's Profit: One Proposal to Solve the Housing Shortage]," *Kokusai kenchiku* 21(1) (January 1954): 67. Translation by Riyo Namigata.

4 Regarding Yosizaka and Team Tokyo, see Rem Koolhaas and Hans Ulrich Obrist, *Project Japan: Metabolism Talks...* (Cologne: Taschen, 2011), 96, 391.

5 Yosizaka, "Jukyo," 67.

6 Quoted in Philippe Boudon, *Lived-in Architecture: Le Corbusier's Pessac Revisited* (Cambridge, MA: MIT Press, 1979), 2.

7 Noboru Kawazoe, *Contemporary Japanese Architecture* (Tokyo: Japan Foundation, 1973), 36.

8 Yosizaka, "Jukyo," 67.

9 See Le Corbusier, *The Radiant City*, trans. Eleanor Levieux et al. (New York: Orion Press, 1967 [1933]), 247.

10 Kawazoe, *Contemporary Japanese Architecture*, 38.

11 The Government Housing Loan Corporation is occasionally given in English as the Housing Financing Corporation, or similar.

12 Takamasa Yosizaka, *Aru Jukyo: Hitotsu no Kokoromi* [*About a House: One Experiment*] (Tokyo: Sagami Shobo, 1960), 94. Translation by Riyo Namigata.

13 Shokan Endo, in conversation with the author, May 15, 2014.

14 See Kenzo Tange, "A Building and a Project," *The Japan Architect* (October 1960): 16; and Kenzo Tange, "A Plan for Tokyo, 1960," *Ekistics* 12(69) (July 1961): 18.

15 Reyner Banham, *Megastructure: Urban Futures of the Recent Past* (New York: Harper & Row, 1976), 47.

16 Regarding Isozaki's dismissal of private houses as architecture, see Thomas Daniell, *An Anatomy of Influence* (London: AA Publications, 2018), 35–36.

17 Indeed, a point of comparison in the original marketing of the capsules was that they costed less than a Toyota Corolla. See *Metabolism—The City of the Future: Dreams and Visions of Reconstruction in Postwar and Present-Day Japan*, ed. Mami Hirose et al. (Tokyo: Mori Art Museum, 2011), 146.

18 Shizuo Harada, in conversation with the author, May 15, 2014.

19 This heterogeneity is emphasized both in Hajime Yatsuka, *Metabolism Nexus* (Tokyo: Ohmsha, 2011) and in Koolhaas and Obrist, *Project Japan*.

20 On Marx's call for a shortening of the work day, see Karl Marx, *Capital: Volume III*, trans. David Fernbach (London: Penguin, 1991 [1894]), 959. Regarding Marx's idea of metabolism as human labor to process nature, see John Bellamy Foster, *Marx's Ecology: Materialism and Nature* (New York: Monthly Review Press, 2000), 157.

21 Kawazoe, "The City of the Future," 99.

22 Kawazoe, "The City of the Future," 100–101.

23 Regarding Marx's position that human metabolism of nature was in no way necessarily rational or benign, see Marx, *Capital: Volume III*, 959.

24 See Foster, *Marx's Ecology*, 155.

25 Kawazoe, "The City of the Future," 104.

26 See "From Household Hardware to Do-it-Yourself, and towards the Age of DIY," http://www.waki-diy.co.jp/about/start_diy.

27 All quotes: Kawazoe, "The City of the Future," 107.

28 See Martijn Vos, "The Foundation for Architects' Research (SAR) in Good Times and Bad," in Koos Bosma et al., *Housing for the Millions: John Habraken and the SAR (1960–2000)* (Rotterdam: NAI Publishers, 2000), 173. Italics in original.

29 Kawazoe, "The City of the Future," 107.

30 See Kenzo Tange and Noboru Kawazoe, *Ise: Prototype of Japanese Architecture* (Cambridge, MA: MIT Press, 1965), 204–206.

31 No precise dates are in my sources for when exactly *hadaka-gashi* emerged.

32 See Kazuo Tatsumi and Mitsuo Takada, "Two Step Housing System," *Open House International* 12(2) (1987): 21.

33 Rem Koolhaas, "Finding Freedoms: Conversations with Rem Koolhaas," interview by Alejandro Zaera in *El Croquis 53: OMA/Rem Koolhaas 1987–1993*, ed. Alejandro Zaera (Barcelona: El Croquis Editorial, 1994), 25. Italics in original.

34 Yositika Utida, "NEXT21," *The Japan Architect* 73 (Spring 2009): 35. With the spread of COVID-19 in 2020, this observation gained particular relevance.

35 For discussion of Dutch influences on Utida and NEXT21, see Casey Mack, *Digesting Metabolism: Artificial Land in Japan 1954–2202* (Berlin: Hatje Cantz Verlag, 2021).

36 See *Osaka Gas Experimental Housing: NEXT21* (Osaka: Osaka Gas Co., 2007), 3.

37 "Parcels": see Stephen Kendall and Jonathan Teicher, *Residential Open Building* (London: E & FN Spon, 2000), 289. Of course, this language transposes a term typically used for terrestrial land to the artificial.

38 For "lifestyle superpower," see Eiko Maruko Siniawer, *Waste: Consuming Postwar Japan* (Ithaca, NY: Cornell University Press, 2018), 238. For scenarios, see *Osaka Gas Experimental Housing*, 24–32.

39 HEXA Architects and Planners, "Tojuso Tokui-Cho Apartments," *The Japan Architect* 58(8) (August 1983): 66.

40 Osamu Ishiyama, "Messages from the Next Generation," in *Takamasa Yosizaka as a Labyrinth*, ed. Takamasa Yosizaka Exhibition Executive Committee (Tokyo: TOTO Publishing, 2005), 138. Translation by Riyo Namigata.

7

MAKI AND DUTCH TEAM X

Step towards Group Form

Kiwa Matsushita

The Metabolism members were respectful to each other's ideas, but by no means did they share the same vision for the future. As a critical reaction to the Congrès internationaux d'architecture modern (CIAM), Kiyonori Kikutake and Noriaki (Kisho) Kurokawa proposed a hierarchical system comprising a core and industrially produced identical and replaceable elements. Their techno-utopian images came to be recognized as the main idea of Metabolism and are often compared with their European contemporaries, such as Archigram and Yona Friedman. Conversely, Masato Otaka and Maki were more concerned with balancing individual freedom with communal identity. Rather than form, they proposed a system of organizing various elements in identifiable unity, which they called *Collective Form*. The idea of Collective Form, which remains relevant even in today's shrinking cities, resonated more with Team X, especially its Dutch members Jaap Bakema and Aldo van Eyck. Maki was closely affiliated with the members of Team X around 1960, during the concept's formative years. Scrutinization of their idea's exchanges would clarify the enduring strength of the concept of Collective Form, which has continued to drive Maki's 60-year career and has developed into his recent proposal, Another Utopia.

Maki between 1958 and 1960

Although Otaka and Maki's idea of Collective Form was first introduced in 1960 in the *Metabolism 1960* booklet, it was presented as a comprehensive principle in *Investigations in Collective Form* (1964) from the Washington University Press.[1] After graduating from Tokyo University (Kenzo Tange Laboratory), Maki studied and worked in the USA from 1952. Such experiences exposed him to a wide variety of progressive discussions on urbanism. In particular, the events between 1958 and 1960 had the greatest influence on his career and thoughts. When Maki was an associate professor at Washington University in St. Louis, he received a generous fellowship from the Graham Foundation of Chicago, enabling him to make a two-year "journey to the West." He traveled to Southeast Asia, India, the Middle East, and Europe;[2]

DOI: 10.4324/9781003186540-8

FIGURE 7.1 The town of Hydra, Greece. Image credit: Fumihiko Maki.

his observations of vernacular and historic settlements in various parts of the world opened his eyes to Collective Form.

The preparation of the World Design Conference and the Metabolism booklet occurred during Maki's travels in his fellowship years. While Maki enjoyed being acquainted with other Metabolism group members, he felt some distance from their techno-utopian vision when he returned to Tokyo between his travels.[3] A person who shared this uneasiness was Masato Otaka, whose undergraduate thesis was on "cluster."[4] Otaka and Maki were interested in how to assemble numerous buildings and maintain order while allowing growth and maximum individuality in architecture. In their *Metabolism 1960* booklet, Otaka and Maki proposed the Shinjuku Redevelopment Project. However, as Maki later confided, their foci for the project were different. Otaka, the oldest Metabolist and a chief designer for various buildings at Kunio Maekawa's office, was concerned with Japan's fragmented land ownership and disorderly streets with modern traffic.[5] Thus, Otaka's focus was more on the artificial land of the project. Maki, whose interest was reflected more in groups of offices and entertainment facilities, drew his idea from the settlements he observed during his travels. In these observations, he saw that "buildings are ingeniously connected to one another to create a small community, and communities are connected to one another to create a town" and "the whole persists even when individual houses are destroyed, and other similar houses eventually take their place."[6] While the group of offices and entertainment facilities did not solve specific problems in Shinjuku as did the artificial ground, it proposed a type of Collective Form that can be considered a universal principle.

During one of his trips overseas, Maki attended a small Team X meeting in Bagnols-sur-Cèze in July 1960 (which Maki was invited to by Peter Smithson at the World Design Conference in Tokyo), the first after the termination of CIAM. Going to the meeting urged him to consolidate his idea on Collective Form and provided an opportunity for him to witness and participate in leading-edge discussions about problems in the contemporary city in the European architectural scene. The themes raised by Candilis-Josic-Woods, the organizer of the meeting, were "the creation of a new habitat, which should be integrated into an existing urban and regional structure" and "the transformation of this structure, transformation of the cities. Transformation of the region."[7]

At this meeting, Aldo van Eyck's Municipal Orphanage and Candilis-Josic-Woods's scheme of the Free University of Berlin were presented for discussion.[8] Van Eyck gave a talk on his concept of part and whole relationships using the metaphor of a tree and leaf, which he later presented using his famous "leaf-tree diagram" at the Team X large meeting at Royaumont in 1962. He also showed a video he took during his research trip to the Dogon villages, which made a strong impression on Maki. Maki felt an affinity with van Eyck's ideas and observations, and considered them to be among the few philosophical ideas that could lead to a new principle.[9]

Despite van Eyck's intriguing proposal and Smithson's remark about the importance of collective space, Team X could not come up with an answer.[10] Maki enjoyed the casual, family-like atmosphere and series of intense discussions at the meeting. However, he was also frustrated that those progressive architects, who criticized and terminated CIAM, could not present any concrete alternatives that could be practically applied to urban design.

Investigations in Collective Form and Dutch Team X

Following his two-year trip, Maki returned to Washington University in the autumn of 1960 and started writing *Investigations in Collective Form* (henceforth *Collective Form*). In *Metabolism 1960*, Maki felt that the members "were looking to develop a new future for Japan at that time" and "weren't trying to spread our ideas to the West."[11] However, *Collective Form*, of which the first chapter was co-authored with Otaka, proposed a universal idea on urbanism. *Collective Form* carefully compared three different types of Collective Form based on Maki's observations of concrete examples throughout the world and at different ages. The first type, "compositional form," is an approach that has often been used throughout history and refers to buildings arranged according to a preconceived master plan. While coherent, compositional form tends toward formal planning, it does not readily lend itself to change. The second type, the "megastructure," is "a large frame in which all the functions of a city or part of a city are housed"[12] and is a new approach made possible with modern-day technology. By prescribing a skeleton with urban-scale infrastructure, order can still be maintained as a whole, regardless of variations in the subsidiary individual elements. The last type of Collective Form is called "group form," which Maki suggested has the most potential. Like historical settlements, group form is composed without a master framework and by the relationships between elements that "have their own built-in link,"[13] such as walls or open spaces. In group form, a system does not rule the whole, but is incorporated within each element, and each element evokes a system.[14] Thus, the elements can readily respond to changes as a collective entity.

Before the book was published in 1964, Maki disseminated the typewritten paper to his extensive network of architects throughout the USA and Europe. He fondly recalled receiving encouraging letters from Walter Gropius, Kevin Lynch, and Jaap Bakema.[15] Maki was frequently in correspondence with Bakema following the Team X meeting

FIGURE 7.2 Three paradigms of Collective Form (from left to right): compositional form, megaform, and group form. Image credit: Fumihiko Maki.

in 1960, distributing the latest developments on group form by Otaka and himself.[16] Maki, Otaka, and Bakema shared a strong belief that people in society should have maximum freedom in living their lives. According to Bakema, architecture "could be realizing everybody's right to full life."[17] In his letter to Maki, Bakema wrote that the study of Collective Form could solve "[h]ow to find what has to be build [sic] publicly in order to give as much as possible freedom for the development of individual (family) initiative for house and workshop."[18] He had a strong belief in a democracy based not only on his interest in US culture, but also on his wartime experience as a Garman camp prisoner in France. Maki was also strongly influenced by the idea of establishing individual subjectivity in mass culture, which was a major topic of discussion among sociologists, such as David Reisman, when he was in the USA. In fact, Maki had declared: "Utopia, to me, is a collaborative society based on the idea of autonomy and is a society that has developed freedom of selection to the utmost degree."[19]

Bakema's reaction to *Collective Form* was not merely personal communication to Maki. A week after the last CIAM conference in Otterlo in 1959, Bakema voluntarily circulated newsletters entitled *Post Box for the Development of the Habitat* as a platform for communication and ideas exchange among CIAM-affiliated members from approximately 90 different cities worldwide. Colleagues could send in their ideas and recent activities regarding the problem of habitat, and Bakema would select and provide brief abstracts. Maki appeared twice in the newsletters—number six in 1961 and number nine in 1962.[20] The number nine newsletter posted an unusually long summary of *Collective Form*,[21] and Bakema openly acknowledged the importance of Maki's idea of Collective Form and promoted it before the book's publication.

Van Eyck and Maki had closer, more profound exchanges on architecture, art, and culture. After the Team X meeting in 1960, they taught at the same studio when van Eyck came to Washington University in 1961 and then at Harvard University in 1963, and spent time traveling and watching movies.[22] *Collective Form* referred to van Eyck's works; in turn, van Eyck responded to *Collective Form* by extensively quoting Maki's works in his book *The Child, the City and the Artist* (henceforth *The Child*), which was written in 1962. Unfortunately, it was not published until 2006, but about one-quarter of the text appeared as articles in *Forum*, the Dutch magazine for which van Eyck and Bakema were the primary editors. So, only recently, their mutual appreciation of each other's ideas became open to scrutiny.

The most apparent similarity between van Eyck's and Maki's ideas was the unification of part and whole. This unification does not depend on a hierarchy or

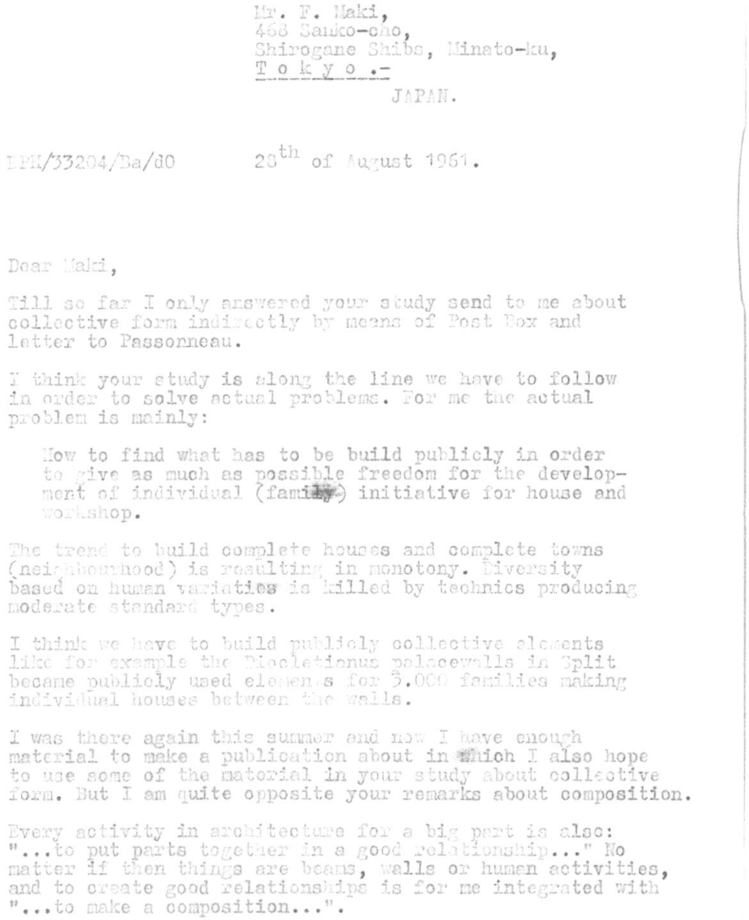

Mr. F. Maki,
468 Sanko-cho,
Shirogane Shibs, Minato-ku,
T o k y o .-
                              JAPAN.

LPH/33204/Ba/d0   28th of August 1961.

Dear Maki,

Till so far I only answered your study send to me about
collective form indirectly by means of Post Box and
letter to Passonneau.

I think your study is along the line we have to follow
in order to solve actual problems. For me the actual
problem is mainly:

     How to find what has to be build publicly in order
     to give as much as possible freedom for the develop-
     ment of individual (family) initiative for house and
     workshop.

The trend to build complete houses and complete towns
(neighbourhood) is resulting in monotony. Diversity
based on human variaties is killed by technics producing
moderate standard types.

I think we have to build publicly collective elements
like for example the Diocletianus palacewalls in Split
became publicly used elements for 5.000 families making
individual houses between the walls.

I was there again this summer and now I have enough
material to make a publication about in which I also hope
to use some of the material in your study about collective
form. But I am quite opposite your remarks about composition.

Every activity in architecture for a big part is also:
"...to put parts together in a good relationship..." No
matter if then things are beams, walls or human activities,
and to create good relationships is for me integrated with
"...to make a composition...".

FIGURE 7.3 Letter from Bakema to Maki, August 28, 1961. Het Nieuwe Instituut/ BAKE_g122-12-1.

predetermined composition, but on the relationship between different elements, evoking organic links that generate the whole system. Van Eyck explained:

It is now possible to invent dwelling types which do not lose their specific identity when multiplied, but, on the contrary, actually acquire extended identity and varied meaning once they are configured into a significant group ... Each individual dwelling possesses the potential to develop, by means of configurative multiplication, into a group (sub-cluster) in which the identity of each dwelling is not only maintained but extended in a qualitative dimension that is specifically relevant to the particular multiplicative stage to which it belongs.[23]

Van Eyck called his concept "configurative discipline," while Maki's idea was described as "group form."

Van Eyck and Maki both considered the idea of vernacular buildings and settlements, which Maki attributed to van Eyck as his predecessor in *Collective Form*.[24] Maki's idea of group form was mostly inspired by his observations. Conversely, van Eyck's concepts were drawn from his extensive sociological and anthropological research on Dogon. He learned that people in Dogon regarded "the village as an organ of the landscape-body, and the house in turn as an organ of the village ... Man is, as it were, himself an organ of the house."[25] Its harmonic equilibrium in Dogon cosmology was maintained by the duality principle, which van Eyck called "twin phenomena." Opposites, such as right and left, male and female, and leaf and tree, generally assumed to be conflicting entities in the Western tradition, were continually alternating and balancing. There was no hierarchy between the two opposite poles, but reciprocity. Francis Strauven, an architectural historian and author of the most comprehensive book on van Eyck, claimed that van Eyck's non-hierarchical and polycentric view of the world "was wholly unique in the architectural world."[26] However, coming from Asia, Maki probably did not feel foreign to this idea. In the mid-1970s, Maki and his staff researched urban Tokyo and its subliminal influences from its old form, Edo, which was compiled in a book called *City with a Hidden Past*. He wrote:

> In the creation of cities in the West, importance has always been attached to the relationship between the parts and the whole. The parts were conceived to be subordinate to the whole ... The relationship between the parts and the whole was not perceived in such a way in the process of urban development in Japan ... the Japanese have long seen small spaces as autonomous microcosms and thus developed the perception that a part was, in fact, also a whole.[27]

Maki, who felt an affinity with van Eyck's concepts of "configurative discipline" and "twin phenomena," was much impressed by van Eyck's masterpiece, the Municipal Orphanage (1955–1960), which was designed as van Eyck conceived these concepts and exemplified them using modern architecture vocabulary. In arranging the groups of rooms to house 125 children, van Eyck attempted to provide a spatial framework for the reciprocal qualities of unity–diversity and individual–collective. In *Collective Form*, Maki placed an image of the orphanage as an example of his idea of Collective Form and "providing a place for every kind of human activity,"[28] and continued to express his appreciation in his essays.[29] When asked by *Architectural Record* in 2016 to provide the name of a single building that had the biggest influence on his thinking and design, Maki said the orphanage continued to inspire his work.[30]

The last chapter of *The Child*, entitled "Some Starting Points and Steps towards a Configurative Discipline," presents 14 works from various architects, including Maki, Tange, and Kurokawa. Van Eyck was deeply concerned about the problem of large quantities in modern cities. Van Eyck admitted that a configurative process alone could not create overall comprehensibility in the urban context of vast plurality. Thus, he considered the need to incorporate an extensive framework: the megastructure. As much as van Eyck appreciated the brilliance of Tange's Tokyo Bay Project (1960), he remained ambivalent. While Bakema considered that both Tange's Tokyo Bay Project and Maki's group form could solve the mass housing problem and provide the residents with the freedom to determine their own living conditions,[31] van Eyck could not agree with the hierarchical system of major and minor structure in Tange's plan.[32]

In his essay in *The Child*, "Step towards a Configurative Discipline" (which was also published in the *Forum* in August 1962), van Eyck extensively quoted Maki's *Collective Form* on megaform to defend his position.[33] Maki did not deny megaform, but questioned whether the fixed framework, made possible by technology, could accommodate a city with unpredictable changes over time. Nobody could foresee that minor elements such as residences would become obsolete more rapidly than major elements like transportation methods. In addition to Maki's point, van Eyck criticized Tange for describing the framework as a major object, as it restricted individual choices and the elements for daily living as minor objects. Van Eyck considered that the technological framework (infrastructure) should be a serving element for people's living. Moreover, van Eyck thought the framework should not have conflicting extremes, as he advocated the "twin phenomena"—that the fundamental human association should not be abstracted into simple opposite poles.[34]

Both Maki and van Eyck were concerned with how to use megaform to design a comprehensive city while allowing for expansibility and diversity. In fact, van Eyck claimed that he was seeking a "configurated megaform ... in which the conflicting extremes ... are not resolved, but are simply not accepted as conflicting categories."[35] In *The Child*, van Eyck quoted the end of Chapter 1 of *Collective Form* under the title "Regionalism and Collective Form," in which Maki stated: "In *both megaform and* group form, the possibility of creating grain elements, hence regional qualities, exists. *In megaform, the frame is a large enough single element to be significant as grain*" (emphasis added).[36] Actually, the emphasized words were edited out in the published version of *Collective Form*; however, at one point, Maki attempted to consider megaform as similar to group form, only larger in scale.

Maki's projects, which van Eyck included in "Some Starting Points and Steps towards a Configurative Discipline" in *The Child*, also described attempts to incorporate megaform without hierarchy. For example, Maki collaborated with Jerry Goldberg, co-author of the second chapter in *Collective Form*, on the Model Traffic System (1962),[37] which used systems of two distinct sizes like Tange's project. However, the large and small systems were expandable and open-ended similar to a web, overlapping and of equal importance. Maki's second project, outlined in *The Child*, Housing with Walls (1962),[38] was a collaborative work with Otaka. This work also appeared in *Collective Form*. It proposed wall-like elements to mediate different city regions, such as busy streets and quiet residential sections or individual houses and a communal place. Walls were a controlling element over the longer term to make a Collective Form without becoming an imposing megastructure.

The difference between Maki and van Eyck in *Collective Form* was the idea of linkage. Van Eyck tended to rely on physical links such as walls between different elements and recognizable and repetitive patterns to create a comprehensive whole. For example, in the Noah's Ark Project (1962) and the competition designs for the Prix de Rome (1962) by his student Piet Blom, which van Eyck considered best illustrations of "configurative discipline," housing units were physically connected to form

FIGURE 7.4 Housing with Walls (1962), a collaborative work with Otaka. Het Nieuwe Instituut/BAKE_ph61-10a.

windmill patterns. Conversely, Maki was not limited to such a configuration, stating clearly in *Collective Form* that "forms in group form have their own built-in link, whether expressed or latent, so that they may grow in a system."[39] In "Linkage in Collective Form," the second chapter in *Collective Form*, Maki investigated different links using historical and vernacular examples. From these observations, he became aware of the importance of open space as an implied link. Hillside Terrace is considered one of the best examples of group form using modern architecture vocabulary. While Maki stated that he was influenced by van Eyck's idea of "place" and "in-between" in its design,[40] the buildings, which were built at different phases, are not physically connected and do not form an identifiable pattern, but small, sequential open spaces with circulations through them create a comprehensive unity.

Maki developed different types of linkage spaces using "three models of the exterior-interior spatial correlation."[41] These models could be a physical connection (e.g., interior), an interiorized exterior (e.g., an atrium), or an exterior in-between space (e.g., a plaza). In particular, under the hypothetical condition of extreme density, the form of these linkage spaces becomes crucial to the framework of programmed spaces. Thus, in the third type, Maki proposed the exterior space, which was normally considered a residue of the interior space, to be determined before the formation of the interior space. This idea was represented as a conceptual model of the Golgi Structure (1967). Here, determined first were the cone-shaped exterior common voids, which served as horizontal and vertical circulations, and serviced core and light wells. At the same time, the programmed interior spaces such as offices were built as needed and

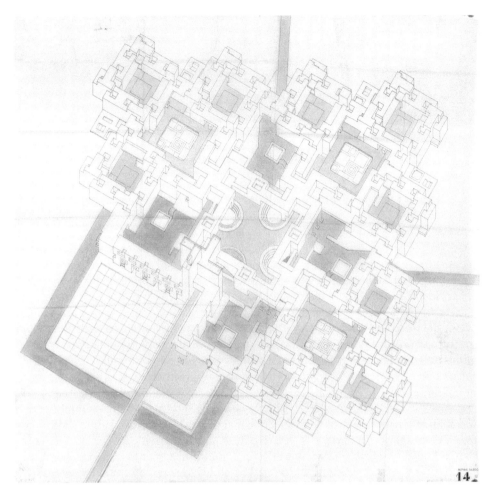

FIGURE 7.5 The competition designs for the Prix de Rome (1962) by Piet Blom, an example of configurative design. Het Nieuwe Instituut/BLOM_17-10.

surrounding the voids so that they would be independent buildings and part of the Collective Form. Instead of regulating the forms of buildings, Maki proposed setting the form of impenetrable public open spaces, which provided services for the public, leaving indeterminant factors to be developed autonomously.

Another utopia-formless megastructure

In the 1960s, when Maki developed the idea of Collective Form, he and van Eyck's close and frequent exchanges strongly influenced each other. Both configurative discipline and group form suggested the profound potential for democratic spatial organization, but there was no specific methodology. Unfortunately, we still need to understand how to apply the system to our city today.

"Another Utopia" (2015) is the latest concept out of group form and linkage when society is facing a population decrease rather than the rapid increase, as was the case in the 1960s. Throughout his 60-year career, Maki has observed that open space—latent

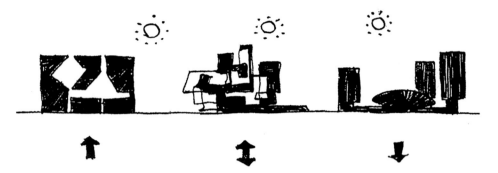

FIGURE 7.6 Three models of the exterior-interior spatial correlation. Image credit: Fumihiko Maki.

linkage—was a strong connection between different urban elements and, in fact, the very entity that composed our experiences of city places. In his essay "Another Utopia," he again emphasized the potential of open space as a place for spontaneous public interactions. He continued to hold a strong belief in the importance of encouraging people in society to participate actively and subjectively in making their own public spaces. However, he realized that they were more inclined to speak out about their individual needs for open spaces than for the form of the built element. Witnessing that the communities present among the residents and visitors were formed autonomously in Hillside Terrace's open spaces and footpaths, Maki proposed prioritizing open spaces as much as, if not more than, building facilities in designing a new community.[42]

Van Eyck's lesser-known works, the playgrounds in Amsterdam, exemplify such kinds of open spaces. From 1947 to 1978, he had designed more than 700 playgrounds for the Public Works Department. These playground sites, which were leftover voids in the existing city fabric, each had a different condition for which he provided a site-specific design with subtle manipulations. The children massed in otherwise-desolate urban niches that became community-gathering places. Observing their effect, many citizens of Amsterdam reacted by petitioning to request playgrounds in their neighborhoods. The enthusiastic public reception changed the mind of Cor van Eesteren, Head of Urban Development for the city of Amsterdam, who was previously an authoritative figure in CIAM and a top-down planner before the war, into becoming an ardent supporter of playgrounds. This master architect started inserting the playgrounds when planning new postwar neighborhoods.[43] Here, critical importance was granted to open spaces as a social connector as much as to housing units.

The gaps growing in our cities could be organized to form the community's foci, in a similar fashion to van Eyck, who had transformed residues of the city into a network of active places with simple interventions. However, the fact that only a handful of his original playgrounds have survived[44] reminds us of the fragility and ephemerality of open spaces. Planning is not enough—places should be protected and nurtured by the community. While immaterial, they need to be treated as independent and permanent public places, impermeable to fickle fashion and economically stronger functions.

Looking back at Hillside Terrace, one may realize that its spatial characteristic is not only due to small open spaces intertwining with the buildings, but that the wide street upon which all buildings face also plays a major role in creating its unique streetscape. Considering the low density of traffic in the early twentieth century on the street, Kyu-Yamate, it was broadened to unusual width of 72 feet and lined with trees by Torajiro Asakura, the landlord and local assemblyman of the area who donated part of his land to the street.[45] The floor area ratio, as well as the height limit of the surrounding area, remained low in contrast to the wide street. Such a condition altogether contributes to the spatial framework of Hillside Terrace; the impenetrable open

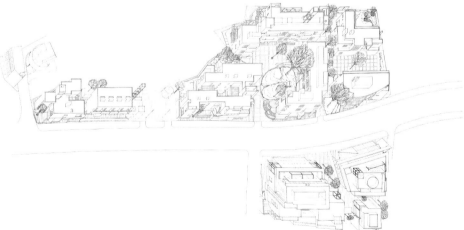

FIGURE 7.7 Aerial view of Daikanyama, with buildings of Hillside Terrace highlighted. Photo credit: ASPI, and Hillside Terrace overview; image: Fumihiko Maki.

space of Kyu-Yamate acts as an implied megaform spine. It provides a spatial order not only to Hillside Terrace buildings, but also to the other buildings around them, which configure part of group form despite their differences in appearance. This example may suggest a sustainable combination of megaform and group form; planning open spaces as formless megastructures and substructures may be the steps needed towards group form today.

Notes

1 Fumihiko Maki, *Investigations in Collective Form* (St. Louis: Washington University Press, 1964).
2 Fumihiko Maki, *Nurturing Dreams* (Cambridge, MA: MIT Press, 2008), 26.
3 Rem Koolhaas, *Project Japan* (Cologne: Taschen GmbH, 2011), 301.
4 Kei Minohara et al. (eds.), *Kenchikuka Otaka Masato no Shigoto* (Tokyo: Ex-Knowledge, 2014), 41. Otaka mentioned his graduate thesis was on "cluster" in the interview, but unfortunately, the thesis was lost.
5 Koolhaas, *Project Japan*, 301. Comments by Masato Otaka.
6 "50 Years since Group Form—Interview with Fumihiko Maki," JA78, 4.
7 Max Risselada and Dirk van den Heuvel (eds.), *Team 10 in Search of a Utopia of the Present* (Rotterdam: NAi Publishers, 2006), 84.
8 Fumihiko Maki, "Modernism tono deai," *Kiokuno Keisho vol. 1* (Tokyo: Chikuma Shobo, 1997), 143.
9 Fumihiko Maki, "Attending the Team-X Meeting in 1960," *Shinkenchiku* (February 1961): 59.
10 Risselada and van den Heuvel (eds.), *Team 10 in Search of a Utopia of the Present*, 85.
11 Koolhaas, *Project Japan*, 303.
12 Maki, *Collective Form*, 8.
13 Maki, *Collective Form*, 19.
14 Fumihiko Maki, "Gunzokei sonogo," *Kindai Kenchiku* (November 1960): 65–66.
15 Maki, *Nurturing Dreams*, 40.
16 Several letters and architectural documents from Maki to Bakema in the early 1960s are archived in the Het Nieuwe Instituut, Rotterdam.
17 Jaap Bakema, "1960–2000," in *Post Box for the Development of the Habitat (B.P.H.)*, ed. Jaap Bakema (no. 5, 27 January 1961), Collection Het Nieuwe Instituut, Rotterdam, 4.
18 Letter from Bakema to Maki, August 28, 1961, Collection Het Nieuwe Instituut, Rotterdam.
19 Maki, "Gunzokei Sonogo," 66.
20 Bakema, *Post Box* 6 (12 May 1961), 1; 9 (1 June 1962): 4–6.
21 Dirk van den Heuvel (ed.), *Jaap Bakema and the Open Society* (Amsterdam: Archis Publishers, 2015), 66.
22 Maki recalls visiting Schroder House, Utrecht, with van Eyck and inviting van Eyck on a tour in Japan after his participation in the Pacific Congress of the Architectural Students' Society of the University of Auckland in September 1963.
23 Aldo van Eyck, "Step towards a Configurative Discipline," *Forum* (August 1962); Aldo van Eyck, *Collected Articles and Other Writings 1947–1998* (Amsterdam: Sun Publisher, 2008); Aldo van Eyck, *Aldo Van Eyck: Writings*, vol. 1 (Amsterdam: Sun Publisher, 2006), 329.
24 Maki, *Collective Form*, 30.
25 Francis Strauven, *Aldo van Eyck: The Shape of Reality* (Amsterdam: Architectura & Natura Press, 1998), 386.
26 Strauven, *Aldo van Eyck: The Shape of Reality*, 459.
27 Fumihiko Maki et al., *City with a Hidden Past* (Tokyo: Kashima Institute Publishing, 2018), 23. The original Japanese version of this book is *Miegakure suru toshi* (1980).
28 Maki, *Collective Form*, 47.
29 The most notable example is "Tadayou Modernism," *Shin-Kenchiku* (September 2012): 40–50.
30 Fred A. Bernstein, "My Favorite Building," *Architectural Record*, last modified September 1, 2016, https://www.architecturalrecord.com/articles/11875-my-favorite-building.

31 Jaap Bakema, "Bouwen voor de anonieme opdrachtgever [Building for Anonymous Clients]," *Forum* 16(2) (1962): 44.

32 Van Eyck, "Steps towards a Configurative Discipline"; *Collected Articles and Other Writings 1947–1998*, 335.

33 Van Eyck, "Steps towards a Configurative Discipline," 336–337; van Eyck, "Collective Form," 8–9.

34 Van Eyck, "Steps towards a Configurative Discipline," 338–339.

35 Van Eyck, "Steps towards a Configurative Discipline," 337.

36 Aldo van Eyck, *Aldo Van Eyck Writings: The Child, the City and the Artist*, vol. 2 (Amsterdam: Sun Publisher, 2006), 159; van Eyck, "Collective Form," 23.

37 Van Eyck, *The Child, the City, and the Artists,* 212–213.

38 Van Eyck, *The Child, the City and the Artist*, 215.

39 Maki, *Collective Form*, 19.

40 Fumihiko Maki, "Tooku kara mita 'Daikanyama syugo jutaku keikaku,' " *Shin Kenchiku* (April 1978).

41 Fumihiko Maki, "Shugotai-Yottsuno Study," *Kenchiku Bunka* (June 1967): 62–63.

42 Fumihiko Maki, "Another Utopia," *Shin Kenchiku* (September 2015). The book was published with the same title by NTT Publisher in 2019.

43 Liane Lefaivre, "Space, Place and Play," in *Aldo van Eyck—The Playgrounds and the City*, ed. Ingeborg de Roode and Liane Lefaivre (Rotterdam: NAi Publishers, 2002), 41.

44 Strauven, "Wasted Pearls in the Fabric of the City"; Lefaivre, "Space, Place and Play," 81.

45 Fumihiko Maki, ed., *Hillside Terrace + West no sekai* (Tokyo: Kashima Publisher, 2006), 31.

8

KIYONORI KIKUTAKE CIRCA 2011

Sustaining Life through Metabolism

Ken Tadashi Oshima

The year 2011 marked the occurrence of the Great East Japan Earthquake on March 11, the staging of the Mori Art Museum retrospective exhibition "METABOLISM, THE CITY OF THE FUTURE" (Figure 8.1) and the passing of Metabolist architect Kiyonori Kikutake (1928–2011). The exhibition's subtitle of "Dreams and Visions of Reconstruction in Postwar and Present Day Japan" sought to highlight the parallel between addressing the contexts of devastation following World War II and the 2011 earthquake and tsunami for the design proposals of Metabolism. The exhibition poster featured Kikutake's vision of Ecopolis, a contemporary reimagining of his original 1958 Tower-Shaped Community proposal.

A fundamental challenge of the 2011 re-examination of Metabolism was to define and assess its meanings, both following the publication of the 1960 manifesto, *Metabolism 1960* and its subsequent evolution through its protagonists. The manifesto asserted:

> "Metabolism" is the name of the group, in which each member proposes future designs of our coming world through his concrete designs and illustrations. We regard human society as a vital process, a continuous development from atom to nebula. The reason why we use such a biological word, the metabolism, is that we believe, design and technology should be a denotation of human vitality.
>
> We are not going to accept the metabolism as a natural historical process, but we are trying to encourage active metabolic development of our society through our proposals.
>
> This volume mainly consists of the designs for our future cities proposed only by architects. From the next issue, however, the people in other fields such as designers, artists, engineers, scientists, and politicians, will participate in it, and already some of them are preparing for the next one.
>
> In future, more will come to join "Metabolism" and some will go; that means a metabolic process will also take place in its membership.[1]

DOI: 10.4324/9781003186540-9

Kiyonori Kikutake circa 2011   **115**

FIGURE 8.1   "Metabolism: The City of the Future," Mori Art Museum, 2011.

In contrast to the original, slender 89-page manifesto, the 719-page *Project Japan Metabolism Talks* by Rem Koolhaas and Hans Ulrich Obrist, together with editors Kayoko Ota and James Westcott of the research and design studio AMO, sought to tackle the issue of Metabolism's meaning through extended interviews and related documents.[2] Beyond the original 1960 featured group members (Kiyonori Kikutake, Noboru Kawazoe, Masato Otaka, Fumihiko Maki, and Noriaki (Kisho) Kurokawa), *Project Japan*'s "cast of characters" included 38 individuals, adding predecessors, collaborators, commentators, Kenzo Tange and his collaborators, family, and research laboratory. The

1960 manifesto features Kikutake as both the first member listed in the group and featured in 35 pages of the publication, which was almost twice that of Maki (17 pages) and Kurokawa (17 pages). Kikutake himself described "Metabolism" both as *taisha kenchiku* 代謝建築 in Japanese and later "as born of renovation" in 2009.[3] In the Metabolism exhibition opening symposium in September 2011, Kikutake acknowledged the evolving meanings of Metabolism between the members as well as his own reconsiderations, asserting that his primary aim was for the "renewal of Japanese wooden architecture."[4] Throughout the multiplicity of the meanings of Metabolism, it could be seen as an organic, ever-evolving design concept to maintain "human vitality."

While the "metabolic" drawings of the "proposals for new urbanism" may appear to be abstract, paper architecture, Kikutake asserted that his Ocean City proposal was a "concrete design" in response to the crowding and paralysis of the contemporary city, as well as the stagnation and contradictions of architecture.[5] Accompanying Kikutake's February 1959 publication of Marine City in *Kokusai Kenchiku*, the journal featured an article on the developing technology vis-à-vis the sea and artificial land through deep concrete piling technology and the calculation of wave currents for marine development.[6] As Raffaele Pernice has pointed out, Kikutake and his Metabolist colleagues built on harbor and coastal engineering that had gained urgency since the 1953 typhoon at Ise Bay for their proposals in Tokyo Bay.[7] In fact, Typhoon Vera had struck on September 29, 1959 as the third-deadliest natural disaster in Japan during the twentieth century, causing approximately 5,000 casualties. For Kikutake, the concern to address these disasters literally struck home with the 1953 North Kyushu flood, in which Kyūshū's longest river, the Chikugo River, flooded in the vicinity of his childhood home in Kurume, resulting in more than 1,000 casualties and 450,000 houses (Figure 8.2). The year 1953 also marked the start of Kikutake's independent architectural practice at the age of 25.

The origins of Kikutake's metabolic vision can be traced back to his formative years growing up in Kyūshū. He was part of the sixteenth generation of a once-large landowning family in Kurume, a former feudal city situated along the Chikugo River, which flows from the volcanic Mount Aso to the Ariake Sea. While the river irrigates some 400 square kilometers of rice fields on the Tsukushi Plain (where wet-rice cultivation was introduced to Japan during the Yayoi Period, 300 BCE to CE 300), it has been prone to frequent flooding. The paddies themselves are filled with water in the spring, denoted by the characters 水田, which Kikutake considered to form his *genfūkei*—an indelible scene from his childhood.[8] Kikutake's family home was located close to the riverbanks and the Suitengū shrine. Here he witnessed how solid shrine structures made of stone could withstand floods, while temporal wooden elements could be easily replaced. Life entailed constantly adapting to the changing natural environment.

Yet it was the post-World War II land reforms rather than natural disasters that led to the loss of the Kikutake family landholdings. Under the 1947 Land Reform Act, 38 percent of Japan's cultivated land was purchased from landlords by the government and resold at low prices to the farmers who worked on it.[9] The Kikutake household thereby lost its social position and historic role in the community. Kikutake noted in his 2005 interview with Rem Koolhaas: "My ancestors were landlords, and in Japan, the landlords were traditionally providers of infrastructure as well as the patrons of culture. They built schools, they built floodgates, they maintained and improved farmland, and they also supported Shinto shrines and Buddhist temples."[10]

FIGURE 8.2   Chikugo River, Kurume, Fukuoka Prefecture. Photo by Ken Tadashi Oshima.

Kikutake's pursuit of architecture thus sought to create a platform for living, raised above the floodplain on land and over the sea, with infinite possibilities for expansion into new territories. As Kikutake wrote in his essay "The Order of Things One Can See: Floors and Columns":

> The first floor surface has a deeper significance than its plain, physical meaning as the base supporting human living. In our country, we have been trained to attach a definite psychological significance to the floor, which is relied upon as a source of stability.[11]

Such plateaus were often the result of great technological feats. Kikutake found particular resonance in the platforms and corridors of Itsukushima Shrine (Figure 8.3) hovering above Hiroshima Bay, originating from the twelfth century; the great terrace of the Kiyomizu Temple in the eastern hills above Kyoto from 1633; or the sublime suspended structure of the Kasamori Temple from 1028 that rests on wooden stilts above a rock outcropping in Chiba Prefecture. Just as the Kasamori Temple has been destroyed by fire three times, the broader challenge for Kikutake was how to reincarnate the essence of such structures to accommodate contemporary needs of "man in the new democratic society [that] … should be neither for the gods nor for the powerful, but must be merely for man."[12] Along these lines, Kikutake believed that the Kiyomizu Temple could be rebuilt and reconceived as the Eiffel Tower of Kyoto. In fact, Kiyomizu Temple was published in 1956 in the contemporary architectural journal *Shinkenchiku,* underscoring its potential for reinterpretation and reincarnation.[13]

FIGURE 8.3 Itsukushima Shrine, Hiroshima. Photo by Ken Tadashi Oshima.

Shinchintaisha: an architecture of change and continuity

Kikutake's earliest independent design work set out to transform and reuse existing wood-frame structures. Such a practice followed the notion of *shinchintaisha* (新陳代謝), which literally translates as "renewal; replacement; metabolism." This practice replaces deteriorated wooden sections with new pieces to resuscitate remaining members. Upon graduating from Waseda University in Tokyo in 1950, Kikutake worked briefly for the Takenaka Construction Company and architect Togo Murano (1891–1984) before establishing his own office at the age of 25 in 1953. His first important client was Shojiro Ishibashi (1889–1976), the founding president of the Bridgestone Corporation, to whom Kikutake's grandfather had lent funds to establish the corporation. Kikutake pursued his pivotal theory of a "system of replacement" for early projects including the Ishibashi Culture Center/Culture Hall (1956) and the Eifukuji Kindergarten (1956) (Figure 8.4). For the former, Kikutake reused gable trusses by cutting them in half and reversing their direction to create a butterfly section. In the latter, he reused the wooden structures while creating a varied rhythm of door and window openings to create a bright and airy new look.[14]

Early work in wood-frame construction housing maintained traditional principles with double-aspect cross-ventilation. Projects such as Kikutake's Bridgestone Tonogaya Apartments (1956) and Bridgestone Mothers' and Children's Dormitory (1957) maintained *tatami*-based flexible living, with the former stacking units within a reinforced-concrete structure. In his Inoue and Ijichi Houses (1954), Kikutake

FIGURE 8.4 Eifukuji Kindergarten, Kurume, 1956. Courtesy of Kikutake Architects.

infused straightforward wood-frame residential construction with a composition of an operable window-wall, with new systems of swinging rather than sliding openings. Kikutake further abstracted the traditional domestic principles within his square-plan Uryuu House (1958), which found its apotheosis in his own Sky House (1958) (Figure 8.5).

Kikutake's Sky House, designed with his wife Norie, was their dynamic platform for the unfolding of family life. The Sky House, in considering the fundamental question of how to accommodate the changing needs of living, built on his previous Uryuu House in pushing the bathroom core from the center to the edge of the house to afford replacement flexibility and lessen the draw on the central living space. The main living space was suspended 6.6 meters above the sloped site from reinforced concrete piers on four sides, with a hyperbolic paraboloid (HP) shell roof above. The design afforded a 360-degree view akin to that from the ninth-century Kasamori Temple that Kikutake admired.

The Sky House design evolved from a pure modeled vision of the postwar single-family house to its built and lived-in reality. First published with the English title "A Plan for a Concrete House," the Kikutake home provided "protection from earthquakes, typhoons, and illness."[15] The Sky House model hovered above the low-rise tile roof houses of the Bunkyō District of Tokyo in the published collage of the unbuilt house. Following the publication of its built form, the Sky House instantly became a masterwork of modern architecture, published with Kenzo Tange's Kagawa Prefectural Building in the January 1959 issue of *Kenchiku bunka*. Noboru Kawazoe

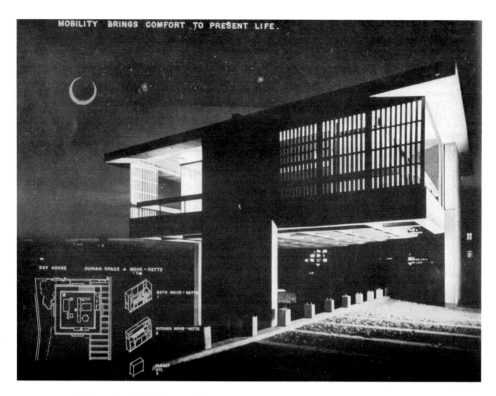

FIGURE 8.5 Kikutake, Sky House. Source: Oscar Newman, *CIAM '59 in Otterlo* (Stuttgart: Karl Krämer, 1961), 184.

(1926–2015), a journalist and soon to be the mastermind of the Metabolist group, praised the two works for establishing a new realm of "humanist" architecture.

Through the design of his own house, Kikutake transformed the application of replaceable wood-frame construction to a reinforced concrete slab/pier structure. This afforded a new mode of flexible living that would serve the family's changing needs through many decades and would come to epitomize the principles of Metabolism *avant la lettre*. The Sky House design followed the teachings of Ken Wajirō (1888–1973), an ethnographic architect and one of Kikutake's professors at Waseda, whose theories of "Modernology" and "Living Science" advocated having few rooms with the sparest possible use of solid walls to divide space.[16] The open living space thus formed the heart of Kikutake's plan, served by his invention of a moveable kitchenette or bath unit that he termed "Movenette," and could be updated as technology advanced. In turn, the living space was modulated by the notion that "the most important feature in a Japanese home is the use of fittings that can be adjusted in highly complex manners according to the change of seasons."[17]

In counterpoint to the facilitation of constant change, the precise proportions of the Sky House provided the framework for lasting beauty. Its 10-square-meter plan, HP shell roof, and slight overhang to protect sliding screens below worked in perfect harmony. For Kikutake, the completed Sky House became a concrete conceptual structure, interchangeable system, and repeatable human-scale living unit to address burgeoning urban problems in terms of inadequate quality and quantity of housing in postwar Japan.

In proposing the Tower-Shaped Community and Marine City (Figure 8.6) in the journal *Kokusai kenchiku* (January–February 1959), Kikutake effectively extended his platform for living vertically and horizontally, from land to sea, rising to the sky. As he explained:

> I realized that [interchangeable architectural systems] would apply to urban environments as well. Would there be any way to add the dimension of replaceability to land, which forms the foundation of urban problems? Why not artificially produce an abundance of floating land, patches of which can be combined in a number of ways to prepare urban spaces.[18]

The Movenettes of the Sky House could be scaled up to form telescoping living units attached to the structural core tower and could be open to views of the sea, sky, and Mount Fuji. Such aspirations informed both unbuilt and built work, including the Hotel Tōkōen (1964–79) (Figure 8.7), the Pacific Hotel (1966), and the Sado Grand Hotel (1967).

The launch of Metabolism

The transformation of building technology at the multiple scales of the Sky House, Marine City, and the Izumo Administration Building formed the ideological basis for Kikutake's pursuit of Metabolism as launched at the 1960 World Design Conference in Tokyo. Following the organic implications of the name "Metabolism," Kikutake expanded on the Marine City to propose the Ocean City "unabara," in which the metabolic city is formed by the process of continual organic cell division. Such a perspective brought together Kikutake's interests in architecture and biology; he had wanted to become a doctor before being encouraged to study architecture based on his drawing skills.[19] Noboru Kawazoe, in supporting Kikutake's organic stance, advocated designing projects to be like a "cell of bacteria which is constantly propagating itself."[20] Kawazoe believed that the will of bacteria to live, like the will of man, would always remain. As he concluded, "the only difference will be men's capacity to dream a magnificent dream."[21] While such assessments may seem naïve or unscientific, they reflect their sincere youthful aspirations and worldview at the time.

With the official launch of Metabolism with the presentation of the *Metabolism 1960* at the World Design Conference in May 1960, Kikutake led the group as its central architectural voice through his core principles articulated in Ocean City/Marine City and the Sky House as the lead projects of the first 40 pages of the group's inaugural publication. Fumihiko Maki (1928–) would later describe the group much like a baseball team coming together for a common cause to address rapidly transforming postwar Japan through an organic architectural/urban strategy.[22] Maki described journalist Noboru Kawazoe as the coach, Kikutake as the ace pitcher, and Kenzo Tange (1913–2005) and Arata Isozaki (1931–) behind the backstop. Thus, Kikutake's Sky House together with his scheme for Marine Cities occupied center stage. For Kikutake, "Metabolism" meant the "introduction into architecture of such a method of replacing and changing the living equipment in accordance with living patterns. At the same time, this method helps us to delineate clearly the main portions of the building which will not change, and which will continue to be the center and predominant part of the building. This also will help the architect to formulate his own goals clearly."[23]

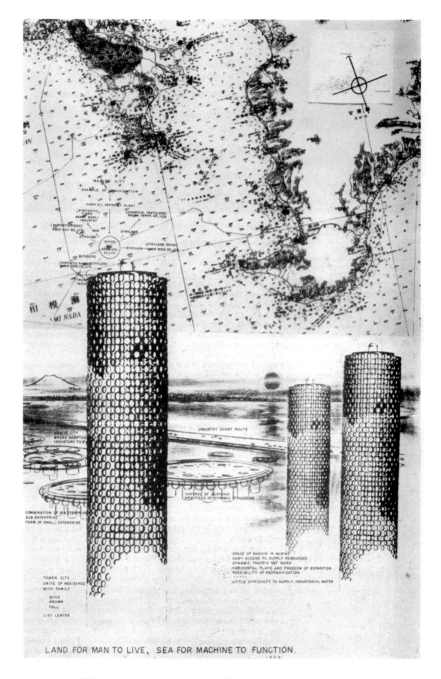

FIGURE 8.6 "Ideas for the Reorganization of Tokyo City, Kikutake Kiyonori," in Oscar Newman, *CIAM '59 in Otterlo* (Stuttgart: Karl Krämer, 1961), 185.

FIGURE 8.7 Hotel Tōkōen, Yonago, Tottori Prefecture, 1964. Photo by Ken Tadashi Oshima.

The Sky House was also a platform for discussing ideas on architecture, including visits by a number of prominent architects from abroad, including Louis Kahn, Peter Smithson, and James Stirling. In particular, the composition of space in the Sky House could be seen to align with Louis Kahn's notion of "served" and "servant" spaces, a topic of heated discussion following Kahn's visit to the house in May 1960 for the Tokyo World Design Conference.[24] Kahn discussed the relationship between the phenomena of form and space, building on his 1955 essay "Order and Form" and his 1957 essay "Architecture is the Thoughtful Making of Spaces."[25] The two discussed fundamental principles of design through elements such the conception of "spoon" as "form made of inseparable parts of a container and an art." As Kahn explained: "If you take the container away you have a handle, if you take the arm away you have a cup. Together they are spoon…"[26] This thinking closely aligned with Kikutake's own developing theory of *ka, kata, katachi*, his tripartite methodology between "imaginative, technological and functional approaches" and "human life/function/space."[27] Moreover, Kikutake noted that Kahn took particular interest in his Tokuunji project and the Izumo Administration Building. While Kahn could be seen to have informed Kikutake's design methodology, Kikutake's designs would find resonance with Kahn, especially in his design of the Salk Institute, in the relationship between concrete walls and wooden louvers. Kikutake and Peter Smithson could also be seen to share common concerns—toward "urban structuring" and in similar expressions of Movenette bathroom units.[28] James Stirling's shared interests with Kikutake in prefabrication and housing could be seen in their respective designs for the PREVI experimental housing project in Lima, Peru (1969) and Stirling's attempt to crawl down through the Sky House floor opening to the children's Movenette space below. However, Kikutake implied the difficulties in establishing universal standards and scale in noting that "the opening was just barely big enough for him to get through."[29]

Creating a floating world

Kikutake's embrace of function and current technology were concomitant tendencies to his "imaginative approach," creating floating space on both land and sea. This could be seen as a "resistance unit" protecting human life from the ravages of flood or fire, as in the Sky House, or a jellyfish floating on the sea as a conceptual motif for his actual Floating City (1971) or his Aquapolis for the 1975 Okinawa Ocean Expo. Kikutake translated the sacred floating planes of the Kasamori Temple and the Itsukushima Shrine to secular contexts, from the elevated office slabs of the Tatebayashi City Hall (1963) to the Kyoto International Convention Hall (1963). The Tatebayashi City Hall maintains the clear *parti* of four cores supporting the office slabs, akin to Louis Kahn's contemporaneous Richards Medical Center, yet on a larger public scale that affords expansive views of the city and surrounding landscape.

In the following decade, Kikutake transformed the conception of a floating artificial ground into three dimensions through the creation of a triangulated, megastructural spaceframe system. Beginning in 1972, he began developing the Stratiform Structure System in collaboration with the Japanese Ministry of International Trade and Industry.[30] The open structural framework allowed for the insertion of gardens and housing units as required. Although the scheme as a whole was not realized, full-scale mockups were constructed to test its fire resistance. This conceptual framework could be seen to evolve into his design of Pasadena Heights terraced housing (1974)

(Figure 8.8), located near the base of Mount Fuji at Mishima and adjacent to the tracks of the Tōkaidō Shinkansen train. The 120 units cascade in a zigzag configuration to accommodate the sloping site and maximize expansive views, notwithstanding the identical minimal 68.3-square-meter units. Each unit is accessed from below via a hanging stair—just as the Sky House originally was—to afford a dynamic spatial experience daily. In fact, Kikutake retained a unit as his own family's second home. Also, just as in the Sky House, the individual units maintain flexible living spaces with the Movenette kitchen and bath units along the front edge for light, view, and ease of replacement. As a complement to the minimal interiors, the exterior private courts are rather expansive, offering a balanced house and garden. In occupying these structures that are open to change and interpretation, the residents have transformed the units over time with a variety of add-ons and personal touches. Finally, the triangulated structural system further evolved into the circular tower schemes known as Amazon Ecopolis (1992) featured on the 2011 "Metabolism: The City of the Future" poster (Figure 8.1).

In parallel with Kikutake's land-based schemes, the early 1970s marked the concretization of Kikutake's Marine City ideals. Upon his appointment as a visiting professor at the University of Hawaii in 1971, Kikutake led an international research team of scientists and engineers to create "Marine City 1971—Project in Hawaii" as a floating city set on two concentric rings. Kikutake found particular inspiration in the Research Platform FLIP (Floating Instrument Platform) as a 355-foot-long ocean research vessel that could pitch backward 90 degrees, with the depth of the partially

FIGURE 8.8 Pasadena Heights, Shizuoka Prefecture, 1974. Photo by Ken Tadashi Oshima.

flooded vessel able to withstand wave currents. The inner ring of high-rise buildings contained housing, hotels, offices, and shops, and the low-rise outer ring served as the platform for the Ocean Expo. The rings sat upon cylindrical "milk bottle" floats, bundled in groups of three as an open-ended, extendable system.

Marine City found its final realization in Kikutake's Aquapolis design for the Japan Pavilion at the Okinawa Ocean Expo '75, which celebrated the return of the Okinawa Islands from the USA to Japan. Kikutake's floating city was towed more than 1,000 kilometers by boats to Okinawa from Hiroshima, where it was built. With a capacity of 2,400 people, the semi-submersible floating Aquapolis was the size of a city block: 100 square meters in plan and 32 meters high, containing exhibition spaces, a banquet hall, offices, an infirmary, a communication room, a post office, residences for 40 staff members, and a computer room. The primary structure termed the "lower hull" consisted of four giant floats that could be pumped with seawater to adjust the draft. In the event of rough seas, the Aquapolis could anchor offshore and could partly submerge to protect the structure.

Aquapolis was a microcosmic realization of an entire sustainable environment.[31] The idea of the Marine City would become a lifelong pursuit; Kikutake authored two full-length books on the subject (Figure 8.9).[32] For Kikutake, this was not science fiction, but rather a vision based on everyday life in which he contemplated the "spectacular experience of the weather and horizon of the sea."[33] In considering the question of "how to live on earth," Kikutake looked to the "great potential of the earth as seen within the universe as a star of glistening blue water."[34] His Marine City followed in the history of great marine cities in the world, including Venice and Mont-Saint-Michel combined with the technology of sea planes and ocean liners. In considering residents' weekly schedules, he contemplated the possibilities of an ocean-based cuisine, "three types of water," "sports and fashion," "three-dimensional movies," and even ocean festivals.[35]

Yet, through the course of Kikutake's career, many of his classic works would face the reality of life and death through their dismantling or demolition. Following Expo '75, Aquapolis could not find a suitable owner and was dismantled. While the Izumo Shrine is rebuilt roughly every 60 years, the adjacent Izumo Shrine Administration building stood for less time, despite extensive preservation efforts (1963–2016).[36] The iconic concert hall Miyakonojo (1966–2019) in the remote area of Miyazaki, Kyushu suffered from maintenance issues, fell into disuse, and was also eventually demolished, despite fervent support for its preservation by Kikutake enthusiasts. Moreover, many of Kikutake's designs for hospitality and retail have suffered similar fates: Hotel SEIYO Ginza (1987–2013) and Hotel Cosima/Sofitel (1994–2003), and the impending demolition of the Seibu Ohtsu Shopping Center (1976) and Sado Grand Hotel (1967) in the aftermath of the COVID-19 pandemic.

Metabolism as resilient change and rebirth

Nonetheless, the ongoing evolution of the Metabolist movement and the ideals of these works (*ka*/*kata*) themselves can be seen through the work of younger generations (*katachi*). The strength of Kikutake's work is in its tectonic construction, human-scaled

海上都市の話

菊竹清訓

FIGURE 8.9 Kikutake Kiyonori, *Kaijō toshi no hanashi* (Tokyo: NHK Books, 1975).

128 Ken Tadashi Oshima

spatial character, and capacity to embrace change over time. These key aspects have been highly influential for those who worked closely with him, including Toyo Ito, Fred Thompson, Itsuko Hasegawa, Hiroshi Naito, and a new generation of young architects. His vision lives on beyond his death in 2011, according to cycles of continued metabolic change. Learning about the Sky House as a young girl inspired Kazuyo Sejima's career in architecture, as she writes in "Recalling Kikutake-*sensei*." Her SANAA partner Ryue Nishizawa has noted his own impression of the Sky House in terms of its efficiency, economy of materials, and almost microcosmic expression of the city.[37] In Toronto, Fred Thompson's scheme for Harbour City (1970) proposed a Marine City on old airport lands and adjacent fill; this project was actually built, in part, on the water as "Ontario Place."[38]

With the devastation of the Great East Japan/Tohoku earthquake and tsunami on March 11, 2011, Kikutake reaffirmed his belief in addressing both the devastating and benevolent forces of nature between land and sea through the creation of public infrastructure. The consequential land subsidence and liquefaction rendered coastal land as sea, giving new relevance for creating marine cities.[39] At this juncture, Kikutake had in fact confirmed his confidence in the viability of the Marine City to withstand forces of such magnitude as a floating built environment.[40] The vision of Kikutake's public architecture has been sustained through Toyo Ito's wood-frame "Home for All" projects in tsunami-ravaged areas (2012–2013)[41]. Itō's scheme for the heavily damaged Kamaishi City in Iwate Prefecture built on Kikutake's A-Frame Stratiform Structure System (1972) and incorporated both *minka* farmhouse-like housing and landscape elements of berms, green belts, and sloped building sites to mitigate future flooding and tidal waves.[42] Moreover, the tsunami's great wake, affecting the entire Pacific Rim, underscores the necessity to look beyond national borders in designing for the constantly changing metabolic world.

While the Sky House has lived on, both physically and as an icon of postwar Japanese architecture, it has in fact proved to be a "resistance unit" to accommodate family changes through multiple generations and respond to an increasingly dense urban environment. In his twilight years, Kikutake once again asserted his vision to create domestic and topographic structures between land and sea, which he noted is expressed vividly in the rice-paddy structures of terraced land such as those of his homeland. Such ecological megastructures that appear to transform from land to sea and back through the seasons thereby situate Kikutake's pursuit within a much longer historical trajectory and confirm his broader lifelong aspiration to sustain human life.[43]

Notes

1 Noboru Kawazoe et al., *Metabolism 1960: The Proposals for New Urbanism* (Tokyo: Bijutsu Shuppansha, 1960).
2 Rem Koolhaas and Hans Ulrich Obrist with Kayoko Ota and James Westcott AMO (eds), *Project Japan Metabolism Talks…* (Cologne: Taschen, 2011).
3 Kiyonori Kikutake, *Taisha kenchikuron [Architectural Theory of Metabolism]* (Tokyo: Shokokusha, 1969); and Kiyonori Kikutake, "Interview: When Metabolism was Born of Renovation/Skyhouse," *Japan Architect*, no. 73 (Spring 2009), 12–27.
4 Kikutake, "The Metabolists on Metabolism," Mori Art Museum, September 18, 2011.

5 Kawazoe, *Metabolism 1960*, 10.
6 Ichiro Ogimachi, "Current Criticism on the Proposals of Artificial Land on the Sea," *Kokusai Kenchiku* (February 1959), 40–53.
7 Raffaele Pernice, "The Issue of Tokyo Bay's Reclaimed Lands as the Origin of Urban Utopias in Modern Japanese Architecture," *Journal of Architecture and Planning (Transactions of AIJ)* (March 2007), 263.
8 Kiyonori Kikutake, "Kenchiku to Mizu," *GA Japan*, no. 70 (September 2004), 112–127.
9 Ibid.
10 Ibid.
11 Kikutake, "The Order of Things One Can See: Floors and Columns," in *Taisha kenchikuron*, published in English in Ken Tadashi Oshima (ed.), *Kiyonori Kikutake: Between Land and Sea* (Cambridge, MA/Zurich: Harvard GSD/Lars Müller), 107.
12 Kiyonori Kikutake, "New Form and Old Tradition," *Arts & Architecture* (December 1964), 34.
13 Isao Motoyoshi, "Kiyomizu dera," *Shinkenchiku*, vol. 31 (November 1956), 2–8.
14 Kikutake, "Interview," 12–13.
15 Kiyonori Kikutake and Norie Kikutake, "Sky House," *Kenchiku bunka*, December 1957, 54–56.
16 Kiyonori Kikutake and Yukio Futagawa, "Sky House, its Background and Significance: Interview with Kiyonori Kikutake," *GA Houses*, no. 100 (2007), 81.
17 Ibid.
18 Kiyonori Kikutake, *Metabolist Kiyonori Kikutake*, special issue, *Space Design*, no. 193 (October 1980), 31.
19 Tatsuo Iso, "Kikutake Yuki shi ni kiku [Interview with Kikutake Yuki]," in Iso Tatsuo, *Kikutake Kiyonori jun rei* (Tokyo: Nikkei BP, 2012), 201.
20 Noboru Kawazoe, "Material and Man," in *Metabolism 1960*, 51.
21 Ibid.
22 Fumihiko Maki remarks at Kiyonori Kikutake's memorial service, April 13, 2012.
23 Kikutake, "New Form and Old Tradition," 16.
24 Kiichiro Fujisaki, "Kikutake sensei, ano yoru, kahn to nani ga attandesuka? [Kikutake-*sensei*, What Happened on That Night with Kahn?]", *Casa Brutus* (July 2004), 74–75.
25 Louis Kahn, "Order and Form," *Perspecta*, vol. 3 (1955), 46–63; Louis Kahn, "Architecture is the Thoughtful Making of Spaces," *Perspecta*, vol. 4 (1957), 2–3.
26 Louis Kahn, "Law and Rule in Architecture," in *Louis Kahn: Essential Texts*, ed. Robert Twombly (New York: W.W. Norton, 2003), 139.
27 Kikutake, "The Great Shrine of Izumo," published in English in Tadashi Oshima (ed.), *Kiyonori Kikutake*, 100–105. The revised complete version of the text has been published as Kiyonori Kikutake, *Taisha kenchikuron ka kata katachi* (Tokyo: Shōkokusha, 1969).
28 "Bath Movenet," *Kenchiku*, April 1965, 86.
29 Kiyonori Kikutake in Koolhaas et al., *Project Japan: Metabolism Talks…*, 139.
30 Mori Art Museum, *Metabolism City of the Future* (Tokyo: Mori Art Museum, 2011), 134.
31 Kikutake, *Kaijōtoshi no hanashi* [*Discussions on the Marine City*] (Tokyo: NHK Books, 1975).
32 Kiyonori Kikutake, *Kaijō toshi* SD84 (Tokyo: Kajima Shuppankai, 1973); Kikutake Kiyonori, *Kaijō toshi no hanashi* (Tokyo: NHK Books, 1975).
33 Kikutake, *Kaijō toshi no hanashi*, 154.
34 Kikutake, *Kaijō toshi no hanashi*, inside cover.
35 Kikutake, *Kaijō toshi no hanashi*,155–185.
36 https://www.sosbrutalism.org/cms/15889529.
37 Ryue Nishizawa, "Kikutake Kiyonori," *Shinkenchiku*, special issue (May 2012), 94.
38 While Fred Thompson was the driving design force for Ontario Place, the design was further developed by Eberhard Zeidler.
39 Tetsuro Imakiire and Mamoru Koarai, "Wide-Area Land Subsidence Caused by 'the 2011 off the Pacific Coast of Tohoku Earthquake,'" *Soils and Foundations*, vol. 52, no. 5 (2012), 842–855.

40 Keita Fukusawa, "Hand Man: Kikutake Kiyonori," *Numéro*, 53, no. 186 (January–February 2012), 185–186.
41 Maria Didero, "Toyo Ito: Re-building from Disaster," *Domus* (January 2012), https://www.domusweb.it/en/interviews/2012/01/26/toyo-ito-re-building-from-disaster.html.
42 "Itō Toyoo shi ga 'gashō zukuri' no shūgō jutaku! Kamaishi shi no fukkoukeikaku ni teaian," *Kensetsu tsūshin shinbun*, March 5, 2012, http://kensetsunewspickup.blogspot.com/2012/03/blog-post_7142.html.
43 Fukusawa, "Hand Man: Kikutake Kiyonori," 186.

9

METABOLISM AS SURVIVAL ARCHITECTURE

Hyunjung Cho

The growing interest in Metabolism owes much to a sense of crisis and vulnerability following a series of natural and humanmade disasters. Architectural historian Yatsuka Hajime has pointed out that the Metabolism retrospective held at the Mori Art Museum, "Metabolism: The City of the Future" (2011), was made more timely by the Great East Japan Earthquake of 2011.[1] As a chief curator of the exhibition, Yatsuka encouraged the younger generation of architects to emulate the "courage" of the Metabolists, who sought to regenerate the country from postwar ruins to prosperity. The lesson learned from the Metabolist movement is an insight into how to survive an apocalypse and regenerate the city. This lesson has surfaced in recent years with renewed urgency and relevance since Anthropocene narratives have posed a complex challenge to the field of architecture and urbanism.

Metabolism has long been understood within the international context of utopian architecture. One of the most influential presentations of Metabolism is Reyner Banham's *Megastructure: Urban Futures of the Recent Past*, which was published in 1976.[2] In this book, Banham characterized Metabolism as an Asian branch of the international megastructure movement by emphasizing their shared interest in megascale infrastructure and advanced technology. However, such an emphasis on the international contemporaneity of the Metabolist movement runs the risk of overlooking the specific postwar conditions to which the group's work responded. In order to compensate for such problems, a recent scholarship has become interested in contextualizing the Metabolist movement within Japan's domestic context.[3] Most of these studies argue that Metabolism represented Japan's glorious era of economic growth, while some scholars have tried to examine Metabolism as an architectural response to Japan's traumatic recent history. Architectural historian Cherie Wendelken, for example, claimed that Metabolism was "a form of cultural nihilism that developed out of the trauma of defeat in war followed by occupation."[4] In a similar vein, Rem Koolhaas and Hans Ulrich, in their recent publication *Project Japan*, implied that it seemed almost impossible for the Metabolists to imagine a technology-driven utopia without considering the wartime destruction and postwar ruins. Slightly changing focus,

DOI: 10.4324/9781003186540-10

Koolhaas and Obrist examined how the Metabolists transformed the national crisis into a rare chance to perform a radical makeover of the entire archipelago.[5]

Pushing these recent interpretations to an extreme, I would like to argue that the essence of Metabolism lies in its survival tactics, the capacity to withstand crises and recover from shocks. To this end, this chapter aims to illuminate the group's under-recognized concerns over impending catastrophe and to examine how the sense of crisis and apocalyptic future scenarios shaped their unique architectural thinking and design. In my previous study, I tried to situate Metabolism within Japan's specific postwar condition, which was closely tied to global Cold War geopolitics.[6] However, rather than overemphasizing Japan's specific context of wartime devastation and nuclear destruction, this chapter aims to present Metabolism as a model of survival architecture whose design tactics can be widely applied.

Noboru Kawazoe's catastrophic future scenario

In May 1960, the Metabolists made a stunning debut at the World Design Conference in Tokyo.[7] Although they presented a manifesto titled *Metabolism 1960: The Proposals for New Urbanism*, the Metabolist group was far from homogeneous, but rather was a collective of diverse and even contradictory voices. Among those disparate voices, critic Noboru Kawazoe requires special attention because he tried to offer a concrete future scenario against which Metabolists proposed their visionary schemes for future cities. Kawazoe was a former editor of the prestigious architectural journal *Shinkenchiku*. Together with Kenzo Tange, Kawazoe played a crucial role in the Japanese tradition debate of the mid-1950s, a collective effort to redefine the nation's tradition to establish a legitimate identity for postwar Japan. As the main protagonist of the Japanese tradition debate, Kawazoe tried to connect Metabolism's organic theory with Japanese indigenous culture and tradition. While his role as an enthusiastic spokesperson for Japanese tradition was well known, little attention was paid to Kawazoe's persistent proposal of a unique vision of the future that was mixed with apocalyptic imagination. In his book titled *The Death of Architecture* (*Kenchiku no metsubō*), published in 1960, the same year as the establishment of the Metabolist group, Kawazoe described a proletarian utopia by drawing on the Marxist principle of social evolution through class struggle.[8] He speculated that, as ordinary people would have more leisure time as result of the help provided to them by new technology, they would build their own houses without relying on the help of elite professional architects. Therefore, he believed that architecture in a conventional sense would come to an end and would be replaced by a flexible system of networks. He employed the metaphor of "death" to think about a totally new concept of architecture that might be more democratic and flexible, and thus suitable for the future society.

Kawazoe's anxiety and fear of impending catastrophe were clearly demonstrated in his essay "Material and Man," published in the 1960 manifesto. The essay starts with the omnipresent prospect of nuclear calamity:

> Everything will come to an end if a nuclear war covers all the Earth with radioactivity. No one on Earth wishes it, but arguments among the best brains of the world are always based on the possibility of a nuclear war. These people use similar logic when they threaten the public by saying that the next war will bring the destruction of mankind, for this approach simply arouses a general feeling of anxiety all over the world.[9]

Such a catastrophic image could not be understood without considering Japan's specific experiences of nuclear bombings at Hiroshima and Nagasaki. However, Kawazoe's concern about a nuclear crisis was not restricted to the Japanese nation, but expanded to a planetary totality threatened by nuclear warfare.

Although Kawazoe accepted the inevitability of catastrophe, he was hardly pessimistic. He argued that only architects and designers could maintain optimism in times of crisis because they were the ones who created things that would remain long after humankind disappears.[10] Kawazoe's optimism resided in his faith in the endless process of Metabolism. The essay ends: "We hope to create something which, even in destruction, will cause a subsequent new creation. This 'something' must be found in the form of the cities we are going to make—cities constantly undergoing the process of Metabolism."[11] Drawing on the biological term "Metabolism," Kawazoe emphasized the ability of architecture to keep growing, transforming, and reproducing in response to continuous changes in its environment. Like a living organism, he believed that architecture could grow, die, and eventually regenerate. By embracing death and decay as a part of the endless life cycle, Kawazoe developed a unique sense of optimism that was radically distinguished from modernism's blind faith in technology and its linear trajectory of moving forward.

In Kawazoe's other essay, titled "The Last Day of the Great Tokyo," published in the architectural magazine *Kenchiku Bunka* in January 1961, the prospect of nuclear calamity was replaced by the gloomy scenario of climate change and natural disaster.[12] The essay predicted the breakdown of the metabolic order of the Earth's system, which had recently been labeled the Anthropocene. This metabolic rift would lead to global warming and the submersion of the great metropolitan cities of Japan and other coastal areas. Kawazoe presented Metabolism's visionary projects, such as Kisho Kurokawa's Wall City, as survival architecture that could function like Noah's Ark for the flood for a while.[13] Despite global efforts to prevent catastrophe, every metropolis would disappear under the sea. However, this was not the end. The sea level would eventually normalize thanks to the continuing metabolic cycle, and ruined cities would finally resurface in the future.

It is worth mentioning that the narrative of a sinking Japan was not unique to Kawazoe's writing, but was a recurrent theme in postwar Japanese fiction.[14] Already in 1959, Kobo Abe's novel titled *Inter Ice Age 4* presented the chilling scenario of the country's submersion due to climate warming. In this story, the Japanese government initiated a project of constructing an underwater city while using genetic engineering to create a race of "aquans" who could live in the ocean. The theme of a sinking island dramatically reappeared in the bestselling novel *Japan Sinks* (1973) by Sakyo Komatsu.[15] Kōmatsu's novel was first published in 1973 and led to numerous remakes in film, TV, and animation, as well as a sequel. Kawazoe retrospectively claimed that the theme of *Japan Sinks* recalled traumatic memories of Japan's recent war: "Kōmatsu and I had a vivid image of the end of the world in that we both belonged to the generation that witnessed the destruction of Japanese cities and the collapse of the Empire."[16] The apocalyptic imagination shared by Kawazoe and Japanese fiction writers was further reinforced by a series of natural disasters that hit postwar Japan and the continuing Cold War nuclear tension.

If Metabolism's future scenario was imbued with the anxiety and fear of natural and humanmade disasters, its future city projects could be discussed as architectural solutions to these imagined catastrophes. Yet, I do not claim that architect members of the Metabolist group were fully sympathetic with critic Kawazoe's God-like position that considered death and destruction as a part of the natural life cycle. Perhaps Kawazoe's cyclical vision appeared too fatalistic to his architect colleagues who had to play a constructive role in rebuilding a country. Unlike Kawazoe, who embraced catastrophe and death as a necessary condition for regeneration, the Metabolist architects attempted to enhance resilience, a technique to manage crises without an endpoint. Given that the concept of resilience means the capacity of a system to withstand a crisis and continue to function, it is defined only in relation to crises. The following sections examine Metabolism's representative design methodologies, megastructure and group form, as two competing modes of resilient, survival architecture.

Metabolism as resilient survival architecture

Megastructure

Metabolism's stereotyped visionary images—cities erected on the sea or spiraling into the sky—can be categorized as a key example of megastructure. A megastructure is a gigantic, self-supporting building that encases all or some urban functions. Yet a megastructure is not all about size; rather, its essence lies in its design tactic that could provide a flexible urban system adaptable to radical urban, social, and technological change. A megastructure takes artificial land that is liberated from the natural ground and can be placed and replaced in any location. To maximize flexibility and changeability, a megastructure differentiates the long-term cycles and the short-term cycles of urban elements. "As trees send out new buds that produce green leaves that then turn red and drop in accordance with the circulation of the four seasons," Kiyonori Kikutake wrote, "each unit in a megastructure was organically linked to the life cycle of the inhabitants and selectively added and removed."[17]

Megastructure's emphasis on changeability and expandability was often discussed in conjunction with the optimism about growth and progress that prevailed in the 1960s. However, the idea of the megastructure was largely stimulated by anxiety and concerns over the radical social, political, and technological transformations taking place at the time. Most of all, it was a Malthusian crisis that drove the Metabolists to try to build technology-driven artificial land in hitherto uninhabitable areas, such as the sea and sky. Japan's geographical condition as an island country made the looming Malthusian crisis look more threatening. Some contemporary commentators pointed out that the Metabolists' idea of a floating city or underwater habitat might have stemmed from the pessimistic premise that population growth could force communities into the sea in the future.[18] They compared Kikutake's floating tower to a "cramped beehive or a bird's nest," the last place on Earth that anyone would want to live in.[19]

However, Metabolism's proposals for megastructures were not merely associated with Japan's land constraints, but responded to the island nation's vulnerability to a series of natural hazards, such as earthquakes, typhoons, and tsunamis. For example, Kisho Kurokawa's Agricultural City was specifically designed as a reaction to the 1959 Ise Bay Typhoon. During the typhoon and subsequent flooding, Kurokawa's family, who then lived in the coastal area of Nagoya, the area most affected by this typhoon, had to take refuge on the second floor of their house for days. Inspired by this horrifying experience, Kurokawa proposed an elevated platform made of a 547-square-yard concrete slab supported by piloti on which a rural community could be built four meters above the ground. Kurokawa was not satisfied with building a high platform to avoid flooding, but aimed to provide a huge, flexible infrastructure needed in such an emergent situation. The artificial land would contain various urban infrastructures, such as roads, monorails, water services, and electrical equipment, on which the survival and well-being of urban populations depended.

Likewise, Kiyonori Kikutake also developed his Marine City project as "a resistance unit" that could emancipate people from the peril of living at ground level.[20] Considering that Kikutake was born and raised in Kurume, Kyūshū, where people's lives were heavily affected by the periodic flooding of the nearby Chikugo River, it was not surprising that disaster prevention was one of his major concerns as an architect. Take, for example, his 1961 redevelopment project for the Koto district, Tokyo's lowland area plagued by flooding during the rainy seasons and after typhoons. Persistent flooding of this area was partly caused by the relentless removal of soil for construction purposes during the construction boom. To prevent annual flooding, Kikutake proposed a lattice-shaped foundation on which residential towers and transportation systems would be built. Each block measured 219 square yards and was capable of holding a 20-story building. What was crucial for the architect was not to build a defensive sea wall that would withstand high waves, but to establish a resilient urban structure that could freely ride the tide. Of this project, Noboru Kawazoe stated: "Even if the Earth sinks, this building will still 'float' on its broad foundation."[21] The floating quality of Kikutake's megastructure deserved close attention as a strategy for survival design. For him, floating cities do not necessarily have to stay in one place, but can be moved to any desired location. Moreover, when it becomes unnecessary, unable to meet public needs, they can be sunk into the deep (Figure 9.1). The architect learned from sea creatures such as jellyfishes and sea plants the ability to drift across the sea and flexibly cope with danger. When the waves are high, and there is a danger that whole structures will be thrown out of the water, they can be designed to be able to sink deeper.

Survivalist rhetoric can be found not only in the gigantic frames, but also in the individual capsule, a prefabricated living unit attached to a megastructure. A capsule is a hyper-interiorized space that protects the occupant from the perilous outside environments of the sky and outer space. As architectural historian Thomas Leslie has pointed out, the origin of postwar capsules can be found in aerospace development, from the military fighter cockpit to a container for astronauts.[22] For him, the Cold War rivalry over the manned space program between the two superpowers had immediate consequences for the capsulization of architectural spaces.

Kurokawa's essay titled "Capsule Declaration" (1969) articulated the survivalist concerns of the capsule as follows:

> The capsule is cyborg architecture. Man, machine, and space build a new organic body which transcends confrontation. The word "capsule" usually conjures up either a capsule containing medicine or the living quarters of an astronaut. The capsule referred to here is a capsule without which what is contained in it would be perfectly meaningless. For example, a spaceship is such a capsule. The capsule, which protects the astronaut from space or from very high temperatures or other hazards, differs in essence from containers such as coffee cups in that it creates an environment peculiar to itself. A rupture in the capsule, however small, would instantly upset the internal equilibrium and destroy the strictly controlled environment in it. Such a device and the life in it depend on each other for their existence and survival.[23]

FIGURE 9.1 Kiyonori Kikutake's Aquapolis floating platform built for the Okinawa Ocean Expo 1975 (model). Image credit: Wikimedia Commons.

The capsule is defined as cyborg architecture, a prosthetic device that enhances the human body's capability to adapt to any environment. Like a spaceship or space capsule, the Metabolists' capsule presents a highly controlled environment that can shield the inhabitant from the dangers outside. In this vein, Kenji Ekuan's Plastic Ski Lodge (1962), a capsule structure located in a ski resort, was conceived as a compact shelter that protected people from snowfall and the cold (Figure 9.2).

Group form

Despite its emphasis on flexibility and changeability, megastructure presupposes a monumental, rigid framework. Therefore, megastructures were destined to become extinct, like giant dinosaurs that could not adapt easily to the changing environment. In reaction to the rigidity of the megastructure, Fumihiko Maki and Masato Otaka put forward a more flexible and adaptable system in their proposal of "group form." Unlike Kikutake's and Kurokawa's provocative futurist schemes, Maki and Ōtaka's proposal for group form, published in the 1960 manifesto, was a more realistic plan for redeveloping the Shinjuku area in Tokyo from a site of water purification plants into a business and entertainment district using artificial land. They further articulated the concept of group form as a new design methodology for the ever-changing contemporary society in the 1964 publication titled *Investigations in Collective Form*.[24]

Metabolism as Survival Architecture   **137**

FIGURE 9.2   Plastic Ski Lodge capsule designed by Kenji Ekuan and GK Design Company Inc. in 1962. Image courtesy of GK Design Company Inc., Tokyo.

Group form is based on a unique understanding of the relationship between the part and the whole. Unlike a conventional building, in which the totality is equal to the sum of all the elements, in group form, the totality is larger than the sum of all the elements. Therefore, the total image would not be affected by continuous changes in its components. Echoing the emerging notion of cybernetics and network theory prevalent in the 1960s, Maki and Otaka claimed that the urgent task of today's designers was to find a "master form which can move into ever new states of equilibrium and yet maintain visual consistency and a sense of continuing order in the long run, at the same time preserving visual integrity."[25] Group form represents a new tendency of post-CIAM urban planning that "surrenders to change rather than imposing mastery, and that asserts interdependence among disparate, even unfinished elements, rather than hierarchy and isolation."[26] Maki and Otaka introduced the concept of temporality and collectivity to overcome the static modernist concept of "master planning." The fundamental difference between megastructure and group form is the presence or absence of a centralized frame. Group form lacks any frame and grows spontaneously and cumulatively over time in response to the changing needs of its residents, the climate, and the regional context. If megastructure is interested in giving a physical and visible order to urban chaos, group form aims to reveal the hidden order that is embedded in the social, cultural, and geographical context. In this regard, group form can be compared to a rhizome, which is a non-hierarchical, divergent, and horizontal structure proposed by Gilles Deleuze and Felix Guattari in opposition to the hierarchical tree structure of the modern system.

To a degree, the idea of group form was largely indebted to vernacular architecture—a type of simple, low-tech, indigenous structures made with available local materials and resources. It was well known that Maki had a chance to travel to various towns and cities in Southeast Asia, India, the Middle East, and Europe as a result of a Graham Foundation Fellowship in 1959. This "grand journey" encouraged him to consider vernacular settlements as an alternative to the top-down planning approach of modern architecture. Maki was not alone in having been inspired by the non-hierarchical and spontaneous approaches of vernacular settlements across the world. Bernard Rudofsky's influential exhibition *Architecture without Architects* (1964), held at the Museum of Modern Art in New York (MoMA), represented a growing interest in the artistic, functional, and cultural richness of vernacular settlements among Western architectural circles.

Unlike Kurokawa and Kikutake, Maki and Otaka did not explicitly refer to a disaster situation in their proposal for group form. However, disasters became a critical issue for Maki much later when he criticized Zaha Hadid's gigantic design for the 2020 Tokyo Olympic stadium. For Maki, the size of Hadid's building is problematic because this megascale building cannot properly address emergent situations such as earthquakes and fires. Maki claimed that "the damaging effects on the historical scenery, the safety concerns for unexpected natural disaster evacuation on a limited site, and the exorbitant construction and management costs are all reasons to question the size of the building."[27] The main problem of megastructures in emergencies derives from the fact that they form a rigid physical system concentrating all functions in one place. In contrast, group form emphasized a soft and flexible system based on the aggregation of various human-scale structures connected by open spaces.

Although group form has long been isolated from the mainstream Metabolist movement in the 1960s, it has consistently broadened its design methodology, as observed in Maki's Hillside Terrace, which grew from 1969 to 1992. Hillside Terrace, a multi-purpose complex located in the trendy Daikanyama district in Tokyo, incorporates several vacant public spaces that link several clusters of buildings built in different phases (Figure 9.3). Since this complex carefully considers the social, geographical, and topographical dimensions of the site, it can better adapt to continuous urban transformation and unanticipated changes, and demonstrates a better capacity to respond to both natural and social challenges. Moreover, encompassing open space has many advantages in times of disaster, in that it can function as an evacuation site and provide a location for temporary rescue camps and medical facilities. Open space can also be expected to help a community to enhance its social resilience by providing a regular meeting place for exchanges and interactions.

The legacy of the Metabolist movement

Today's Japan is quite different from that of the 1960s when the Metabolists proposed their ambitious future visions. Japan's economy fell into recession after the collapse of the bubble, and its population has been rapidly shrinking and aging. The Great East Japan Earthquake of 2011 further intensified a sense of crisis that had already prevailed in Japanese society and forced many architects to engage critically with various social issues. As architectural historian Igarashi Tarō has pointed out, 3.11-related architecture is characterized by "widening the scope of architects' roles beyond the limited radius of an individual building."[28] Architects' ambitions for rescuing society from a crisis resurrected Metabolism's nation rebuilding project of the past. However, the younger generation of architects has tried to distance itself from Metabolism's

FIGURE 9.3 The Hills Side Terrace residential complex designed by Fumihiko Maki. Image credit: Wikimedia Commons.

megalomaniac vision, which seemed to have lost its social relevance. If the Metabolists undertook the technocrats' role in laying the foundations of urban infrastructure in the era of expansion and growth, contemporary practitioners tend to regard themselves as "social reformers" or "social designers" who are presenting an alternative model of living in the era of shrinkage and recession. In this regard, post-3.11 architecture has emphasized small-scale, bottom-up, "soft" aspects of community building rather than megascale, top-down, "hard" infrastructure.

Nevertheless, Metabolism's organic vision of architecture has been widely and persistently revisited as the art of living in today's shrinking society because it embraces not only growth and expansion, but also decay and regeneration. Ambitious architects have turned to Metabolism's notion of cyclical transformation as a way of dealing with aging urban infrastructures and abandoned houses. Yoshiharu Tsukamoto, a founder of Atelier Bow-Wow, for instance, tried to intervene with residential buildings whose life cycle is about 26 years on average. His tactic for revitalizing a city was to incorporate void spaces to enhance urban vitality, communal sense, and social tolerance. Emphasizing its connection with the historical Metabolist movement and at the same time distancing it from the Metabolists' technocratic vision, Tsukamoto termed his new design approach "void Metabolism."[29] The concept of "void Metabolism" became the theme of the Japanese Pavilion exhibition at the Venice Biennale of Architecture in 2010, curated by Tsukamoto together with Koh Kitayama and Ryue Nishizawa.

The legacy of Metabolism has gone far beyond Japanese architecture in this era of ongoing crises. A good example is the "New Metabolism" project launched by the

Massachusetts Institute of Technology Media Lab in 2015.[30] This project focuses on new materials and structures that could be easily decayed and recycled, like a living organism. Here, the idea of "Metabolism" is loosely equated with sustainability and resilience—values needed to respond to global climate change. Metabolism is an ongoing process.

Acknowledgement

This work was supported by a National Research Foundation of Korea (NRF) grant funded by the Korean government (MSIT) (NRF-2018R1A5A7025409).

Notes

1 Hajime Yatsuka, "The Structure of This Exhibition: Metabolism Nexus' Role in Overcoming Modernity," in *Metabolism: The City of the Future* (Tokyo: Mori Art Museum, 2011), 10.
2 Reyner Banham, *Megastructure: Urban Futures of the Recent Past* (New York: Harper & Row, 1976).
3 Hajime Yatsuka and Hideki Yoshimatsu, *Metaborizumu: 1960 nendai nihon no kenchiku avuangiyarudo* [*Metabolism: Architectural Avant-gardes of the 1960s*] (Tokyo: INAX Publisher, 1997); Hajime Yatsuka, *Metabolizumu Nexus* (Tokyo: Ohmsha, 2011); Zhongjie Lin, *Kenzo Tange and the Metabolist Movement: Urban Utopias of Modern Japan* (Abingdon: Routledge, 2010).
4 Cherie Wendelken, "Putting Metabolism Back in Place," in *Anxious Modernisms: Experimentation in Postwar Architectural Culture*, ed. Sarah Williams Goldhagen and Réjean Legault (Cambridge, MA: MIT Press, 2000), 281.
5 Rem Koolhaas and Hans Ulrich Obrist, *Project Japan: Metabolism Talks* (Cologne: Taschen, 2011).
6 Hyunjung Cho and Chunghoon Shin, "Metabolism and Cold War Architecture," *Journal of Architecture* 19, no. 5 (October 2014).
7 Noboru Kawazoe (ed.), *Metabolism 1960: The Proposals for New Urbanism* (Tokyo: Bijutsu Shuppansha, 1960).
8 Noboru Kawazoe, *Kenchiku no metsubō* [*The Death of Architecture*] (Tokyo: Gendai shichō-sha, 1960).
9 Kawazoe, *Metabolism 1960*, 48.
10 Kawazoe, *Metabolism 1960*, 48.
11 Kawazoe, *Metabolism 1960*, 49.
12 Noboru Kawazoe, "Dai Tōkyō saigō no hi [The Last Day of Tokyo]," *Kenchiku bunka* 16, no. 171 (January 1961): 5–12.
13 Interestingly, the idea of a floating megacity reminiscent of Metabolism's futurist schemes also appeared as a temporary living space in Kōmatsu Sakyō's *Japan Sinks: Part II*, the belated sequel to the aforementioned *Japan Sinks* that described a diaspora after the catastrophe.
14 For the commonality of the future scenario shared by Japan's science fiction and Metabolism, see William O. Gardner, *The Metabolist Imagination* (Minneapolis: University of Minnesota Press, 2020).
15 For further discussion on disaster narratives in postwar Japanese literature, see Thomas Schnellächer, "Has the Empire Sunk Yet? The Pacific in Japanese Science Fiction," *Science Fiction Studies* 29 (2002): 389–393; Susan Napier, "Panic Sites: The Japanese Imagination of Disaster from Godzilla to Akira," *Journal of Japanese Studies* 19, no. 2 (1993): 327–351.
16 Kawazoe, *Interview with Naito*, 31.
17 Kawazoe, *Metabolism 1960*, 19.
18 Ada Louise Huxtable, "The Architect as a Prophet," *New York Times*, October 2, 1960, 21.
19 Huxtable, "The Architect as a Prophet," 21.
20 Ken Tadashi Oshima (ed.), *Kiyonori Kikutake between Land and Sea* (Zurich: Lars Müller Publisher, 2010), 20.

21 Noboru Kawazoe, "A New Tokyo: In, on, or Above the Sea?," *This is Japan*, no. 9 (1962): 62–64.
22 Thomas Leslie, "Just What is it That Makes Capsule Homes So Different, So Appealing? Domesticity and the Technological Sublime, 1945 to 1975," *Space and Culture* 9, no. 2 (2006): 181–182.
23 Kisho Kurokawa, *Metabolism in Architecture* (London: Studio Vista, 1977), 75.
24 Fumihiko Maki and Masato Otaka, "Collective Form: Three Paradigms," in *Investigations in Collective Form* (St. Louis: University of Washington, 1964).
25 Fumihiko and Otaka, "Collective Form: Three Paradigms," 11.
26 Fumihiko and Otaka, "Collective Form: Three Paradigms," 11.
27 AP, "Architects Clash over Japan Olympic Stadium," *Al-Jazeera*, October 16, 2013, https://www.aljazeera.com/sports/2013/10/16/architects-clash-over-japan-olympic-stadium.
28 Taro Igarashi and Ryo Yamazaki, *3.11 iko no kenchiku: shakai to kenchika no atarashii kankei* [*Architecture after 3.11: New Relationship between Society and Architecture*] (Tokyo: Gakuei Shuppan, 2014).
29 Koh Kitayama, Yasuhiro Tsukamoto and Ryue Nishizawa, *Tokyo Metabolizng* (Tokyo: Toto, 2010), 29.
30 David Benjamin, who led the "New Metabolism" project at the MIT Media Lab, shared his findings and insights with Japanese architects and planners at the International City Forum held in Tokyo in 2015.

10

METABOLISM ADVENTURE

A Personal View

Philip Drew

> Metabolism was dedicated to a new world pervaded by creative endlessly expanding architecture. It was led by Kiyonori Kikutake, then aged thirty-two, with Noriaki Kurokawa and the critic Kawazoe. Other architects including Asada, Oe and Maki, as well as some planners, painters and allied designers, followed along in spirit ... the British Archigram Group ... has collaborated with the Metabolists ... Both create images of megastructures, buildings big enough to carry a city's population, but so basic and adaptable they may be no more than skeletons or masts to carry mechanical services. Both are concerned with a noticeable inconsistency in current technological development the disproportional rate of progress between the mass-manufactured items and the individually constructed shells that house them.
>
> Robin Boyd, New *Directions in Japanese Architecture*, 1968, p. 15

On June 17, 1967, I joined a converted freighter at Pier 21 Pyrmont Wharf, Darling Harbour, on a grand architectural adventure in the land of Madame Butterfly. Four days out from Nagoya, a typhoon whipped up huge Hokusai-size seas that buried the plunging bow of the *Aramac*'s forward deck and confined passenger to their cabins.

In the wake of the 1964 Tokyo Olympics, Japanese architecture emerged as a world leader and a must-see for young architects.[1] Only now as I write, viewed from a perspective more than half a century later, does it register fully. The experience proved overwhelming as well as transformative. Japanese culture was so inconceivably different from anything I had known—the very antithesis of Australia. It has taken a lifetime to fully take in its meaning. In this chapter I will examine what I found 50 years ago in the context of present-day Japan with a declining population of 126 million people, under circumstances in which humanity is faced with its greatest environmental and existential challenge. This begs the question as to whether Metabolism still has lessons for us today. Are Metabolism, Japan, its culture and architectural traditions relevant?

In 1967 I knew almost nothing concerning Metabolism. Frank Martin, my university travel companion, subscribed to the *Japan Architect* magazine, which published the best modern Japanese architecture, and was much better informed, and he insisted

DOI: 10.4324/9781003186540-11

we visit the modern besides the traditional architecture. We divided our daily sorties between the two. This worked out well. In time, I came to see they were linked, Modern Japanese architecture could only be understood viewed through the lens of tradition and not exclusively through its Western models; both Maekawa's Corbusian Brutalism and Tange's carpentry stylization of modernism were inflected with Japanese color.

From the very earliest times, the chief difference between Western and Japanese architecture is explained by one being stone masonry and the other wood; one statically flexible in highly unstable earthquake prone Japan, and the other permanent and fire-resistant. Stone is quarried in blocks, while wood is split or sawn into lengths; one by piling stone upon stone to form cells and the other by joining lengths of timber to create open spatial frames.[2] Masonry produced an architecture of additive closed cells, there was no spatial concept in Japan which instead evolved into a traditional concept of architectural space structured by columns that minimized the distinction between building the interior and exterior landscape. Japan developed a fire-prone lightweight carpentry architecture whose flexibility helped it to survive earthquakes. Its carpentry traditions decisively shaped Japanese architectural style and its spatial perception psychologically. A meaningful understanding of Japanese architecture depends upon recognition of the pervasive role played by the perfectionism of a refined carpentry technique. The assimilation of Western industrial materials such as concrete, steel, and glass, in the nineteenth century entailed a profound technological shift, which led in turn to an important cultural reorientation of which, I will argue, Metabolism was but one symptom. Metabolism contains a curious mixture of Corbusian Rationalism and Western ideology, embalmed in traditional Japanese sentiment.

Ancient Greek temples began as timber constructions that later underwent fossilization that converted carpentry construction to stone. In the 1950s, modern Japanese architecture underwent a similar mimetic process from a carpentry style expressed in poured stone, also known as concrete. Joseph Rykwert in *Dancing Column* (1996) followed the evolution of the column in ancient sacred Greek architecture whose Japanese symbolic equivalent was the central post, both in traditional and including Metabolism, whose role was to orient and organize interior architectural space.[3]

Japanese culture was conditioned by Buddhism and an unstable geology to regard human existence as cyclical and ephemeral, unlike in the West, which stressed values of permanence and monumentality. Western tradition seeks to retain the original material; the Japanese do not and instead periodically reconstruct the original. The Ise Shrine is a memorable example of periodic renewal whereby the form rather than the material is retained in an unending cycle of reconstructions.

Western and Japanese architectural canons are not entirely opposed. Metabolism should be viewed as the Japanese response to Western modernism under conditions that made it necessary for modernism to be reconciled with existing Japanese tradition, in the face of unrelenting rapid technological change pressing in on the national psyche, during a period of economic prosperity at the beginning of the Korean War that elicited a creative urban response founded on organic additive cellular replication.

Two existential concepts and cultures collided, each with their separate ways of dealing with rapid urban change: in Europe, the model was inspired by science and industry as expressed by Italian Futurism and Soviet Constructivism; in Japan, the model adopted was based on biology and nature in a hierarchical combination of permanent supports and ephemeral capsules to deal with racing technology. The Metabolists were not shy in taking ideas from the USA and Europe.

FIGURE 10.1 Unlike monumental masonry in the West, Japanese architecture is a post-and-beam carpentry tradition, insulated from earthquakes by an elaborate shock absorbing bracket system, resulting in an open flexible lightweight architectural aesthetic. Photo by Philip Drew.

FIGURE 10.2 Le Corbusier. National Museum of Western Art, Ueno, Tokyo, 1957–1959. The stay of Juzo Sakakura and Kunio Sakakura as assistants in Le Corbusier's Paris studio (Sakakura for many years) ensured an authentic interpretation from the source filtered through their Japanese sensibility. Photo by Frank Martin.

To properly understand Metabolism, it is first necessary to recognize the confrontation of Japanese tradition and Le Corbusian rationalism as the bridge over which modern architecture reached Japan for a number of its most influential Japanese architects, namely Junzo Sakakura and Kunio Maekawa. Metabolism acted as an intermediate staging post in the merger of diametrically opposed technical and artistic design philosophies, Japanese tradition and Western revolution.

Le Corbusier wrote his assessment of Japanese character in 1941 outside Paris at Vézelay, during the German occupation of France, published after the war in *The Four Routes*:

> To begin with the Japanese. On the plan of one of our large public halls, it was necessary to draw some fourteen thousand seats—a circle inked-in by compass indicating each seat. Just the work for a Japanese! He [Juzo Sakakura][4] made a superb job of it, and of many another also, and finishing up, after four years, designing the Japanese pavilion at the Paris Exhibition of 1957. He, and all his compatriots who preceded him, were actuated by the same driving will power; they have uniquely sensitive hands; their politeness amounts almost to solemnity. They seem able to follow a line of continuity, but sometimes fall into a hole; their ingenious assimilation of Western ideas nevertheless still leaves them Orientals, which is all good. They have great integrity of technique. They first appear, sweating with fright, with presents in both hands: generally a book, or engravings of their national art. To one of them, turning over pictures of their perfect traditional tea-houses, I exclaimed: "Why are you coming to acquire our barbarities, you who once upon a time made such perfect poems of your houses?"[5]

Why indeed?

Kenzo Tange's Tokyo gymnasia for the 1964 Olympics at Yoyogi was the first to excite my enthusiasm for architecture in Japan. His recapitulation of Eero Saarinen's Yale Hockey Rink as a swept-steel tent on posts and silhouette seemed such a deliberate, quite conscious, reference to the traditional Japanese emphasis of the roofs, imposed upon the Corbusian Brutalist sculptured seating platforms.

The first visit in 1967

I arrived in Nagoya in July 1967 determined to see every new building of importance. First stop was Fumiko Maki's Toyoda Auditorium at Nagoya University (1960). It looked drab and forlorn through the persistent drizzle, unexpectedly American, and not obviously Metabolist. The Toyoda Auditorium was Maki's debut project. Even then, Maki seemed at pains to distance himself from the Metabolists. The administrative building at Izumo (1963) by Kiyonori Kikutake (1928–2011), which I visited next a month later, was, by comparison, tiny. I now see them as having a similar hierarchical organization with a main or primary framed structure that is infilled by secondary subordinate non-structural infill panel units, inherited from the legacy of Japanese timber frame carpentry, was a delicate modernist reincarnation of the larger timber Izumo-Taisha. The complex jewel-like perfection is unforgettable. Large size alone is relatively unimportant; what truly matters when judging architecture, which came as

FIGURE 10.3 Kenzo Tange and Yoshikatsu Tsuboi, National Olympic Gymnasium No. 1 (Swimming), Yoyogi, Tokyo, 1964. The roof adopted the same ridge tent form as Saarinen's earlier Yale Hockey Rink supported on two masts and anchored at either end above the entrances, unlike Gymnasium No. 2 which is supported on a single mast that repeats the traditional symbolism of the central post. Photo by Philip Drew. ID: 4662.

a complete surprise were its qualities of refined sculptural coherence and elegance in what was a Brutalist concrete, though tiny work.

My first building in Kyoto was Sachio Otani's Kyoto International Conference Centre (ICC Kyoto), which opened the previous year in 1966. I was struck by its distinctive trapezoidal cross-section and linear form to accommodate large auditoria and smaller service spaces and offices. The geometry was reminiscent of Kikutake's earlier Izumo miniature. Completed a year before the release of the George Lucas 1977 cinema classic *Star Wars*, the ICC perfectly anticipated its Futuristic Baroque imagery.

As a traveler, it is impossible not to fall under the spell of Japan, its mystery and rituals. On the climb to Kiomizu-dera Temple, anxious for a long life and clarity of thought, I drank from its spring and later gazed out at the pagoda opposite it from the sloping deck high above the valley. What impressed me most was the enormous column supports underneath the deck, which I now consider anticipate Tange's cylindrical Metabolist cores at Yamanashi.

Katsura Imperial Villa seemed perfection itself. Cleverly contrived and consummately maintained, it sublimely epitomized the refined surrender to nature as one of humankind's greatest artistic accomplishments. Ever so gently, it invites us to melt into a state of oneness with nature. Separate from the outside world and recalling a time of courtly love and romance from *The Tale of Genji*, the palace pavilion and garden frames architecture and life in perfect harmony.

FIGURE 10.4 Sachio Otani, Kyoto Conference Centre (ICC Kyoto), 1966. Its distinctive trapezoidal cross-section responded to the variety of large and small interior spaces, which like the Izumo-Taisha administrative building was at once evocative of the past and Futuristic in its Baroque imagery. Photo by Frank Martin.

On my return to Tokyo on Friday, July 28, I climbed Mount Fuji. Uncannily symmetrical, Fuji was a necessary, if physical exertion I undertook to fully enter into the spirit of Japan.

At Kamakura, the Junzo Sakakura Museum of Modern Art (completed 21 years after his stay in Le Corbusier's Paris studio in 1951) levitated, a strangely pure horizontal orthogonal of white in suspension above an irregularly shaped jade green lake. Sakakura and Maekawa both spent time in Paris with Le Corbusier at his studio and were transformed by the experience—this was more the case for Maekawa than for Sakakura, but it was Maekawa's Japanese sensibility that survived and was most forcibly fused with the modern. There is a very telling detail in the museum where Sakakura inserted a flat stone beneath the main stair which does not reach the floor and instead is suspended above the stone. No one can possibly miss the symbolism of a modern structure inverted over a Japanese connection to nature—modernism tiptoeing, filtered, and adjusted by Japanese sensibility, and Western technology in tension with Japanese spirit.

Nearing the end of my stay, I managed to talk my way into Kenzo Tange's Tokyo office. An assistant showed me an entire floor of balsa models of the office's current projects, including a recently completed kindergarten, after which he led me downstairs to meet other staff working on the Sports Centre at the New York World's Fair and a new Kuwait International Airport. By August 1967 Tange had moved on and had discarded Eero Saarinen's tensile expression in favor of Louis Kahn monumentality. The newest projects organized by circular service cores that supported connecting floors were evidence of a renewed interest in Metabolism. Days later, I left for San Francisco. Afterwards, I found myself questioning whether Japan actually existed—it seemed in retrospect so weirdly improbable and strange a country.

The second visit in 1978

The purpose of my second visit in June 1978 was to conduct research on Arata Isozaki. *A + U*'s Editor-in-Chief, Toshio Nakamura,[6] arranged for me to meet the rising generation of Post-Metabolists previewed in the October–November 1977 edition of *Japan Architect*.[7] Nakamura was well informed, had been an active participant in the early days of Metabolism, and confided to me the inside political background and individual maneuvering. I did not meet any of the founding Metabolists during my 1967 visit. This was my chance 11 years later and I was about to be thrown into the bear pit of Tokyo's architectural politics.

Toshio Nakamura arranged a party at the office of *Japan Architect*. Isozaki, Kikutake, Kurokawa, and Maki were being challenged by a new younger generation comprising Minoru Takeyama, Masayuki Kurokawa, Hiromi Fuji, Makoto Suzuki, Itsuko Hasegawa, Kazuhiro Ishii, and Takefumi Aida, and arranged visits to examine their work. I met the Metabolists soon after. *Japan Architect* editor Shozo Baba was deliberately stirring the pot.

I was interested in *minka* houses so Nakamura introduced me to Professor Teji Itoh who generously advised me on their location for my upcoming road trip that took me to small towns in the wild Alps of central Honshu. This was a journey that widened my appreciation of the spiritual ethos behind the Japanese aesthetic considerably, which Isozaki had only just begun to explore in preparation for his Paris exhibition on "Ma, the Japanese Sense of Place."

FIGURE 10.5 Kenzo Tange. Shizuoka Press and Broadcasting Centre, Shimbashi, Tokyo, 1966–1967. Tange adapted the symbolism of the sacred central post to the requirement for flexibility of Metabolism by leaving spaces for additional cantilevered bracket-floors. Photo by Philip Drew. ID: 4681.

FIGURE 10.6   The October–November 1977 issue of *Japan Architect* examined trends post-1970 and posed the question of who would succeed Kenzo Tange (hidden top right in a darkened sky of clouds) with the rise of a new post-Metabolist generation. Arata Isozaki (upper left) and Kisho Kurokawa (upper right) hover below Tange, and below them a group of young samurai is seen rising (*Japan Architect*, no. 247 (October–November 1977), 12 and 13).

I saw Kikutake at his office. Kikutake was affable and courteous—urbane perhaps sums him up best. He was preparing material to send to George R. Collins for inclusion in the "Visionary Drawings and Architecture and Planning" at the MoMA exhibition (1960).[8] Kikutake presented his Pasadena Housing, Floating Hotel Tokyo Bay, Village Centre for Euphrates River Iraq, Mobile Factory for Libya near Benghazi. The recent work disappointed me considerably; it was flimsy and lacked Kikutake's customary panache. He talked about a new Izumo building which was to be cast iron because of fire requirements.

Fumihiko Maki was next. I met him in his office in the Green Building opposite the Bridgestone Gallery. I was shown slides of his recent building projects, including the Central Facilities Building at Tsukuba University, the Aquarium at Okinawa, the Austrian Embassy, and Kato Gakuin Elementary School Shizuoka. Maki was cool and was clearly influenced by American place-making theory (importing squares inside and exporting rooms outside in an exchange of public and private) that was intended to create distinct precincts. He was looking at post towns and their Japanese expression of place. His contribution to the 1960 Metabolist manifesto was a theoretical essay on "group form," but he now appeared to distance himself from this.[9] I was impressed by his moderation—he made no attempt to dazzle. Of the architects I met, he was least extreme, the most serene and calm. Withdrawn and sensible, Maki seemed

FIGURE 10.7   View of the Central Alps, Honshu. Many outstanding examples of *Minka* are found there, including spectacular A-frame Gassho-style houses at Kamitaira Village, Toyama Prefecture, which were the model for Kenzo Tange's 1960 Tokyo Bay Proposal. Photo by Philip Drew. ID: 4804.

quite indifferent to the rivalry promoted in the architectural media between himself, his friend Isozaki, and Kurokawa, as prospective challengers to Tange.

Driven and ambitious, Kurokawa was temperamentally the opposite of Maki. Accompanied by Nakamura and Baba, I was entertained by Kurokawa at Kocku, a spectacular restaurant re-creation of a traditional Kyoto farmhouse and garden at night deep underground below an office tower. "Bell-sound" insect mating calls accompanied by images of the mythical butterfly from China were projected onto the upper parts of the walls. A boyish and elegantly attired, Kurokawa reveled in his current success and excitedly mentioned his recent association through the Red Cross building to the Japanese Royal Family. He talked expansively about technology and architecture, pointing to Kocku restaurant as an example of technological theatricality.[10]

After conferences with Professor Teiji Itoh,[11] I set off in a rented Honda. The journey from Tokyo took me across the Honshu Alps through gorgeous mountain scenery. Prior to setting out, I traveled by train to Children's Land between Tokyo and Yokohama. It was in a sad dilapidated condition, and the buildings by Kikutake and Kurokawa were rusted wrecks. The first stop on leaving Tokyo was Tange's Yamanashi Press and Broadcasting Centre at Kofu (1966). A colossal Lego castle in concrete and stucco, set against a stunning mountain backdrop, it was more of a static mechanistic trope than anything suggestively organic. By its very nature, architecture is static, yet everywhere technology races ahead and outpaces it. For a structure that purported to be flexible, it was anything but flexible or open to revision and change. When I

FIGURE 10.8 Yoshijima House, Takayama, twentieth century. The combination of primary and secondary posts is both functional as well as highly symbolic. The posts carry the entire load of the heavy roof, yet are symbolic, as evidenced in the sacred post of the famous Kasuga Shrine in Kyoto Prefecture. Photo by Philip Drew. ID: 4837.

Metabolism Adventure **153**

FIGURE 10.9 Kiomizu-dera Temple, Kyoto. The huge timber post-and-beam supports under the veranda deck presaged Tange's core-node structure of the Yamanashi Building. Photo by Philip Drew. ID: 4951.

FIGURE 10.10 Kenzo Tange, Yamanashi Press and Broadcasting Centre, Kofu, 1966. Too small to qualify as a megastructure, the Yamanashi structure is Tange's frozen manifesto for the Metabolist vison of a remade world. Photo by Philip Drew. ID: 4718.

154 Philip Drew

examined it up close, the very opposite seemed true—it was a monument and Metabolism in name only. Futuristic drawings of cities such as those by Archigram depicting walking cities and by Isozaki of Greek columns superimposed on a ruined Hiroshima after the atomic bomb were nothing more than fanciful musings lacking even a shred of reality. The drawings were romantic dreams, not real buildings, suggestive and evocative in their own special way, but Tange's Yamanashi Press and Broadcasting Centre demonstrated the enormously wide gap between such dream-like ideas and actual performance.

I enjoyed Isozaki's newly completed Kamioka Town Hall (1978). For all its sixteenth-century Italian-inspired Mannerism, it was more human and sane than I had anticipated. This included a pop profile of Marilyn Monroe's nude body over the entrance. The Shugakuin Branch of Kikutake's Kyoto Community Bank (1971) said little that was new. The Tange Kagawa Prefectural Government Office at Takamatsu (1958), with its massive stone information desk, magnificent tile mosaic, and deliberate juxtaposition of broken rock against concrete structure, looked stunningly like every bit traditional carpentry.

The resurrected 1972 Ise-Shima Inner Shrine was out of bounds and the old mirror shrine had yet to be dismantled. The ancient grove of sacred trees was shrouded in a thin mist; every now and then between the trunks, I caught a glimpse of an ancient carpentry-and-bark shrine structure veiled in mystery and magic. The Ise Shrine is unforgettable, so perfect yet so primitive in its purity and simplicity, impregnated with emotion and ecstasy. As a Westerner, I was forced to ask whether the Greek temple was equally a stone survival and replica of such a contiguous shrine arising from its sacred landscape.

By end of June, I reached Maki's Kuragaike Commemorative Hall for Toyota outside Nagoya. A play on paired triangles, ground-hugging centre housed a whizz-bang James Bond-inspired VIP Reception room the outside of which was clad in stone from Italy and India. Sited on the top of a heavily wooded hill, Kikutake's Pasadena medium-density housing (1972), experiment in "Group Form" had weathered badly, as had his Pacific Hotel at Chigasaki (1966).

After my family flew back to Sydney, I resumed research in earnest, meeting Kurokawa and Isozaki followed by project visits commencing with Gunma Prefecture Museum of Art at Takasaki whose gleaming surface of square aluminum panels and glass produced an abstract Cartesian grid with deceptive "there not there" ambiguity confirming my Mannerist thesis.

Tange's most recent project, the Hanae Mori Building near Omote-Sando, which doubtless inspired by Philip Johnson, was dazzling staggered glass that projected a perfect image of anonymous American corporatism behind showy Formalism.

Kurokawa's best recent work was in Osaka. The National Museum of Ethnology (1977), near the Expo site, hid technology behind a classical mask of extravagant stone contrasted with polished aluminum interiors, stone and tile having now replaced the beton-brute concrete of the 1950s, which had blackened in the meantime. Hidden and tucked away, Kurokawa' shiny stainless steel capsule video rooms had become by then a signature.

Work was proceeding to clear the Expo '70 site. Kikutake's Capsule Tower remained painted in red-and-white stripes for greater aircraft visibility, but Tange's airy space-frame roof had been removed by then. Expo '70 was Tange's his final attempt to retain lordship of Metabolism. Only Isozaki's giant pop-action figure now survived—it grinned grotesquely as a potent symbol and reminder of a failed vision.

Kurokawa's 30-meter-high Osaka Sony Tower (1976), with service nodes and toilet capsules in stainless steel and fiber-glass, exposed copper plumbing, arrived too late, yet was especially impressive as a demonstration of Archigram's 1960s plug-in techno-Metabolism. The open space tower interiors, offering free access to a bewildering array of electronic gadgetry for young enthusiasts to play with, were truly visionary in a practical hands-on way. From concept to the final result, nothing had been left to chance—everything was so convincingly realized and far in advance of anything so far envisaged by Archigram in England.

Isozaki came from Oita and his early buildings were there. The city is on the north coast of Kyushu facing the Inland Sea and was proud of its famous son. There were many buildings in Oita by Isozaki, a list that included a large Audio-Visual Centre under construction to replace his formidable 1966 brute concrete Library building which was listed for demolition, the Oita Branch of the Fukuoka Sogo Bank, Oita Medical Hall, and Dr. Nakayama's four-cube house.[12]

The Kitakyushu Museum of Art straddles a ridge overlooking the city, with its twin massive beams directed threateningly like a shotgun at the city below.[13] Compared to the Oita Library, the Kitakyushu Art Museum beams are colossal manic Mannerist overstatements and inflated fossilized carpentry, magnified to a terrifying extent reminiscent of Boulée in a manner that seems quite un-Japanese.

Italian Mannerism attenuated and distorted form, engaged in visual tricks with mirrors, and through various devices played up contradiction and emptiness to unbalance

FIGURE 10.11   Arata Isozaki: Oita Prefectural Library, Oita, Kyushu, 1966. Isozaki began with post-and-beam Japanese carpentry, hollowed out and enlarged the Library beams, then further enlarged them to the point of extreme giantism for the Kitakyushu Museum of Art, 1974. Photo by Philip Drew. ID: 5452.

156 Philip Drew

and unsettle and enhance a sense of ennui. By the 1970s, with his international practice rapidly growing, increasingly turned to Western and especially eighteenth-century neoclassical sources to expand the vocabulary of his *manniera*.

As I left Tokyo for the USA, I had the impression that Isozaki had unwillingly become trapped in a contest with Kurokawa for artistic leadership which he regarded as pointless. No longer the undisputed reigning shogun of Japanese architecture, Tange was increasingly seen as a once great modern master whose time had passed. Isozaki's friend Maki remained coolly detached and uninvolved. My arrival in Japan coincided with the opening hostilities. As an outsider, a *gaijin*, my independence counted for something. Without fully appreciating my position, I unwittingly allowed myself to become involved, if only for a short while, and this undoubtedly effected my interpretation of events and colored my observation.

At the time, Kurokawa was the most politically active and dominant figure. He was ambitious and determined on commercial success, more so than on stylistic eminence such as Isozaki and had gone out of his way to cultivate links with heads of major business corporations, including the Imperial Family. Isozaki was the more influential artist. His Oita Library, Gunma Museum Stage II, Fukuoka Bank interiors, Kamioka City Hall, and Mijima Country Club were greatly admired, while his friend Kazuo Shinohara was a secret force.

By 1978, Metabolism had lost much of its allure and was no longer considered to be avant-garde. Maki's urbanity and good sense limited his influence. In their assessment of the Kōhai frontrunners in the October–November 1977 issue of *Japan Architect*, the journal editors mostly failed to pick the winners. Isozaki would go on, never settling for a length of time on a new manner, always on the lookout for the next coming wave. Maki remained unfathomable, unperturbed, and consistent in his devotion to group form plus technology.

The act of publishing a manifesto in 1960 was itself more Western than Japanese. I have set out to show the connections between Japanese tradition and Metabolism as a continuous unbroken phenomenon. The emergence of Metabolism at a critical moment when modernism was being assimilated directly into Japanese architecture while attempting to deal with key problems arising from the interface with industry and a rapidly changing technology which consistently raced ahead of architecture, doubtless created a need which Metabolism sought to answer before historicist post-modernism.

The biological analogy that underpinned Metabolism is itself contentious, although in recent years, biomimicry has become a prominent scientific field, with Frei Otto as one of its most prominent early exponents. Some would say it is fallacious—the transfer of natural process and their imitation by technology is extremely complex and far from straightforward. Metabolism's reductionism simplified everything and had a number of distinct strands and evolved along several contrasting lines: in one, deploying megastructure with impermanent capsules and infill elements, the rigid repetitive geometry produced an excessively brutal and authoritarian uniformity; in another different formulation based on additive forms of vernacular sources, results such as Moshe Safdie's Habitat '67, Montreal and Jorn Utzon's courtyard housing, the outcomes were far more human and varied, indicative of a more palatable democratic sensibility, and hence was more acceptable.

Humans are not separate and above nature, but are a part of it, with all that this implies, as the COVID-19 pandemic has so forcibly reminded us. David Attenborough's *A Life on Our Planet* (2020) presents a plan to meet the crisis of climate change and

FIGURE 10.12 Garden of the "Blissful Mountain" at the Zuho-in Zen Monastery, Kyoto. At its best, the Japanese capacity to emote with nature set it apart from the West's need to dominate and exploit nature. Photo by Philip Drew. ID: 5493.

argues that we must take our knee off nature's neck in order for it to recover by rewilding the planet. Of the world's nations and cultures, the Japanese, with their traditional reverence and love of nature, are better equipped spiritually than most to accept and follow the blueprint wisely advocated by David Attenborough.[14]

Notes

1 The German architect Bruno Taut came to Japan in 1933 and his publication *Houses and People of Japan* (Tokyo: Sanseido Press, 1937) was instrumental in promoted his discovery of Japanese houses, and more directly in the West, as having affinities with modern functional theory and minimalist abstraction. The 1964 Olympics brought modern Japanese architecture and notably Kenzo Tange to the attention of the world at large.
2 "Nature, Space and Japanese Architectural Style," *Japan Architect* (Special Issue, June 1964), 99. Yasutaka Watanabe wrote in his conclusion: "The first point in Japanese style is wooden construction. As we have seen, Japanese architecture is consistently wooden, and the basis of the structure is posts, beams, and lintels. Such things as Western stone construction, arches and piling up of ridge tiles have never been attempted in Japanese architecture."
3 Joseph Rykwert's approach was to provide a context which was anthropological rather than historical, within which the orders were formed, showing why they were differentiated and why it was that their configurations later acquired a kind of timeless validity. The central post, though entirely different, operates as an ordering device that creates stops in continuous Japanese spaces. In the West, space is contained by walls; in Japan, space quietly flows and it is the columns that control and organize space abstractly and socially, a phenomenon which Le Corbusier recognized when he placed a post support under the triangular-shaped skylight in the middle of the central hall, which is the emotional focus,

158 Philip Drew

yet obstructs movement, of his National Museum of Western Art at Ueno Park, Tokyo (1957–1959).

4 Junzo Sakakura (1901–1969) entered Le Corbusier's studio in 1930, the same year as Kunio Maekawa, but unlike Maekawa, who returned to Japan to work for Antonin Raymond, he stayed on and rose to become chief of studio. He was involved in the Villa Savoye and Swiss Pavilion projects. Maekawa's pavilion design was initially favoured, but when it was judged to be too modernist, the project was handed to Maeda Kenjiro. When the French insisted that only French materials and labour were to be employed, Sakakura received the commission.

5 Le Corbusier, *The Four Routes* (London: Dennis Dobson, 1947), 150.

6 Toshio Nakamura joined Kajima Institute Publishing in 1970, when he was invited to join *A + U* as its editor. He indicated later that he knew the "inside story" of Tange's distant influence on events, i.e., on the Metabolism group. This confirmed my suspicion that Arata Isozaki acted as the link and catalyst between the two on Tange's behalf. Tange selected Isozaki's first wife (they were by that time divorced). This may have moderated criticism of Tange later when Isoaki went out on his own. Toshio spoke about this at his home at Chitose Karasuyama on July 9, 1978. Nakamura assisted and helped publicise the group, and suggested that Noboru Kawazoe. Kikutake was singled out and targeted, and suffered the most from infighting within the group. Tange repaid Isozaki for his loyalty with the Festival Plaza at Expo '70, the Osaka World Fair. See Kenneth Frampton, *Arata Isozaki, Vol. 1 1959–1978* (Tokyo: A.D.A. Edita, 1991), 86–87.

7 Kazuhiro Ishii and Hiroyuki Suzuki, "Post-Metabolism," *Japan Architect*, no. 247 (October–November 1977), 7–108. Shozo Baba introduced the issue with a statement that "In the past, Japanese society was—and is today—arranged in a pyramidal hierarchy of orders of inferiority and superiority," which he interpreted to apply equally to architects in an open system, before asserting that "in the field of architecture, the pyramid began to crumble a little over a decade ago when Arata Isozaki and Kisho Kurakawa left Tange at URTEC, and set out on their own courses of activity." To further strengthen his point (at 13–14), Baba published a montage showing a god-like Tange hovering above Mount Fuji, among heavenly beings, and below him Isozaki on the left, and Kurokawa on the right, as demon-like rival challengers for the title of architectural shogun; on the next level below them are the young samurai who await their turn to challenge Isozaki and Kurokawa.

8 George R. Collins, *Visionary Drawings of Architecture and Planning: 20th Century* (MoMA, 1960) comprised 131 drawings. It was developed for travel and circulated by the Smithsonian Institution Travelling Exhibition Services (SITE) and was later published as a book by MIT Press in 1979.

9 It was republished in 1964 in Collective Form with Masato Otaka. Maki distinguished three different categories of 'group form': (1) the compositional mode (modernist space); (2) the megastructure (Tange's Tokyo Bay project); and (3) group form. Maki defined group form as a type of additive form (much like vernacular building and Jørn Utzon housing), whereby single units could be removed or added without destroying the balance of the totality. It did not have a fixed concept as in a megastructure, but was an open-ended non-hierarchical humanmade landscape.

10 Philip Drew, "Travel Diary 1978," unpublished, Tokyo, July 10, 1978, 57.

11 Itoh was a descendant of the eleventh-century Ise Fujiwara clan (who were rulers of Japan) who, besides being the authority on *minka*, was planning to write a history of Japanese architecture as his next project.

12 Dr. Nakayama treated Isozaki as a teenager for a nasal infection and knew the Isozaki family. Isozaki's father was a businessman and was well known in Kyushu as a haiku verse poet. At his local high school, Isozaki was a conscientious student who showed early talent in his paintings. Dr. Nakayama observed that even then, his art displayed individualism and was clearly identifiable for its idiom. The Nakayama house was originally intended as a clinic and residence for the doctor and his parents. Thought was given for his son to live there later, which resulted in wood partitions in the interior which could be removed in the future. Dr. Nakayama introduced Isozaki to the local medical fraternity and influenced his selection to design the Oita Medical Centre. He clearly had considerable affection for Isozaki. (Drew, "Travel Diary, 1978," Oita, July 26, 1978, 77).

13 Many interpretations of Mannerism exist. See David B. Stewart, *The Making of Modern Japanese Architecture 1868 to the Present* (Tokyo: Kodansha, 1987), 248, who rejected the Mannerist style label identification of Isozaki based on John Shearman's definition, who took it to mean facility and style agility, which Isozaki certainly has. My interpretation came from Arnold Hauser, who describes Mannerism as "virtuosity that is always a piece of bravura, a triumphant conjuring trick, a firework display with flying sparks and colours. The effect depends on the defiance of the instinctual, the naïvely natural and rational, and the emphasis laid on the obscure and problematic, and ambiguous, the latent, and the ambiguous ... Beauty too beautiful becomes unreal, strength too strong becomes acrobatics, too much content loses all meaning, form independent of content becomes an empty shell." Arnold Hauser *Mannerism* (London: Routledge & Kegan Paul, 1965), 13.

14 In *A Life on Our Planet: My Witness Statement and a Vision for the Future* (London: Witness Books, 2020), 220–221, David Attenborough recommends: "We can yet make amends, manage our impact, change the direction of our development and once again become a species in harmony with nature ... Our future on the planet, the only place so far as we know where life of any kind exists, is at stake."

11

THIS IS YOUR CITY

The Pop Future Foretold by Metabolism

Yasutaka Tsuji

The history of Metabolism has been examined in two recent exhibitions: "Metabolism: The City of the Future" at the Mori Art Museum (September 17, 2011–January 15, 2012)[1] and "Tectonic Visions between Land and Sea: Works of Kiyonori Kikutake" at the Harvard University Graduate School of Design (August 24, 2012–October 16, 2012).[2] However, the scholarship has tended to ascribe the start of the group to the staging of the World Design Conference (May 11, 1960–May 16, 1960) and thereafter follow its members who participated in the conference and their works: as well as members Kiyonori Kikutake 菊竹清訓, Kishō Kurokawa 黒川紀章, Masato Ōdaka 大髙正人, Fumihiko Maki 槇文彦, Kiyoshi Awazu 粟津潔, and Kenji Ekuan 榮久庵 憲司. However, this conference cannot be thought of as the only initial impetus for the group known as Metabolism.[3]

Moreover, narratives on the context in which Metabolism began have tended to refer to the debate over tradition instigated by the "spokesman" of Metabolism, Noboru Kawazoe 川添登, as the editor of *Shin Kenchiku* 新建築. However, it is difficult to say whether there has been sufficient attention paid to the fact that, with the binary opposition between the International Style and regionalism in mind, he started the debate to clarify on which side those who participated in it belonged. Further, this binary opposition was brought to Japan via the translation by Ryūichi Hamaguchi 浜口隆一 and Tsutomu Ikuta 生田勉 of Lewis Mumford's discourse, which favored regionalism over the International Style. In addition, referencing this discussion concerning regionalism, Kawazoe attempted to demonstrate that Metabolism had a unique character that was not present in other countries. Yet this declaration of being a group representing Japan has been accepted at face value, even in historical examinations of Metabolism.

As a result, Metabolism came to be viewed as a representation of rapid Japanese industrialization and economic growth, which were different from that in other countries. Taking the example of the 1964 Tokyo Olympics and the 1970 Osaka Expo, it is possible to argue that in imagining the future, Metabolism shared the state's drive toward developing national lands. However, I would like to examine Metabolism from a

DOI: 10.4324/9781003186540-12

different perspective than simply asking whether the members of this group were able to create a future for the city or whether that future was actually realized. In this text, I would like to argue that it was the demonstration of the power of images visualizing a techno-utopia that was the contribution of Metabolism group, using the cases of the 1960 "Visionary Architecture" exhibition at the Museum of Modern Art (MoMA), New York and the 1962 "This is Your City: Urban Planning and Urban Life" exhibition 都市計画と都市生活展 あなたの都市はこうなる at the Seibu Department Store in Tokyo.

Immediately after the group Metabolism was organized, Kiyonori Kikutake and Kisho Kurokawa sent in their works for the "Visionary Architecture" exhibition. First, I would like to clarify how their works came to be an exhibition, starting with an overview of the exhibition itself. Next, I would like to examine the exhibition curated by Metabolism two years later, "This is Your City," and demonstrate how it expressed a "scientific future" using comics (manga) and animation.

Further, "Visionary Architecture" was exhibited two years later in the Seibu Department Store, just as "This is Your City" was. So, lastly, I would like to focus on this circulating exhibition and examine how Metabolism attempted to represent a society in which people came together in the city, without the growth narrative from their present reality to the ideal future.

Sculpture as an architectural model: the "Visionary Architecture" exhibition

In the "Architecture and Imagery: Four New Buildings" exhibition, Arthur Drexler displayed drawings and models of the Sydney Opera House, designed by Jørn Utzon, and the Trans World Airlines Flight Center by Eero Saarinen.[4] In this exhibition, Drexler presented structural expressionism in architecture as an argument through images of buildings not yet completed. In further exhibitions, he also focused on the visuality of architecture (Figure 11.1).

In curating "Visionary Architecture" (September 29, 1960–December 4, 1960), instead of simply selecting projects that had not actually been constructed, Arthur Drexler chose "project[s] [that] usually combine[d] a criticism of society with a strong personal preference for certain forms."[5]

First, at the entrance of the exhibition hall were drawings by Leonardo da Vinci, Giovanni Battista Piranesi, Hugh Ferriss, and Étienne-Louis Boullée displayed in panels. These were collected under the heading of "Introductory Historical Section." Next, passing this section through gaps in the walls, one saw works by leaders of twentieth-century art movements, such as Hans Poelzig, Bruno Taut, Antonio Sant'Elia, and Frank Lloyd Wright. Continuing into the next large room were plans and models by El Lissitzky, Louis Kahn, and Anne Tyng. That said, more than Arthur Drexler, those who shaped the entirety of the exhibition were likely Buckminster Fuller and Frederick Kiesler.[6]

"Visionary Architecture" was Fuller's third exhibition at MoMA in two years, after "Three Structures by Buckminster Fuller" (September 22, 1959–March 1, 1960) and "Buckminster Fuller" (October 27, 1959–November 22, 1959). "Visionary Architecture" showed his Partial Enclosure of Manhattan Island, a massive dome enclosing

162 Yasutaka Tsuji

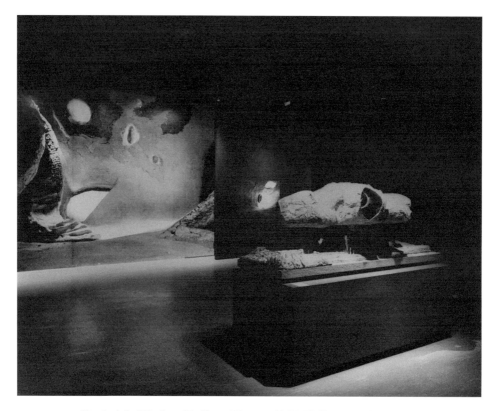

FIGURE 11.1 Frederick Kiesler, Endless House, 1947–1960. MoMA Exhibition Records, 670.11. MoMA Archives. © 2021. Digital image: MoMA, New York/SCALA, Florence.

Manhattan.[7] Like an overzealous engineer trying to control temperature and humidity with machines artificially, Fuller's scheme left people to either revel in a dream or suffer in a nightmare.

Further, a special room was given to Frederick Kiesler, who, calling the reciprocal forces of seeing and non-seeing "correalism," proclaimed that "Form does not follow function. Function follows vision. Vision follows reality." It can be said that it was this room that contained the main attraction of the exhibition. Thus, for Frederick Kiesler too, this exhibition was an opportunity to display his long-conceived ideas as drawings and models in the hope of realizing them.

Of course, to simply cry out that the construction of continuously curved surfaces, which was difficult or impossible in the past, had been made possible with the concrete shell—that is, that engineering had changed society—was not the aim of this exhibition. At the time, functionalism was supported by most architects on the East Coast. For instance, the wall and the floor were viewed as elements with singular functions, and the building was understood as the collection of these elements. Conversely, functionalism separated the structure of the building from ornament, which could not be functionally quantified and was thus unnecessary. However, Frederick Kiesler continued to object to the awkwardness of judging design elements according to their function only through his design of exhibition spaces and theatrical sets that unified the floor with the walls and ceiling.

In addition, as in the "Visionary Architecture" exhibition, the architectural works on display were not intended to be constructed. This meant that they could eliminate political and economic limitations from architecture to emphasize its autonomy. Yet, Kiesler and Drexler did not use the models to demonstrate the autonomy of architecture; instead, they attached to the gallery walls enlarged photographs of their interiors. The visitor could look into these models and, when looking up, experience the illusion that the gallery itself is within the model. Here inside the Endless House, the divisions between interior and exterior were not clear; this confused the perception of visitors, forcing them to question how a sculpture might be defined as a sculpture, or if the three-dimensional body is architecture, what it is that makes it differ from a sculpture. In other words, "Visionary Architecture" aimed to reorganize the artistic institution of the museum through the visual layering by extension from the museum's floor to the city.

"Visionary Architecture" saw the city as a techno-utopia, and the exhibition did not present anything especially new, insofar as praising this ideal, compared to other experiments of the time. However, rather than placing reality in opposition to this ideal, it can be said that the exhibition was epoch-making to show these two as part of a continuum.

Exhibitions are not only for self-promotion

Kiyonori Kikutake and Kisho Kurokawa sent a letter to Arthur Drexler soon after the World Design Conference because they had heard about plans for the "Visionary Architecture" exhibition.

In an article titled "The Plan for K," Kurokawa presented his concept for revitalizing his hometown of Kanie, which had been hit by the Ise Bay Typhoon of September 1959. In this plan, Kurokawa had a pedestrian deck in the air unified with all infrastructure, and arranged educational and agricultural facilities along the ground. In doing so, he established a 547-yard grid to form the unit of a new city for 2,000 inhabitants. This plan not only showed buildings, but tried to innovate by showing farmworkers together with the land, that is, people as inhabitants of the buildings. At the time of the World Design Conference, Kurokawa divided this concept into two works, Mushroom-Shaped House and Agricultural City.[8] However, he put them back together again as a panel for "Visionary Architecture," which he sent to New York (Figure 11.2).

In addition, in January 1959, Kikutake published Tower-Shaped Community in Kokusai Kenchiku, consisting of artificial lands extending into the sky. Inside cylindrical towers of reinforced concrete were prefabricated residences using standard-sized materials. These were attached to the towers formed of units. The construction of the architecture was to proceed at the same time as the production of its parts, creating a system for self-reproduction across the ocean. This was published the following month as Marine City. For the World Design Conference, Kikutake unified these with other projects, naming them together as "Ocean City." Yet, for "Visionary Architecture"

FIGURE 11.2 Kisho Kurokawa, Agricultural City, 1960. Photograph by George Barrows. International Council and International Program Records, I.A.1082. MoMA Archives, New York. © 2021. Digital image: MoMA, New York/SCALA, Florence. Yasutaka Tsuji, *Postwar Japan as Dullness: A History of Art Movements and Exhibition Installations* (Tokyo: Suisei-sha, 2021): 161.

he returned to the title "Marine City." This Marine City was displayed together with Michael Webb's project (Figure 11.3).

Michael Webb presented Office Building with individual rooms as units contained within an exposed skeleton frame, which later became the Furniture Manufacturers' Association Headquarters. Webb joined Archigram the year after the exhibition. Archigram and Metabolism together illustrated the 1960s using not only architectural drawings, but also combining photographs and graphics.

For Kikutake and Kurokawa, and Metabolism, the "Visionary Architecture" exhibition was an opportunity to boast that they had been praised along with Western movements.[9] So, Kurokawa spoke proudly of having accepted the invitation to the exhibition. That said, it cannot be forgotten that most of the architects whose works were exhibited were Western, and that the selection of Kikutake and Kurokawa from Japan was somewhat unexpected.

Directly after the conference, Kikutake sent a letter to MoMA.[10] First, having heard of a project called Fantasy of Architecture, he tried to sell his works for exhibition in a letter dated June 7, 1960.

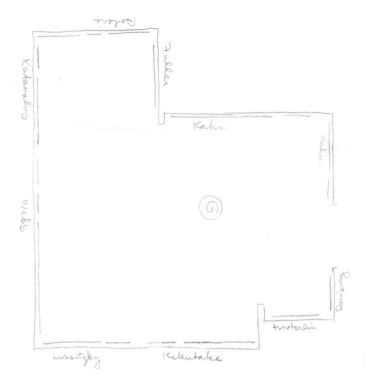

FIGURE 11.3 The Plan of "Visionary Architecture." MoMA Exhibition Records, 670.11. MoMA Archives, New York. © 2021. Digital image: MoMA, New York/SCALA, Florence. Yasutaka Tsuji, *Postwar Japan as Dullness: A History of Art Movements and Exhibition Installations* (Tokyo: Suisei-sha, 2021): 162.

Arthur Drexler, who received this letter, had curated numerous exhibitions relating to Japan: "Japanese Household Objects" (April 17, 1951–June 18, 1951), "Japanese Exhibition House" (June 16, 1954–October 15, 1955) and "Japanese Calligraphy" (June 22, 1954–September 19, 1954). These exhibitions were held as part of US–Japanese cultural diplomacy supported by Blanchette Rockefeller, who had already been involved before then in MoMA's management in various ways.

For these reasons, Drexler could not ignore the offer from the young Japanese architects. Drexler explained the concept of the "Visionary Architecture" exhibition, using that title in a letter dated June 21. Having heard of this from Kikutake, Kurokawa wrote to Drexler on September 5 that he would be sending panels used in the World Design Conference as exhibition pieces. Yet, at this point, there was only a month before the exhibition would start, so they were lucky that their panels arrived in New York on time.

To summarize this sequence, Drexler was clearly open to Metabolism, but this probably had more to do with MoMA being influenced by this cultural diplomacy than with the fact that their projects were appealing. In other words, Kikutake and Kurokawa's panels were chosen due to MoMA's interest in Japan and the debate over regionalism, as mentioned above. Obviously, it cannot be said that members of Metabolism arrived at their projects independently; the visualization of their projects depended on the involvement of others.

Kikutake and Kurokawa changed the names and dates of many of their works. This was to organize their ideas, but also to complete with the novelty of works from other countries. From this point onward, Japanese architects would repeatedly speak of the World Design Conference as if it were proof that they had achieved equal status with foreign architects. Kikutake, Kurokawa, and members of Metabolism declared that they represented Japan, having achieved international approval. However, Kikutake and Kurokawa had only sent a few panels to MoMA but had not taken notice of the issue, which Arthur Drexler and Frederick Kiesler tried to raise in the exhibition. At this point, Metabolism was not yet able to pay attention to the debate over this issue.

This is my city: a world for architects

After "Visionary Architecture," Kiyonori Kikutake and Kisho Kurokawa continued to address the real problems they encountered with their own representations of an ideal future in which they had already solved. Metabolism presented a series of proposals in trade journals both within and outside Japan,[11] and attempted to publish a follow-up issue to *Metabolism 1960*.[12] However, it would not be published during this period, and the next occasion on which the members of Metabolism came together was the exhibition at the Seibu Department Store, "This is Your City: Urban Planning and Urban Life" (October 12, 1962–October 17, 1962). An article in *Kindai Kenchiku* 近代建築 served as a catalog for this exhibition. Using photographs by Osamu Murai 村井修, I would like to go into more detail on what was in "This is Your City."[13]

This exhibition was curated by Metabolism. Yet actually, Noboru Kawazoe was its main organizer, who was credited as a "collaborator" on the entrance wall (Figure 11.4).

Kawazoe gave each of the plans a one-word label. This unified the exhibition in terms of the issue of how to solve the problem of cities in Japan. At the entrance was a massive model by Kikutake, and to its left was his panel "The City Plan for Ikebukuro" (Figure 11.5).

This model, tall enough to nearly reach the gallery ceiling, showed replaceable residential units at a tactile distance to visitors. This proposal by Kikutake was labeled "Exchange" 交代. To the side of this model was Fumihiko Maki's The D Plan and K Plan, which took up urban renewal in Dōjima and Kinshichō, respectively, and Masato Otaka's Artificial Land, which added floor space to Ōtemachi using reinforced concrete. These two panels were labeled "Organization" 組織 and "Communities" 群生. Following this was Kurokawa's Helix Plan, which imitated the structure of DNA and was labeled "Coexistence" 共存, as it was a proposal in which people would congregate autonomously in clusters.

Further, this exhibition also displayed works by others who were not members of Metabolism. One of these was The Plan for Shizuoka, an attempt at reorganizing an existing shopping district labeled "Breaking Convention" 脱皮 by Eika Takayama 高山英華. This was a detailed concrete plan dependent on government authority, and this was to show that the plans of Metabolism were not just fantasies. There was also A Plan for Tokyo by Kenzo Tange 丹下健三 labeled "Growth" 成長. Also displayed were

FIGURE 11.4 "This is Your City: Urban Planning and Urban Life," Seibu Department Store, Ikebukuro, October 12–17, 1962. Photo: © Osamu Murai.

the Σ Plan for a property in Kōjimachi by Sachio Otani 大谷幸夫 and Shinjuku Project by Arata Isozaki 磯崎新. These were labeled "Unit" 単位 and "Structure" 構造.

The labels were keywords representing the ideal life in the future and how to achieve them through planning. This aimed to demonstrate how different the stance of Metabolism was from other architects of their generation.

Collective images

When he was playing the role of organizer for Metabolism, Noboru Kawazoe was conscious of the discourse in other countries also dealing with recovery after World War II, just like Japan, such as the special issue on functionalism in *Architectural Review* edited by James Maude Richards,[14] *L'architettura* edited by Bruno Zevi, and *Zodiac* edited by Bruno Alfieri.[15] At the same time, Kawazoe helped those around him in terms of getting hired by trade journal publishers. Among these were Isamu Kurita 栗田勇 and Toshio Nakamura 中村敏男, who published many of the plans by Metabolism.[16] One of these, for instance, was the transcript of a discussion titled "Metabolism against Kenzo Tange." In these publications, how much the Metabolism practice differs from the earlier generations is emphasized, and the movement is described as having a unique character. Further, Kawazoe emphatically wrote that meeting Alison and Peter Smithson, who came to Japan for the World Design

FIGURE 11.5 "This is Your City: Urban Planning and Urban Life," Seibu Department Store, Ikebukuro, October 12–17, 1962. Photo: © Osamu Murai. Yasutaka Tsuji, *Postwar Japan as Dullness: A History of Art Movements and Exhibition Installations* (Tokyo: Suisei-sha, 2021): 165.

Conference, was very important.[17] The Smithsons participated as the Independent Group, and one can imagine that they would have discussed exhibitions the "Parallel of Life and Art" (September 11, 1953–October 18, 1953) and "This is Tomorrow" (August 9, 1956–September 9, 1956),[18] which would later come to be viewed as important exhibitions involving popular culture and Pop Art. Also examining popular or mass culture, and titled beginning "This is," the "This is Your City" exhibition was part of a series of plans by Kawazoe to bring together Metabolism, inspired by the Smithsons. With this in mind, in a narrow sense, Metabolism was the generation of critics of functionalism who wanted to replace it with a different practice.[19]

However, Kawazoe's plans were also aimed at placing Metabolism on the same level as Team X, with its critique of the Congrès Internationaux d'Architecture Moderne (CIAM). This positioning ultimately came from the discourse of Metabolism.[20] For this reason, we cannot accept their words at face value.

While the architects who came together in these conferences would use the word "urbanism" broadly to include even civilization, they would use the word "architecture" limited to individual buildings, as if to express the limits of their powers.

This rhetoric of "architecture and urbanism" 建築と都市 had a certain force during the period of high economic growth, in which the occupation of the architect had been accepted by society, and the state and industry greatly demanded construction.

Yet, for the historical examination of Metabolism today, is it valid to use this rhetoric, which is only comprehensible by architects?

In order to answer this question, let us examine their initial attempts without using *a+u* rhetoric. To begin with, Metabolism was not just architectural design, but, like its predecessor, the Japan Design Committee, a group that valued collectivity among those involved in graphics and product design, industries which are not part of the *a+u* rhetoric.[21] For instance, when Metabolism began, Kikutake designed the exhibition "Today's Focus: From Primitive Art" (June 11, 1960–July 27, 1960) at the Early National Museum of Modern Art in Tokyo, collaborating with Ikkō Tanaka 田中一光. This was because it was not only architects who were eager to be considered on equal terms with the West; this sentiment was shared by many artists in Japan. In other words, the doubt about whether they were viewed as equals to those practicing in the West was not felt only by architects who were developing their practice from the rhetoric of architecture and urbanism.

Moreover, aside from the "Today's Focus" exhibition, Kiyonori Kikutake also designed displays of "This is Your City" with Kiyoshi Awazu and Hiroshi Manabe 真鍋博. Later becoming a member of Metabolism, Awazu designed the group's symbol for the publication of *Metabolism 1960*. Although it is unfortunately difficult to determine how much he was involved in "This is Your City," it is clear that Hiroshi Manabe contributed greatly to this exhibition. Manabe drew freeform manga on the gallery's walls and columns, with curves contrasting with the orthogonal architectural drawings exhibited.

FIGURE 11.6 Murals by Hiroshi Manabe. Photo: © Osamu Murai.

At the time, Hiroshi Manabe was part of a group of three animators along with Yoji Kuri 久里洋二 and Yanagihara Ryōhei 柳原良平, who presented a "moving manga" in 1960 at the Sogetsu Kaikan in Tokyo. Conversely, Kawazoe also sought photographer Shomei Tomatsu 東松照明 and graphic designer Kōhei Sugiura 杉浦康平 to join Metabolism. With this in mind, it makes sense that Kawazoe would have intended to bring in science-fiction artist Manabe as a new member of Metabolism. The ideal life in the "This is Your City" exhibition was made not only by architects but also by the graphics of collaborators Kikutake, Awazu, and Manabe.

When they came to design buildings, Kikutake and Kurokawa began referring to the extent of their practice as "architecture" 建築 and that which was beyond their control as "city" 都市. Perhaps seeing it as an insignificant problem, these first steps were gradually forgotten as an unrecallable past. To repeat, the utopia presented in "This is Your City" was not an image limited to the rhetoric of "architecture and urbanism"; it was a composite image expressed through graphics, photographs, comics, and animation made by a collective group of artists in many fields.

Vision and reality might then coincide

"This is Your City" treated the visuality of architecture by combining photographs, comics, and animation, and this was also the case with the "Visionary Architecture" exhibition. However, when looking at Endless House, "Visionary Architecture" emphasized the relationship between artist and audience, along with questioning the idea of perception. In contrast, "This is Your City" exhibition presented the enlightening message of "this is your city," a future made by the subject of the architect. So lastly, it is necessary to examine how the "Visionary Architecture" exhibition was held in Japan in 1964.

After being held at MoMA, New York, "Visionary Architecture" traveled throughout North America.[22] In addition, it traveled to Berlin, Edinburgh, and Zagreb, as well as Sydney, Manila, and Tokyo, and then on to Central and South America, before returning to New York in 1969.[23] The Tokyo exhibition titled "Architectural Vision" 建築ビジョン (January 10, 1964–January 22, 1964) was held in the same Seibu Department Store as "This is Your City."[24] "Visionary Architecture" was a visualization throughout the East and West under the Cold War of architectural works that would normally not be visible without visiting their sites.[25]

For the circulating exhibition, Arthur Drexler oversaw the production of 49 explanatory panels for 74 works. An exhibition catalog was later published using these panels.[26] He ended the catalog's introduction with the strong phrase: "Vision and reality might then coincide." This was because he aimed not only to foretell his ideal future but also to demonstrate the issue of perception by unifying vision and reality.

Kiyonori Kikutake and Kisho Kurokawa were also involved in this exhibition. It was in 1964, the same year that "Visionary Architecture" came to Japan, that Metabolism was introduced as a representative of Japan in *World Architecture One*, edited by John Donat.[27] Also, in October 1964, an article about Metabolism by Günter Nitschke appeared in *Architectural Design*, edited by Monica Pigeon and Kenneth Frampton.[28] Certainly, these were not only influenced by the "Visionary Architecture" exhibition. Yet, it was a significant opportunity for members of Metabolism to position their work as a symbol of the Japanese state to foreign audiences.

In the end, Metabolism was not able to acknowledge the issue raised in "Visionary Architecture" between the creating self of the architect and the observing masses. However, it is not the masses that build the city of the future, but architects. Yet, it is possible that Metabolism over-estimated their ability to take part in the creation of the future. That said, Metabolism should not be judged on whether their proposals came to be realized or not. Its contribution is that its members demonstrated the imaginary power of a "pop" vision that was easily understandable, even by the masses, without the rhetoric of architecture and urbanism.

The proposals of Metabolism were derided by some architects, engineers, and politicians as a cartoon, lacking reality. Against these criticisms, Japanese architects might have been able to claim that the recovery from the war until then had created a certain reality, following the thinking that conglomerations of architecture had apparently amounted to more than the sum of their parts. Those outside Japan might argue that Metabolism foretold early twenty-first-century problems such as surveillance society or climate change. However, when discussing urban problems, few architects go beyond giving interpretations that serve the needs of their own projects. Whether Metabolism had the means of anticipating the future is doubtful and, in fact, whether this question should be asked at all might also be questioned.

Metabolism should not be judged on whether its proposals became realized. Rather, the contributions of its members demonstrated the power of images of pop vision that were easily understandable at a glance—even by the masses who lacked expertise in architecture and urbanism.

Conclusion

The "Visionary Architecture" exhibition called for the unification of reality before one's eyes and the ideal that could not yet be perceived through a representation of unconstructed buildings with drawings and models. Thus, there is no doubt that the exhibition, like other experiments of its time, tried to express the future of cities as a techno-utopia. Metabolism, too, tried to visualize this techno-utopia in the later "This is Your City" exhibition. However, this was not necessarily only expressed through drawings and models utilizing architects' jargon in relation to architecture and urbanism.

The influence of architects cannot be judged solely on the basis of whether or not their works have been realized. It is how they visualize the collectivity of cities that matters. Metabolism was a group that embodied pop images consisting of photographs, comics, and animation.

Notes

1　Hajime Yatsuka, *Metabolism Nexus* (Tokyo: Ohmsha, 2011).
2　Ken Tadashi Oshima (ed.), *Kiyonori Kikutake: Between Land and Sea* (Cambridge, MA: Harvard University Graduate School of Design; Zurich: Lars Müller Publishers, 2016).
3　Following the publication of *Metabolism 1960*, the group assumed the name "Metabolism," and thereafter few members referred to themselves as Metabolists, even though the term has continued to be used outside of Japan. At the time, they were criticized for technological determinism, and some members tried to separate themselves from the group. On the other hand, as the group's work began to be known abroad, Noboru Kawazoe began to use the name "Metabolists" as representing Japan. Thus, I believe it is important to use the official

name of the group rather than the one attached later by Noboru Kawazoe. See Masato Otaka and Noboru Kawazoe (eds.), *Metabolism and Metabolists* (Tokyo: Bijutsu Shuppan-sha, 2005).

4 Museum of Modern Art, New York, "Architecture and Imagery: Four New Buildings," press release, February 11, 1959.

5 Museum of Modern Art, New York, "Visionary Architecture Exhibition," press release, September 29, 1960.

6 Arthur Drexler, "Visionary Architecture," *Arts and Architecture* 78, no. 1 (January 1961): 10–13.

7 Following "Visionary Architecture," Buckminster Fuller was invited to Japan by the *Yomiuri* newspaper and Nippon Television from February 3, 1961 to March 2, 1961. See Noboru Kawazoe, "Fuller's Concept," *Yomiuri Shimbun* (March 1961): 3.

8 The first edition was April 1960. See Noboru Kawazoe (ed.), *Metabolism 1960: The Proposals for New Urbanism* (Tokyo: Bijutsu Shuppan–Sha, 1960).

9 Noboru Kawazoe, "Interview with Kisho Kurokawa," *Bijutsu Techo*, no. 186 (March 1961): 81–84.

10 "Visionary Architecture: Correspondence," Museum of Modern Art Exhibition Records 1960–1969, 670.15, Museum of Modern Art Archives, New York.

11 Kiyonori Kikutake, "Design Hypothesis," *Kindai Kenchiku*, no. 15 (November 1961): 72–79.

12 Noriaki (Kisho) Kurokawa, "Deux Propositions de Tours Hélicoidales," *L'Architecture d'Aujourd'hui*, no. 101 (April–May 1962): 86–87.

13 "This is Your City: Urban Planning and Urban Life Exhibition," *Kindai Kenchiku* 16, no. 11 (November 1962): 31–40.

14 "Functional Tradition," *Architectural Review* 107, no. 637 (January 1950): 3–5.

15 Noboru Kawazoe, "Modern Japanese Architecture Confronts Functionalism," *Zodiac*, no. 3 (November 1958): 117–148.

16 Kenzo Tange, Masato Otaka, Noboru Kawazoe, and Kisho Kurokawa, "About Metabolism," *Kindai Kenchiku* 14, no. 11 (November 1960): 67–72.

17 Noboru Kawazoe, "Afterword," in *This is Design* (Tokyo: Kadokawa Publishing, 1961): 213–215.

18 Held at the Whitechapel Art Gallery and partially designed by Richard Hamilton, John McHale, and John Voelcker. See Theo Crosby (ed.), *This is Tomorrow* (London: Whitechapel Art Gallery, 1956). Reprinted in 2014.

19 Noboru Kawazoe, "A New Tokyo: In, on or above the Sea?," *This is Japan* no. 9 (January 1962): 56–65.

20 Kisho Kurokawa (ed.), *After CIAM* (Tokyo: Shokoku-sha, 1971).

21 Yasutaka Tsuji, "From Design to Environment: 'Art and Technology' in Two 1966 Exhibitions at the Matsuya Department Store," *Review of Japanese Culture and Society* 28 (December 2016): 275–296.

22 "C/E 61–47: Visionary Architecture, 'Misc. Memos and Lists,'" Department of Circulating Exhibitions Records, II.2.132.11.2, Museum of Modern Art Archives, New York.

23 International Council and International Program Records, I.A.1059–I.A.1096, Museum of Modern Art Archives, New York.

24 Arthur Drexler, "Visionary Architecture," *Kokusai Kenchiku* 30, no. 10 (November 1963): 40–43.

25 It was sponsored by the Mainichi Shimbun and MoMA, New York. Hartzell Lincoln Dake of the United States Information Service was involved in the shipping. See "Visionary Architecture," *Mainichi Shimbun*, January 10, 1964, 3.

26 Arthur Drexler, "Introduction," in *Visionary Architecture: An Exhibition Prepared and Circulated by the Museum of Modern Art, New York, under the Auspices of the International Council* (n.p., 1963).

27 Noriaki (Kisho) Kurokawa, "Metabolism: The Pursuit of Open Form," in *World Architecture One*, ed. John Donat (London: Studio Vista, 1964): 10–13.

28 Gunter Nitschke, "The Metabolists of Japan," *Architectural Design* 34 (October 1964): 209–524.

12

SPACESHIP EARTH

Metabolist Capsules, the Petro-economy, and Geoengineering

Yuriko Furuhata

One notable aspect of Metabolist architecture is its use of plastics and other synthetic materials as construction materials, along with the more well-known use of concrete. This chapter puts these plastic uses in metabolism's capsule architecture of the 1960s and 1970s in dialogue with recent debates on geoengineering and the planetary scale metabolic rift that manifests in anthropogenic climate change. Famously, Metabolists borrowed the term "metabolism"—the group's namesake—as mediated by labor from Marx and Engel's discussion of material exchanges between humans and nature.[1] Reading the work of Metabolist architecture through the lens of contemporary Marxist theories of anthropogenic ecological crisis—the so-called metabolic rift—allows us to view Metabolist architecture concerning their work's ecological impacts.

As a biochemical concept, *metabolism* refers to a set of life-sustaining chemical interactions maintaining living organisms. These interactions include conversions of matter into energy and vice versa from food to air to sunlight. It also refers to the body's regulatory mechanisms, such as the respiratory and endocrine systems that regulate the flows of oxygen, hormones, and other biochemical elements. Therefore, metabolism as a metaphor implies a cyclical and even holistic process of organic life and its constant renewal. These holistic connotations of organic growth, renewal, conversion, and maintenance of life are theoretically implied in the renewable and sustainable design of Metabolist capsule architecture. However, the idea of metabolism points to something more troubling when considering the materiality of construction materials and finances that made Metabolist architecture possible.

This chapter focuses on the material history of plastics in Japan to analyze how Metabolist architectural design, and particularly the work of Kisho Kurokawa, intersects with the growth of the petrochemical industry, the oil economy, and environmental pollution. I argue that Kurokawa's conceptualization of metabolism—the eponymous concept that defines the group—and his experiments with plastics point to the fundamental ecological dilemma of Metabolist architecture. In other words, there is a contradiction between the ecological aspiration of Metabolist theory and the ecological degradation produced by the theory's material execution. Metabolism's

DOI: 10.4324/9781003186540-13

architectural experiments and the political economy of petrochemicals meet in geoengineering's revival as the ultimate technological fix for climate change today.

The effects of anthropogenic climate change are palpable everywhere, from the accelerating speed of global warming, environmental pollution, and rising sea levels to increasingly catastrophic droughts, wildfires, and extreme weather patterns. In response to this deepening climate crisis, some scientists and engineers have called for the geoengineering of Earth's atmosphere.[2] I want to situate Metabolist architecture's contradictory relations to ecology within this planetary context.

The popularity of plastics in architecture

In the mid-1950s, the petrochemical industry started to mass-produce cheap plastics. Some became the iconic plastic commodities of the 1950s onward, such as Tupperware. Other cheap plastics became new construction materials for architects and industrial designers to experiment with lightweight, flexible, and prefabricated modular forms.[3] A salient example of Metabolist capsules is Kenji Ekuan's Plastic Ski Lodge (1963). He built this capsule assisted by Kasei Komatsu, a manufacturer of polyvinyl chloride (PVC) pipes. This project was followed by Yadokari Hermit Crab Capsule Lodge (1969), a compact orange capsule, which Ekuan built in collaboration with Kasei Nikko, a manufacturer of thermoplastic resins.[4] Another iconic example is Kisho Kurokawa's Capsule House (1970) and Nakagin Capsule Tower (1972). Both projects were made from fiberglass-reinforced polyester and implemented newly available synthetic materials (i.e., plastics). Kurokawa imagined that these capsule housings would sustain the metabolic cycle of the city. Instead of demolishing the entire building when wear and tear occurs, Kurokawa imagined residential units of prefabricated capsules as replaceable. Once every few decades, new capsules could be manufactured and plugged back into the tower's core. This periodic replaceability was key to Kurokawa's holistic vision of Metabolism as an ecologically sustainable architectural practice.

Beyond polyester capsules, there was an international boom of pneumatic domes, polyester roofs, and tensile canopies made with synthetic fabrics in the 1960s. For example, the pneumatic roof of the Festival Plaza at Expo '70 used layers of translucent polyester films filled with air, designed by a team of Tange Lab architects.[5] Polyester, plexiglass, synthetic rubber, vinyl, polyethylene terephthalate, and other kinds of plastic materials entered urban and domestic spheres in the form of walls, roofs, bathtubs, furniture, clothes, toys, insulations, and food packages as Metabolist and Tange Lab architects began experimenting with these new construction materials.

Plastics, to quote Heather Davis, are "the substrata of advanced capitalism." Their pervasive presence in our daily environment—from utensils to clothes to smartphone cases to shopping bags—has become habitual.[6] However, these commonplace plastics hold a close ecological relationship to the material processes of fossil fuel extraction, greenhouse gas emissions, the internal organs of living organisms, and the pollution of air, water, and soil. From this perspective, capsule architecture made of plastics is connected to the planet's changing geological and climatic conditions intimately. By extension, the futuristic aesthetic of Metabolist architecture exemplified by its shiny plastic capsules is ecologically bound to the planetary future's macroclimate.

I suggest that we need to closely examine the biochemical concept of metabolism (*shinchin taisha* or *taisha* in Japanese) in order to unpack the contradictory relationship between Metabolist architecture and ecology. As often noted by Kawazoe Noboru, one of the founding members of the Metabolist group, the very turn to the term "metabolism" by the group was motivated by Friedrich Engels's use of the term in *Dialectics of Nature* (1883).[7] Metabolism signifies the biochemical renewal of cells and tissues within living organisms in biology's conventional sense, including their growth and death. The group's use of capsules to accommodate the organic growth of buildings, megastructures, and cities expressed the idea of metabolic renewal. In so doing, they analogized the architectural process of designing built structures to the biochemical process of growing organic cells. Buildings and cities were conceived as living organisms whose metabolic activities could be regulated by design more efficiently.

Metabolic rift

The Marxist inflection of metabolism allows us to re-evaluate the Metabolist architectural movement's ecological vision, particularly Kurokawa's vision, in light of its reliance on plastics and the oil economy. The Marxist perspective allows us to shift the term "metabolism" away from its associations with a holistic view of nature–human relationships. In doing so, we can focus on production's political economy, the rift between humans and nature, the ecological consequences of petrochemical and chemical industries, and the real environmental footprint of Metabolist architects.

The term *metabolic rift*, coined by sociologist John Bellamy Foster, and its associated idea of the material historical separation between humans and nature have been widely adopted by Marxist thinkers interested in addressing anthropogenic climate change and expanding industrial capitalism's ecological critique within Marx and Engel's work.[8] According to Foster, Marx responded to German scientist Justus von Liebig's metabolic analysis of the impoverishment of soil nutrients by formulating a historical materialist critique of industrial capitalism. For Marx, the displacement of nutrients from the soil is a symptom of the larger historical condition of capitalism, causing the metabolic rift between humans and the earth.[9] Therefore, Marx's use of the metabolism concept gave him "a more solid—and scientific—way in which to depict the complex, dynamic interchange between human beings and nature, resulting from human labor. The material exchanges and regulatory actions associated with the concept of metabolism encompassed both 'nature-imposed conditions' and the capacity of human beings to affect this process."[10]

Put simply, industrial capitalism's development relied on the colonial practice of dispossessing the land, natural resources, and bodies through transatlantic slavery and indentured labor. It also relied on the systematic displacement of the agrarian population through enclosures of the commons, private ownership, and other expropriation means.[11] As industrial capitalism developed, workers migrated to urban centers where they consumed crops and clothes made of organic fibers (e.g., cotton) grown in the countryside. Yielding these agricultural products required fertile soil. Soil loses its fertility over time without regularly replenishing essential nutrients (e.g., nitrogen, phosphorus, and potassium). There was a more or less metabolic balance between the soil's fertility and agricultural production in the preindustrial era since human waste and used clothes would often return to the land where the crops were produced. However, with increased human population concentration in urban centers, more crops were brought to the cities and turned into waste. Consequently, these soil nutrients never returned to the countryside. According to Marx, this metabolic rift in nature is structurally related to the metabolic rift in society. In other words, the rift manifests as biochemical imbalances in the soil and politico-economic problems of social inequities.[12]

In the case of Japan, arguably, the spread of chemical fertilizers more than urbanization brought this problem of the metabolic rift into sharp focus. In the early twentieth century, chemical fertilizers in the form of factory-produced nitrogen and phosphate became popular and reduced human excrement's value as a natural fertilizer.[13] In other words, the development of petrochemical and chemical industries in Japan was central to the metabolic rift in the soil's biochemical balance. Further, these industries were behind the production of plastics, becoming the construction materials of the Metabolist capsules.

Industrial pollution

The historical connection between the development of chemical fertilizer, petrochemicals, and plastics is directly linked to the material and economic conditions leading to Metabolist architecture's reliance on plastics and oil. The systematic dislocation of chemical elements is at stake in the metabolic cycle, such as nitrogen, mercury, sulfur dioxide, and carbon dioxide moving through the soil, water, air, and bodies of living organisms. This systematic dislocation of chemical elements is also inseparable from the capitalist economy of fossil fuel extraction, petrochemical production, and subsequent environmental pollution. The local effects of this industrial metabolism capitalist cycle became glaringly visible through pollution-related diseases in Japan in the 1960s and 1970s.

By the late 1960s, Japan was a leading global producer of plastics. At this time, Metabolist architects turned to plastics to build iconic capsules. Further, the severity of industrial pollution caused by petrochemicals began to gain public attention. The petrochemical complexes built along coastal cities were the principal culprits of infamous cases of devastating industrial pollution in the 1960s and 1970s.[14]

A notorious case of industrial pollution from this era was a form of methylmercury poisoning known as Minamata disease. Chisso Corporation, one of the principal producers of chemical fertilizers and plastic ingredients, was directly responsible for this case. Chisso used inorganic mercury as a catalyst to produce acetaldehyde, which was a toxic chemical compound used to manufacture plastics. Methylmercury was a byproduct of the chemical reaction. Consequently, Minamata disease caused severe neurological damage among its victims, many of whom were directly or indirectly engaged in the fishing industry in Kyūshū, where Chisso Corporation's factory was located.[15]

I highlight the Chisso Corporation case to overturn harmonious connotations of renewal and equilibrium associated with the metabolism concept that Metabolist architects like Kurokawa proposed. Metabolist architecture, especially its compact design of brightly colored plastic capsules, is deeply implicated in this chain of chemical displacements due to its reliance on manufacturing plastic-based construction materials and the oil economy. In other words, when we thoroughly examine the materiality of plastics and industrial metabolism, including the effects of environmental pollution, they undercut the Metabolists' holistic vision of organic growth and the renewal of buildings and cities. Considering these material and economic conditions of biological and industrial metabolisms, the metaphor of metabolism loses its harmonious connotations.

Indeed, Metabolism's holistic vision of renewable architecture and the sustainable growth of cities as living organisms is further contradicted by its reliance on the extractivist oil economy flows, directly contributing to global warming and environmental pollution. We could fully grasp their ecological dilemma if we consider these two sides of extraction and environmental pollution together, mediated by the flows of oil and money, which provided the material and financial support for Metabolist architects in the 1960s and 1970s.

The oil economy

The 1970s was also a decade when the domestic financing of large-scale architectural projects by Tange Lab and Metabolist architects in Japan dwindled. However, Kenzo Tange and Metabolist architects received invitations to work on architectural and urban planning projects in the Middle East, North Africa, and Southeast Asia, having already established an international reputation as starchitects. Many of the projects were financed by the petroleum sector.[16]

For instance, Tange worked in Saudi Arabia, while Kikutake was involved in the tourist industries of oil-exporting countries, making megastructure projects in Abu Dhabi (1975), such as floating luxury hotels. Meanwhile, Kurokawa opened a local office in Abu Dhabi to expand his architectural business networks in the Middle East and North Africa. The continuation of Kurokawa's capsule design principle is evident in many of these projects, including developing luxury capsules in Iraq (1975).[17]

Many of these projects were never completed due to political and geopolitical instabilities. Nonetheless, they attest to Tange Lab architects' deep entanglement with the global oil economy. In other words, Tange and Metabolist projects were directly implicated in the unsustainable practices of fossil fuel extraction and the petroleum industry. Therefore, plastics used to build capsules are not the only material connections these architects had with petroleum and petrochemical industries, significantly contributing to environmental pollution, greenhouse gas emissions, melting of polar ice, sea-level rise, and other symptoms of climate change. Metabolist projects are ecologically inextricable from the biochemical and economic flows of oil and petrochemicals.

However, it would be remiss to conclude that the ecological dilemma of Metabolist capsule architecture was driven by the architects' material and financial reliance on plastics and oil. Indeed, their metabolic renewal theory of buildings and cities was also conditioned by the nascent planetary understanding of Earth as an enclosed ecosystem. I want to discuss this last point briefly before concluding this material historical analysis of Metabolism.

The Spaceship Earth

The term "capsule" "conjures up either a capsule containing medicine or the living quarters of an astronaut," as Hyunjung Cho suggested in her analysis of Metabolism.[18] Just as the synthetic membrane of space capsules and spacesuits protects the lives of astronauts in vacuum conditions, Earth's atmospheric membrane protects the lives of living organisms on the planet.

Importantly, this similarity between the enclosed spaceship and the enclosed planet was captured by the analogy of Spaceship Earth, which gained popularity in the mid-1960s and critically intersected with Kurokawa's holistic view of metabolism.

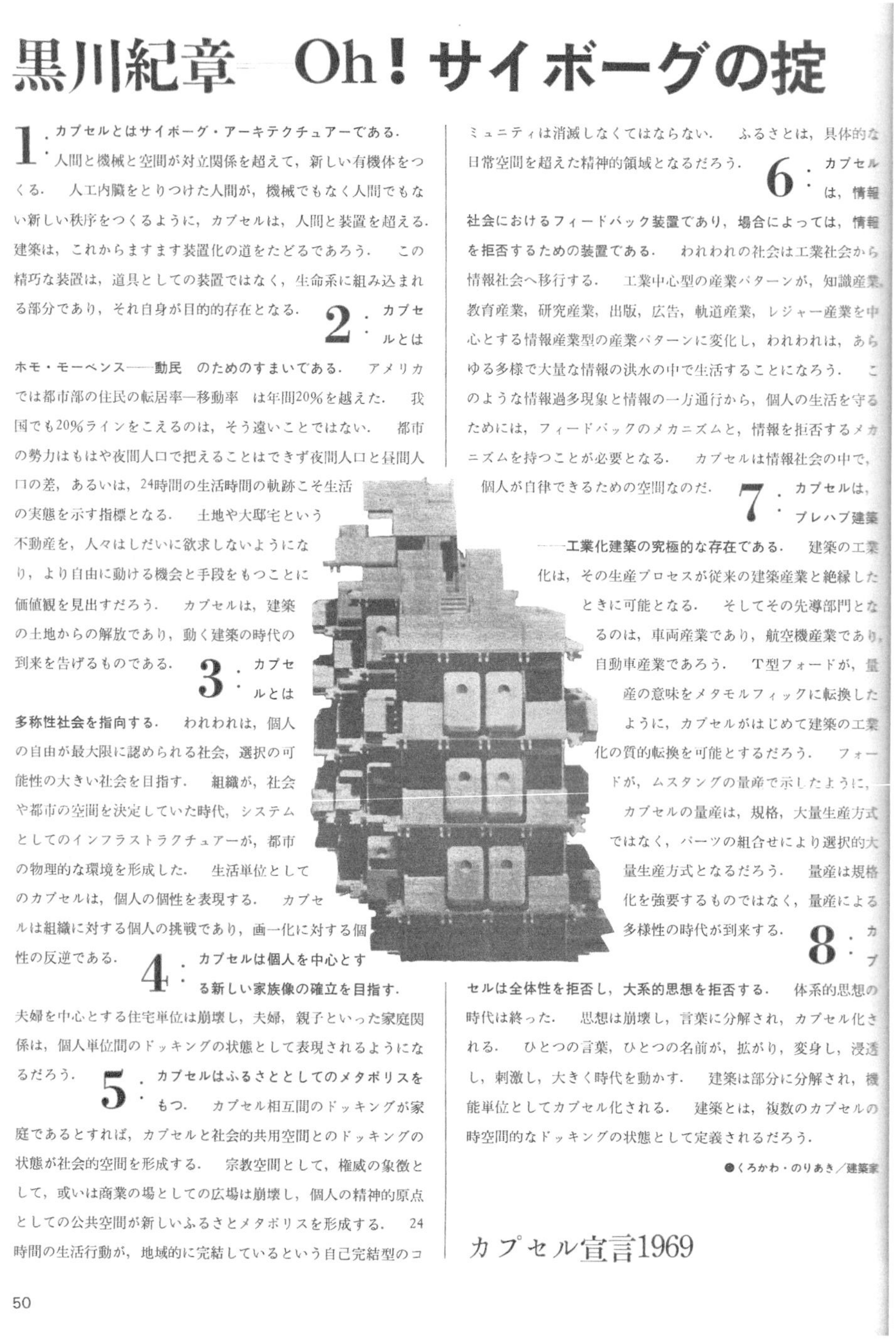

黒川紀章　Oh！サイボーグの掟

1．カプセルとはサイボーグ・アーキテクチュアーである．人間と機械と空間が対立関係を超えて，新しい有機体をつくる．　人工内臓をとりつけた人間が，機械でもなく人間でもない新しい秩序をつくるように，カプセルは，人間と装置を超える．建築は，これからますます装置化の道をたどるであろう．　この精巧な装置は，道具としての装置ではなく，生命系に組み込まれる部分であり，それ自身が目的的存在となる．

2．カプセルとはホモ・モーベンス――動民　のためのすまいである．　アメリカでは都市部の住民の転居率―移動率　は年間20％を越えた．　我国でも20％ラインをこえるのは，そう遠いことではない．　都市の勢力はもはや夜間人口で把えることはできず夜間人口と昼間人口の差，あるいは，24時間の生活時間の軌跡こそ生活の実態を示す指標となる．　土地や大邸宅という不動産を，人々はしだいに欲求しないようになり，より自由に動ける機会と手段をもつことに価値観を見出すだろう．　カプセルは，建築の土地からの解放であり，動く建築の時代の到来を告げるものである．

3．カプセルとは多称性社会を指向する．　われわれは，個人の自由が最大限に認められる社会，選択の可能性の大きい社会を目指す．　組織が，社会や都市の空間を決定していた時代，システムとしてのインフラストラクチュアーが，都市の物理的な環境を形成した．　生活単位としてのカプセルは，個人の個性を表現する．　カプセルは組織に対する個人の挑戦であり，画一化に対する個性の反逆である．

4．カプセルは個人を中心とする新しい家族像の確立を目指す．夫婦を中心とする住宅単位は崩壊し，夫婦，親子といった家庭関係は，個人単位間のドッキングの状態として表現されるようになるだろう．

5．カプセルはふるさととしてのメタポリスをもつ．　カプセル相互のドッキングが家庭であるとすれば，カプセルと社会的共用空間とのドッキングの状態が社会的空間を形成する．　宗教空間として，権威の象徴として，或いは商業の場としての広場は崩壊し，個人の精神的原点としての公共空間が新しいふるさとメタポリスを形成する．　24時間の生活行動が，地域的に完結しているという自己完結型のコミュニティは消滅しなくてはならない．　ふるさとは，具体的な日常空間を超えた精神的領域となるだろう．

6．カプセルは，情報社会におけるフィードバック装置てあり，場合によっては，情報を拒否するための装置である．　われわれの社会は工業社会から情報社会へ移行する．　工業中心型の産業パターンが，知識産業，教育産業，研究産業，出版，広告，軌道産業，レジャー産業を中心とする情報産業型の産業パターンに変化し，われわれは，あらゆる多様で大量の情報の洪水の中で生活することになろう．　このような情報過多現象と情報の一方通行から，個人の生活を守るためには，フィードバックのメカニズムと，情報を拒否するメカニズムを持つことが必要となる．　カプセルは情報社会の中で，個人が自律できるための空間なのだ．

7．カプセルは，プレハブ建築工業化建築の究極的な存在である．　建築の工業化は，その生産プロセスが従来の建築産業と絶縁したときに可能となる．　そしてその先導部門となるのは，車両産業であり，航空機産業であり，自動車産業であろう．　T型フォードが，量産の意味をメタモルフィックに転換したように，カプセルがはじめて建築の工業化の質的転換を可能とするだろう．　フォードが，ムスタングの量産で示したように，カプセルの量産は，規格，大量生産方式ではなく，パーツの組合せにより選択的大量生産方式となるだろう．　量産は規格化を強要するものではなく，量産による多様性の時代が到来する．

8．カプセルは全体性を拒否し，大系的思想を拒否する．　体系的思想の時代は終った．　思想は崩壊し，言葉に分解され，カプセル化される．　ひとつの言葉，ひとつの名前が，拡がり，変身し，浸透し，刺激し，大きく時代を動かす．　建築は部分に分解され，機能単位としてカプセル化される．　建築とは，複数のカプセルの時空間的なドッキングの状態として定義されるだろう．

●くろかわ・のりあき／建築家

カプセル宣言1969

FIGURE 12.1 Kisho Kurokawa's manifesto, "Capsule Declaration 1969." Published in the journal *Space Design – SD* (March 1969), 50.

Capsule architecture emerged when plastics gained wide attention as a novel construction material and source of environmental toxicity. It also emerged when the atmospheric enclosure of Earth was analogized to that of a spaceship.

The analogy of Spaceship Earth caught the attention of Metabolist architects. Kisho Kurokawa was particularly fond of this comparison between Earth and the spaceship. While Buckminster Fuller popularized this spaceship metaphor in his book *Operating Manual for Spaceship Earth* (1968), Kenneth Boulding was the first to analogize Earth's closed ecosystem to a spaceship in his 1966 essay "The Economics of the Coming Spaceship Earth." Along with Ludwig von Bertalanffy, Boulding is known as one of the early proponents of the general systems theory and served as the inaugural President of the Society for General Systems Research (1957–1958).[19] From 1963 to 1964, Boulding also visited a professor at the International Christian University in Tokyo. He returned to Japan in 1970 to give a series of talks at the invitation of the public broadcast company NHK.[20]

Boulding's call to shift our understanding of economic productivity from the image of the open frontier (where "cowboys" and other colonial settlers pillage and kill) to the image of the enclosed capsule (where astronauts are trapped) advocated for the sustainable development of capitalism. One Japanese architect on whom Boulding's vision had a strong impact was Kurokawa. Commenting on Boulding's work, Kurokawa wrote: "Boulding's ecosystem approach is based on the theory of Earth as a closed system composed of ecological, economic, and social circulations. When combined with a theory of environmental metabolism, his approach offers an important hint on how to address and resolve the fundamental problems of pollution." Kurokawa argued that architects must learn from Boulding and his critique of the cowboy economy's non-sustainable logic, presuming that land and resources are limitless. Instead of following the expansionist model of cowboys, Boulding argued that we must live like astronauts (or spacemen), who manage to survive with limited resources and recycled air inside the enclosed environment of a space capsule.

Boulding's theory paralleled Kurokawa's theory of architectural metabolism, emphasizing renewal and recycling.[21] Therefore, the optimized management of the biochemical processes of metabolism inside the sealed envelope of an extraterrestrial capsule provides a holistic model of recycling terrestrial capsules and other resources on Earth. Architectural metabolism in cities shares the ecosystem view of managing resources and waste inside the enclosed environment, as imagined by Kurokawa. To be sure, the ecological conditions inside the space capsules, architectural capsules, and Earth operate differently, and this managerial vision of an enclosed ecosystem cannot be scaled up easily. However, attending to the mediating role of Boulding's theory of Spaceship Earth in Kurokawa's theory of metabolism allows us to make sense of the otherwise counterintuitive leap in his 1960s and 1970s writings from metabolic metaphors of connectivity operating at the scale of bodies or buildings to the planet. In addition, it draws our attention to the political implications of enclosure and containment that the image of the capsule evokes. This image of the capsule as a hermetically sealed envelope, creating a controlled environment, motivated Boulding's analogy of Spaceship Earth and Kurokawa's Metabolist vision of capsule architecture.[22] According to Kurokawa, the philosophy of Metabolist architecture shares an ecological-economic perspective with Boulding regarding the optimal management of waste.[23]

Here I highlight the influence of Boulding's theory on Kurokawa's conceptualization of architectural metabolism in order to speculate on the resonance between the

Geoengineering

Recently, this ecosystemic model of managing Earth, exemplified by the work of Boulding, has come back in the contemporary discourse on geoengineering. Take, for instance, Paul Crutzen, a Dutch atmospheric chemist who popularized the geological concept of the Anthropocene epoch. He was one of the most vocal proponents of solar geoengineering to reset the planetary thermostat.[24] His proposal was to inject sulfur dioxide—the same material that causes air pollution—into the stratosphere to reflect solar radiation away from Earth's surface. From fertilizing the ocean with iron to growing more carbon-absorbing algae to refreezing the Arctic ice by seeding the clouds with salt particles to blocking the incoming sunlight, various proposals to mitigate the future impact of climate change have been tabled and debated over the past decade.[25]

At the base of these geoengineering proposals is the same assumption: Earth as a closed ecosystem analogous to a spaceship, needing constant management and intervention through design. Geoengineering is a project of designing an enclosed capsule similar to architecture. However, a paradox of geoengineering is that it often relies on the same chemicals and industrial mechanisms that have caused anthropogenic climate change in the first place. For example, the toxic particles of sulfur dioxide, which Crutzen and others proposed injecting into the stratosphere to cool Earth, are emitted by burning fossil fuels and create smog. Many cities worldwide are combating the problem of air pollution. Still, some contend that this pollution is helping to cool the planet and that cleaning up the air would, over a brief decade, lead to an unprecedented increase in global temperature.[26] Scientists supporting planetary climate engineering such as Crutzen have thus counterintuitively proposed injecting sulfate aerosols into the stratosphere to cool the atmosphere. In other words, geoengineering proposes continuing the same metabolic cycle of displacing chemicals from one sphere to another without radically challenging the underlying problems of extraction and pollution—and capitalism.

Therefore, I see a parallel dilemma between the current discourse on geoengineering and the earlier discourse on Metabolist architecture. Both are based on the same metaphors of an enclosed capsule and the planet as an enclosed ecosystem. Further, both see the metabolic rift as fixable through design. Design becomes the ultimate solution. From this perspective, the historical lesson of Metabolist architecture goes beyond the field of architecture. It draws our attention to the ethical and political stakes of imagining our planet as a gigantic capsule. Metabolist architecture made of plastics reminds us of the danger of imagining and designing capsules without considering their oil-based materiality and toxicity. Both result from the industrialized mode of resource extraction. In the absence of such attention, dangers arise less in a breach of the capsule's seal and more in the matter that allows the seal to adhere.

Acknowledgement

The present essay is a modified excerpt of Chapter 4 from Yuriko Furuhata's *Climatic Media: Transpacific Experiments in Atmospheric Control*, 104–132. Copyright: 2022, Duke University Press. All rights reserved. Republished by permission of the copyright holder. www.dukeupress.edu.

Notes

1 This is referencing Engel's *Dialectics of Nature*, where Engels argues that the fundamental mode of life existence is metabolism. Kawazoe notes that they chose this term since it would be legible to European Americans. Hyunjung Cho commented on Kawazoe's explanation of Metabolism and linked it to John Bellamy Foster's discussion of the metabolic rift: "Kawazoe has made it clear that the concept of metabolism derived from Marx and Engels' ideas about the material exchange between nature and humans, the fundamental relationship between external conditions and human society. Marx and Engels employed the term 'metabolism' in their key publications including *Capital* to suggest a dialectical interaction between nature and society. As sociologist John Bellamy Foster has pointed out, Marx and Engels relied on the concept of metabolism to criticize humankind's alienation from nature and the ecological crisis caused by capitalism and to restore the relationship between nature and human society to its rightful form through socialism." See Noboru Kawazoe, "Metaborisuto tachi to mananda toki to ima," in *Metaborizumu to Metaborisuto tachi*, ed. Masato Otaka and Noboru Kawazoe (Tokyo: Bijutsu Shuppansha, 2005), 15; Hyunjung Cho, "Competing Futures: War Narratives in Postwar Japanese Architecture 1945–1970" (PhD. diss, University of Southern California, 2011), 194–195; Brett Clark and Richard York, "Carbon Metabolism: Climate Change, and the Biospheric Rift," *Theory and Society* 34, no. 4 (August 2005): 391–428; John Bellamy Foster, Brett Clark, and Richard York, *The Ecological Rift: Capitalism's War on the Earth* (New York: Monthly Review Press, 2010).
2 Paul J. Crutzen, "Albedo Enhancement by Stratospheric Sulfur Injections: A Contribution to Resolve a Policy Dilemma?", *Climate Change* 77, no. 3 (2006): 211–219.
3 Simone Jeska, *Transparent Plastics: Design and Technology* (Basel: Birkhäuser 2008), 12; "Environmental Wind-Baggery," *Whitney Moon, e-flux Architecture*, accessed July 3, 2019, https://www.e-flux.com/architecture/structural-instability/208703/environmental-wind-baggery.
4 Rem Koolhaas and Hans Ulrich Obrist, *Project Japan: Metabolism Talks*, ed. Kayoko Ota and James Westcott (Cologne: Taschen, 2011), 486.
5 Kamiya Koji, "Ōyane," *Shinkenchiku* 45, no. 5 (May 1970): 171; Nakawada Minami and Atmosphere Ltd., *Expo' 70: Kyōgaku Osaka hakurankai no subete* (Tokyo: Daiyamondo Sha, 2005), 59. Kurokawa's Capsule House is comparable to an all-plastic prefabricated *yunitto basu* (bath module), a combination of a bathtub, toilet, and sink in one modular unit. Japan developed it for Hotel New Otani, anticipating foreign visitors coming to the Tokyo Olympics. It is often made of fiber-reinforced plastics.
6 Heather Davis, "Life and Death in the Anthropocene: A Short History of Plastic," in *Art in the Anthropocene: Encounters among Aesthetics, Politics, Environments and Epistemologies*, ed. Heather Davis and Etienne Turpin (London: Open Humanities Press, 2015), 349; Heather Davis, *Plastic Matter* (Durham, NC: Duke University Press, 2022).
7 Kawazoe, "Metaborisuto tachi to mananda toki to ima," 15.
8 The idea of the metabolic rift has both material and ontological connotations. On the one hand, it manifests as the material separation between humans and nature, mediated by labor. Conversely, the rift also manifests as the ontological state of alienation or estrangement from nature experienced by these humans. See Foster, Clark, and York, *The Ecological Rift*, 241–242. John Bellamy Foster and Paul Burkett also argued that Marx borrowed the dialectical pair of the organic and inorganic concepts from Hegel. The organic concept is etymologically associated with the Greek term *organon* (tools). Therefore, Hegel aligned the realm of human consciousness with the organic concept. Foster and Burkett wrote: "The organism (particularly the animal organism), in other words, comes to stand for subjectivity and self-dependence—that is, for rational life connected to the life of the spirit within nature. Here, animate species are the means by which the spirit discovers itself in nature and overcomes its estrangement." See John Bellamy Foster and Paul Burkett, "The Dialectic of Organic/Inorganic Relations: Marx and the Hegelian Philosophy of Nature," *Organization & Environment* 13, no. 4 (December 2000): 410.
9 John Bellamy Foster, "Marx's Theory of Metabolic Rift: Classical Foundations for Environmental Sociology," *American Journal of Sociology* 105, no. 2 (1999): 370.
10 Foster, "Marx's Theory of Metabolic Rift," 381.

11 Karl Marx, *Capital*, accessed July 12, 2019, https://www.marxists.org/archive/marx/works/1867-c1/ch27.htm.
12 John Bellamy Foster and Paul Burkett, *Marx and the Earth: An Anti-critique* (Chicago: Haymarket Books, 2017), 23–25.
13 Brett L. Walker, *Toxic Archipelago: A History of Industrial Disease in Japan* (Seattle: University of Washington Press, 2010), 157. For more on this history, see Yuriko Furuhata, *Climatic Media: Transpacific Experiments in Atmospheric Control* (Durham, NC: Duke University Press, 2022). The chapter is excerpted from this book.
14 Walker, *Toxic Archipelago*, 208.
15 Masazumi Harada, "Minamata Disease: Methylmercury Poisoning in Japan Caused by Environmental Pollution," *Critical Reviews in Toxicology* 25, no. 1 (1995): 4.
16 Koolhaas and Obrist, *Project Japan*, 606. For instance, Tange cultivated a friendship with the Saudi royal family, particularly Faisal bin Abdulaziz Al Saud (the King of Saudi Arabia from 1964 to 1975). Faisal commissioned Tange to work on several unfinished projects, including the monumental stadium in Riyadh and temporary accommodation facilities for pilgrims visiting Mecca. For the latter project, Tange enlisted the help of Ekuan. See Kenzo Tange, *Ippon no enpitsu kara* (Tokyo: Nihon tosho sentā, 1997), 121. After Tange designed the Kuwait embassy in Tokyo, he also developed a close relationship with the Kuwaiti government. Moreover, Tange and his team also worked on projects in Syria, Iran, and Qatar in the 1970s.
17 Koolhaas and Obrist, *Project Japan*, 622–626. In 1979, he also won a competition to master-plan Sarir New Town in the desert of Libya, located near an oil field. Kurokawa Kishō, *Shin kyōsei no shisō* (Tokyo: Tokuma shoten, 1996), 579.
18 Cho, "Competing Futures," 216; Koolhaas and Obrist, *Project Japan*, 388. The capsule as the envelope of a sealed environment differs from other kinds of containers, such as a coffee cup: "A rupture in the capsule, however small, would instantly upset the internal equilibrium and destroy the strictly controlled environment in it."
19 Robert Scott, *Kenneth Boulding: A Voice Crying in the Wilderness* (New York: Palgrave Macmillan, 2014), 92. In his 1966 essay, Boulding put forward the following memorable analogy: "For the sake of picturesqueness, I am tempted to call the open economy the 'cowboy economy,' the cowboy being symbolic of the illimitable plains and also associated with reckless, exploitative, romantic, and violent behavior, which is characteristic of open societies. The closed economy of the future might similarly be called the 'spaceman' economy, in which the earth has become a single spaceship, without unlimited reservoirs of anything, either for extraction or for pollution, and in which, therefore, man must find his place in a cyclical ecological system which is capable of continuous reproduction of material form even though it cannot escape having inputs of energy": Kenneth Boulding, "The Economics of the Coming Spaceship Earth," in *Environmental Quality in a Growing Economy*, ed. H. Jarrett (Baltimore: Johns Hopkins University Press, 1966), 7–9.
20 Kisho Kurokawa, *Metaborizumu no hassō* (Tokyo: Hakuba shuppansha, 1972), 309.
21 Kurokawa, *Metaborizumu no hassō*, 309.
22 In addition, Kurokawa specifically highlighted waste management as the number one ecological challenge of his generation. He argued that his architectural theory of metabolism addressed waste management, including the need to recycle plastics. Recycling wastes binds his earlier conceptualization of capsules as organic cells to his later conceptualization of capsules as miniature ecosystems. Kurokawa cites Boulding's notion of Spaceship Earth to support this vision of the global metabolic (re)cycle of wastes as commodities. Just like the efficient management of waste inside the enclosed environment of the spaceship is crucial to the successful survival of astronauts in outer space, the industrial waste on the planet must be carefully managed. See Kisho Kurokawa, "Metaborizumu to kyōsei no shisō," in *Metaborizumu to Metaborisuto tachi*, ed. Masato Otaka and Noboru Kawazoe (Tokyo: Bijutsu shuppansha, 2005), 222. For instance, Kurokawa argued that the challenge he took up in the 1960s by participating in the Metabolist group was to think about the system of recycling from the perspectives of architecture and urban planning: "Life maintains a dynamic balance through the cycle of the birth of new cells and the death of old cells. Halting this cycle means death. The cessation of blood flow due to cardio-respiratory arrest also means death. The same can be said about Earth's ecosystem, whose equilibrium is maintained by the climatic cycle and food chain of living organisms."

23 Kurokawa, "Metaborizumu to kyōsei no shisō," 224.
24 Crutzen, "Albedo Enhancement by Stratospheric Sulfur Injections," 211–219.
25 James Rodger Fleming, *Fixing the Sky: The Checkered History of Weather and Climate Control* (New York: Columbia University Press, 2010), 253–255. See also Clive Hamilton, *Earthmasters: The Dawn of the Age of Climate Engineering* (New Haven: Yale University Press, 2013); "Geoengineering the Planet? More Scientists Now Say It Must Be an Option," *Yale Environment 360*, published May 29, 2019, https://e360.yale.edu/features/geoengineer-the-planet-more-scientists-now-say-it-must-be-an-option.
26 Hamilton, *Earthmasters*, 15–16. Hamilton is referencing the situation that Paul Crutzen has called Catch-22. See also Crutzen, "Albedo Enhancement by Stratospheric Sulfur Injections," 211.

13

AN ETERNAL RETURN?

Considering the Temporality and Historicity of Metabolism

Julian Worrall

They might be giants

From our situation today, in the chastened aftermath of the COVID-19 pandemic of 2020, the ambitions of the Metabolist architects appear superhuman, Herculean, even incomprehensible. There is something of the wonder and awe that those in the medieval and early modern eras experienced when seeing the ruins of Ancient Rome: the work of giants rather than men. The Metabolist visions of great platforms on the sea from which enormous urban extensions rose, or giant inhabited lattices of high-rise towers linked by inhabited crossbeams today seem audacious to the point of naïveté. Yet the distance that separates us from them is not one of scale, or capability, or even will. The urban transformation of contemporary China and India, the fantastical visions of artificial islands and instant cities in the Gulf, and the ubiquity of powerful computing devices in every hand may have exceeded even the Metabolists' imagination. I suggest that their strangeness to us lies elsewhere—in their relationship with the future and their past. It is in this temporal dimension that Metabolists feel most distant from us, and perhaps here that a reconsideration of their agenda has the most potential for insights into our own contemporary situation.

This chapter considers the ways in which time has figured in Metabolist conceptions of architecture and cities, and in the reception of these ideas.[1] Three scales of temporality are considered: the modalities of change in architecture and urban space; general perspectives on the larger historical situation at the national or global level; and the unfolding life cycle of the movement and its animating ideas. Each of these levels affords a number of distinct temporal geometries and rhythms. In their interaction is found the specificity of the historical formation that the Metabolists occupy, as is that of ours.

The mutable city

The Metabolist manifesto begins with the recognition of eternal change. The first page of *Metabolism 1960* states: "We regard human society as a vital process, a continuous development from atom to nebula."[2] The frontispiece shows an ambiguous image that

DOI: 10.4324/9781003186540-14

could be a stellar nebula or biological cell. Two recognitions are evident here: the appeal to *life*, as displayed in the dynamic forms of natural phenomena; and the emphasis on *process* rather than form. Notably, the Metabolist analyses based on this recognition are active rather than descriptive, and prescriptive rather than merely diagnostic. "We do not see metabolism as a natural historical process; [rather] we are trying to encourage active [metabolic] development of our society through our proposals."[3] There is a conscious avant-gardism on display in these pronouncements.

Surveying the projects and ideas that populate the Metabolists' repertoire from the most fertile period of their existence during the 1960s, we can identify a number of distinct conceptions of architectural and urban change. These include growth and energy, cycles, and evolution. To these an additional external category can be identified: ruin. Each of these modes has its principal theorist and champion in the group.

Growth and energy

The overwhelming challenge of the contemporary Japanese city at the end of the 1950s was its condition of unmanaged growth. The rapid urbanization that accompanied the end of the postwar reconstruction era and the rapid industrialization of the high growth period led to dire warnings of congestion, pollution, and lack of housing and transportation. The Metabolist manifesto reflects this: "Tokyo … is worn out with bad sickness … [having] lost proper control because of her mammoth-like scale … The city has lost its direction, has broken its balance, and has given up its hope."[4]

These words were written by Kiyonori Kikutake, whose work, of all the Metabolists, displayed the most tenacious and earnest engagement with the dilemmas and opportunities of urban growth. However, in his analysis, the existing city was almost beyond saving. Its growth only resulted in "confusion and paralysis."[5] The best way to deal with this situation was to strike out on new ground, literally. In every opportunity to build, Kikutake sought to establish a purified territory upon which a rational and ordered urban pattern could be implemented.

The key method to achieve this goal was the production of "artificial land." On existing land, the natural foundation was multiplied through stacked decks and platforms supported by vast megastructures, as exemplified by the Stratiform Structure Module (1972), creating what Kikutake called the "City Floor."[6] Although this project wasn't built, another realized project, Pasadena Heights (1974), applied the principle of suspending a layer of artificial ground above the real terrain, adapting it into a sloping site. Dwellings are arranged over five stepping levels in a linear form snaking around the contours of the land, stopping only at the site boundary, but potentially endlessly extendable. The dwellings are knitted into this terraced structure in an interlaced pattern, such that the roof of one dwelling becomes the garden courtyard of the one above.

A more emblematic domain upon which this new territory could be constructed is the ocean. This yields the fantastical spectacle of Kikutake's successive schemes for aquatic urbanism, such as Ocean City (1960) and Marine City (1963), incorporating large floating structures, amoeba-like islands of reclaimed land, and proliferating cylindrical towers bristling with prefabricated housing units. For Kikutake, to build on the sea was a lifelong project[7] pursued with utopian enthusiasm. There were two other dimensions in play in this obsession: one personal and the other geopolitical. Kikutake's memories of the devastating floods of the Chikugo River in his hometown of Kurume in Kyushu nourished his sense of mission to build structures that could overcome the destruction of nature's disasters.[8] Second, Kikutake never lost his indignation over his family's fate at the end of the war: the occupying authorities broke up his family's substantial landholdings following the postwar land reforms. For Kikutake, the ocean represented an unbounded and utopian realm beyond the ceaseless conflicts that arose from the terrestrial competition for scarce land: "the sea is waiting for a new discovery … which will promise a true happiness of human beings."[9]

If artificial land provided the spatial extension for *growth*, movable equipment was Kikutake's proposition to accommodate *energy*, that is, flexibility in patterns of life. His own house, the Sky House, incorporated "movenettes," movable service elements for kitchen and bathroom on the perimeter, and children's rooms suspended beneath the main floor, which theoretically could be relocated according to shifts in the life stage of the family. In the 1960 manifesto, Kikutake outlines "three movable things," at the scale of the room, the dwelling, and the urban block.[10] Dwelling-sized flexible units are a prominent feature of Kikutake's theoretical housing proposals, such as the two-story-high steel drums that populate the cylindrical Tower Shaped Community. Explicitly linking the life cycle of the dwelling to that of the family, Kikutake writes that "in accordance with the cycle of the four seasons, the living unit will belong together with the inhabitants' life."[11]

Cycles

Consideration of the natural waxing and waning of the lifespan leads directly to the temporal concept of *cycles*, repeating patterns of activity. If this perspective seems stereotypically Japanese with its traditional emphasis on seasonal rhythms, the repetition of defined processes also underpins the economic activity of mass production, and the replication and interchange of modular elements is an emblematic strategy in Metabolist design.

The Metabolist exponent most associated with this approach is Kisho Kurokawa. He once said that his "biggest dream is to design time"[12]—a beautiful and unexpected proposition for an architect, the pre-eminent shaper of space. Temporality is manifest in Kurokawa's Metabolist work in a variety of ways, but the architectural concept with which this period of his work is most closely associated is the "capsule": the interchangeable element or "cell" that underpins his concept of an organic urbanism. It is surely not coincidental that Kurokawa's deployment of the term "capsule" emerges in parallel with the "space capsule" of Project Mercury, the component of the US human spaceflight program which first sent an astronaut into orbit in the early 1960s. The image of a lone individual in space, protected and sustained by the artificial environment of the capsule, presents a powerful symbol both of technological capability and of the private cocoon to a world in which the individual is increasingly becoming the dominant social unit.

Just as an automobile is an industrially mass-produced product for individual mobility, the capsule was conceived to be an industrially mass-produced product for individual living. Underlying the technique of mass production is a system for the ceaseless repetition of the same, a combination of novelty and permanence. There is an echo in this formulation, in a technological guise, of the Ise Shrine, rebuilt in identical form every 20 years since 674. Simultaneously ancient and intact, unblemished by decay, the shrine is the visible manifestation and ostensible premise concealing its real objective: the preservation of the craft skills, tacit knowledge, and artisanal lineages of its makers. Paradoxically, the Ise Shrine, despite the planned obsolescence of its component parts, signifies permanence through the principle of cyclical renewal.

Kurokawa's Nakagin Capsule Tower, built in 1972, remains the most recognizable built icon of Metabolism, and the built demonstration of the concept of the capsule approach to providing residential space. An assemblage of 144 capsules, each 2.5 m x 2.5 m x 4.0 m, attached to two central cores providing access and services, the building was designed for bachelor businessmen working in downtown Ginza. Each capsule was a self-contained living pod, equipped with a bathroom, built-in furniture, the latest audio-visual equipment of the era, and a porthole to the city beyond. The vertical cores were the durable element, built of high-performance concrete designed to last for centuries, while the capsules were bolted on to this core and designed to be replaced every couple of decades. This exhibits the characteristic design strategy of Metabolist schemes: a durable megastructure (the "core") providing a flexible framework supporting replicable transient elements in constant flux (the "capsules"). It was conceived as a building that moves with, rather than resists, the flow of time.

All visionary propositions conceal a particular conception of the relationship between the present (or "reality") and the future (or "vision"). In 1967, Kurokawa drew an interesting distinction between the temporality of the Metabolists and that of the English Archigram group: "The Metabolist group sows seeds of the future on the earth as it exists today. [We] despair of the future but not of reality … Archigram, on the other hand, despairs of reality, which is why the group is trying to realise the future. Archigram objectifies the future as 'things that have the potential to realise the future.'"[13] Kurokawa here highlights how Archigram's visions were *images* that gave the future a form and generated a desire, but that were never designed to be built, whereas the Metabolists sought to "futurize" present-day reality. Despite the audacity of its propositions, the Metabolist future was embedded in the latent potentials of what was already in existence.

Evolution

Kikutake and Kurokawa were futurists, seeking in their projects to erect an arena of action or clear a space of the residues of the past, allowing new ideas and structures to rise. This approach entails a rejection and separation from what currently exists, in favor of the sense of possibility—that which *could* exist. However, others in the constellation expressed a more gradualist, evolutionary approach to the existing city. Fumihiko Maki is the exemplar of this approach.

Maki is ostensibly more a spatial than a temporal thinker, and his work exhibits an enduring concern with composition: the patterning and balancing of formal elements such as solid and void, figure and field. This formal concern is already announced in the title of his contribution (co-authored with Masato Ōtaka) to the Metabolist manifesto, "Toward Group Form,"[14] which presented a proposal for Shinjuku. But the temporal dimension is deeply embedded within Maki's interest in urban form, as is demonstrated by his career-long experiment of Hillside Terrace (1969–1992), which over three decades unfolded buildings and spaces gradually along a Tokyo street to form a loose and flexible congregation.

Maki's concept of "Group Form" describes a patterning of generative elements that accrete organically to produce urban space. This is distinguished from "Compositional Form," consisting of balanced, static arrangements in the manner of Brasilia or Chandigarh, and "Mega Form," in which functional components are plugged into large frameworks. The cores and capsules of Kurokawa and the megastructures of Kikutake are examples of "Mega Form" urbanism; Group Form does not require an independent organizing structure, the preparation of which requires large concentrations of power and resources; rather, formal coherence is generated from the elements themselves. As Maki writes: "Space within and space without is developed simultaneously."[15] The totality of such a form embraces its elements, but it is not their summation, and it can tolerate the removal or addition of new elements.

This principle is illustrated in the proposal for Shinjuku that Maki and Ōtaka produced for *Metabolism 1960*, in which the cultural facilities are configured as radial "petals," which can tolerate the absence of several elements without losing the overall flower: "Accepting certain accidental design results, we shall be able to express the feeling of concentrated urban energy in the group form."[16] It is the Hillside Terrace project in Daikanyama, Tokyo, a loosely unfolding aggregation of buildings and interlaced open spaces which progressively developed over seven phases across three decades, that forms the most enduring and convincing demonstration of the potential of Maki's conception. This project exemplifies a resonant modernist urbanism that is sympathetic to the texture of the existing city.

At the core of Group Form is an idea of evolution, understood as a kind a quasi-genetic unfolding, in which processes of urban change never arrive at a completed form, but manifest emergent and durable patterns, which are most evident in urban open spaces and the human activities they sponsor and embrace. Among his Metabolist colleagues, Maki's conception of urban form is most sensitive to the existing city and is based on a nuanced reading of social reality: "Group Form evolves from the people of a society, rather than from their powerful leadership. It is the village, the dwelling group, and the bazaar which are Group Forms, not the palace complex, which is compositional in character."[17] This modesty makes Group Form at the same time the least radical and the most durable of the urban concepts to emerge from the Metabolist moment, one whose possibilities continue to have relevance to the work of a younger generation of architects and urbanists who are active today.

Ruin and oblivion

The incessant growth and eternal change of the city was the principal subject of the Metabolists' sense of temporality. Their propositions described and responded to the vibrations of the *life* of the city. Another temporal perspective, existential and tragic, concerns not the life but the *death* of cities. This is the view that Arata Isozaki brings to bear on Metabolist temporality.

Isozaki always understood that the essence of the avant-garde is criticality, and never counted himself directly among the Metabolists, but always formed their "loyal opposition," shadowing their development. Isozaki has said of his Metabolist colleagues: "These architects had no skepticism toward their utopia ... They really believed in technology, in mass production; they believed in systematic urban infrastructure and growth."[18]

Isozaki's figuration of time was powerfully marked by the experience of catastrophe and the inevitability of ruin. During the last months of the Pacific War, Isozaki, aged 14, witnessed both the tragic death of his mother in an accident and the destruction of his family's house along with the rest of his hometown Oita in one traumatic night of fire and chaos.[19] The devastated ash plains of Japan's firebombed cities were seared into Isozaki's memory and formed the starting point for his architectural imagination. This is the modernist tabula rasa as scorched earth: a field of ruin, death, and ghosts.

Entwined with this memory of apocalyptic erasure is that of the "cloudless blue" of the sky of surrender day:

> [T]hat instance of total tranquility, when everything seemed to have stopped, that I experienced on the day of the Japanese surrender. The houses and buildings that we had considered mainstays of our way of life; the established belief of the national state with the Emperor at its head; and the social system that controlled even the smallest daily activities, had been destroyed and vanished, leaving behind only the void of the blue sky overhead.[20]

This was the void from which new futures and other times were born. Where in the march of time Kikutake saw progress and Kurokawa saw heroism, Isozaki saw its dual nature, an eternal dance of creation and destruction locked in a fatal embrace.

This pairing is encountered repeatedly throughout Isozaki's works of the 1960s. His distinctive perspective is initially announced dramatically, if cryptically, in his short elliptical text of 1962 entitled "City Demolition Industry, Inc.," consisting of a dialogue between two characters "Arata" and "Shin," two alternative readings of Isozaki's first name,[21] discussing the establishment of an enterprise to both build and destroy the city. The fact that the ideograph of Isozaki's given name signifies "new" indicates how deeply this conception of time is embedded in Isozaki's identity. In a later essay, "Space of Darkness" (1964), he probes more deeply into the philosophy of time, developing the idea that as the experience of architectural space only occurs by a corporeal being embedded in time, space itself can only be regarded as "specific, concrete, flickering, and never fixed."[22]

Isozaki's contributions to the visual and urban repertoire associated with Metabolism include projects such as the City in the Air/Joint Core System (1960), Clusters in the Air (1962), Marunouchi Project (1963), and later, as a kind of portent of a ruined future, Re-ruined Hiroshima (1968), part of the Electric Labyrinth installation at the Milan Triennale in 1968. A commitment to the power of symbolic form is evident throughout these projects. Elements are not merely technologies to be deployed, but bearers of meaning. The suspended modules of Clusters in the Air consciously recall the *hijiki* roof brackets of Buddhist temples. Such semantic reframings could also be self-referential. In a 1962 photomontage entitled Incubation Process, Isozaki refigured the cylindrical cores of his Joint Core System of 1960 as ruined classical columns from Ancient Rome, provoking a *memento mori* meditation on oblivion entirely absent in the techno-utopian enthusiasms of Kikutake and Kurokawa.

190 Julian Worrall

Destruction and ruination is latent in all these projects. As an accompaniment to the Incubation Process image, Isozaki composed a poem of the same name, from which this couplet is drawn:

> Ruins are the style of future cities
> Future cities are themselves ruins[23]

This couplet expresses the intimate link in Isozaki's temporal imagination between the concepts of the future, ruin, and oblivion. In this imagination, underlying all existing and future cities, there lies the darkness and emptiness of a "state of undifferentiated being."[24] As both a coda to the unrealized ambitions of a Metabolist future and an evocation of the originary scene of Japan's postwar creative imagination, Isozaki's curation of the Japan Pavilion at the 1996 Venice Architecture Biennale, entitled "Fractures," exhibited the rubble from the 1995 Great Hanshin Earthquake.

Afterlife

As with Charles Jencks' dating of the "death" of Modernism to the precise moment of the demolition of the Pruitt-Igoe project in St. Louis on July 15, 1972,[25] the demise of Metabolism is often located at the moment of its greatest apotheosis, the Osaka Expo in 1970. The narrative of decline traces the co-option of radical energies by the developmental state, the defeat of the radical idealism of the generation who barricaded the streets of Paris and stormed the Milan Triennale of 1968, and assembled at Shinjuku Station West Exit singing folk songs protesting the Vietnam War in 1969. The episode of Arata Isozaki's psychic collapse on the morning of the opening of the Expo when he was about to meet the Emperor carries the potency of an omen.[26] And the oil price shock of 1973 served the coup de grace on the city-shaping and nation-building ambitions of the movement.

However, if Metabolism died a natural death in the early 1970s, since then, it has enjoyed an active afterlife. The architectural activity of the protagonists moved on to a global stage, operating in various arenas of the developing non-West (the Middle East, Africa, the former Soviet states, and China). In the West, Metabolism appears to continually return, in the form of discourse, memory, and nostalgia. Interest in the Metabolists increased in the 2000s; the steady ministrations of a number of dedicated scholars and enthusiasts were given a significant boost with the anointing of the Metabolist legacy by Rem Koolhaas and Hans Ulrich Obrist in their monumental oral history *Project Japan* of 2011,[27] which provoked an ongoing fascination with the audacity of the work of the Metabolist generation to this day (of which this publication is another manifestation). However, for Koolhaas, the interest was both critical and elegaic—a condemnation of the impoverishments imposed by the contemporary domination of the private sector over the architectural imagination, and a lament for the loss of the ideal of the public mission of architecture, in which the state works hand in glove with architects to construct a long-term vision for a nation.

Project Japan coincided with the "Metabolism: The City of the Future"[28] exhibition at the Mori Art Museum that opened in Tokyo in September 2011—a retrospective to a legacy that suddenly seemed immensely relevant in the aftermath of the 3.11 triple disaster, the earthquake, tsunami, and nuclear disaster of March 11 of that year. The word "reconstruction" (*fukkō*) was back in vogue, just as it had been in the postwar years after 1945 and earlier in the years after the Great Kanto Earthquake of 1923.[29] The temporal echoes resonating across historical time since the publication of *Metabolism 1960* were consciously evoked as Koolhaas timed the release of *Project Japan* to coincide with the opening of the exhibition in Tokyo. In a potent but poignant piece of stagecraft, Koolhaas presented the book to an audience of the professors and students at the University of Tokyo, successors and descendants of the Metabolists, in the very same auditorium that Kenzo Tange and his assistant Takashi Asada had convened the initial group over half a century before.

Other registrations of the Metabolist legacy included Koh Kitayama, Yoshiharu Tsukamoto, and Ryue Nishizawa's "Void Metabolism" exhibition, shown in Venice in 2010 on the 50th anniversary of the Metabolist manifesto.[30] In a provocative inversion of Metabolist tabula rasa utopian urbanism, this exhibition focused on the ordinary suburban hinterland of the Japanese metropolis and the slow continuous churn of its sites. The urban element of concern here is the private house, between which a network of small voids and spatial reserves are maintained. These urban grains have an average lifespan of 26 years, and as they are progressively renewed, the pattern of voids between them fluctuates but persists. In contrast to the rigid vertical "cores" of Metabolist structures, it is this soft and permeable void that becomes the enduring layer of the city. Here, the authors suggest, is the true metabolic renewal of the city.

A decade after the triple disaster of 3.11, what is evident is that the disaster did not kick off a new Metabolist-inspired fervor of state-led reconstruction. Among architects, it led in a completely different direction: toward community building and participatory urbanism, exemplified by the Home-for-All project led by Toyo Ito.[31]

FIGURE 13.1   Rem Koolhaas presenting his book *Project Japan. Metabolism Talks* to an audience of professors and students at the University of Tokyo, 2011. Image: Julian Worrall.

192 Julian Worrall

This collaborative effort drew on a roster of talented younger architects to respond in concrete ways to alleviate the suffering of the communities devastated by the tsunami, through building structures that accommodated community-gathering spaces. This work—collaborative, small-scale, patient, caring, and slow—is the antithesis of the Metabolist approach to reconstruction and the hubris that accompanies it. "I am amazed by the fragile state of things despite all the economic and technological 'strength' Japan has been so proud of," Ito writes in a wistful coda to *Project Japan*. "Was our achievement of the past several decades a house of cards?"[32] Let us remember that these are the words of a disciple of Kiyonori Kikutake. What seems clear is that, notwithstanding the presence of the elements of disaster, crisis, technology, and political disquiet, the time of the Metabolists is not our time.

New times

What are the characteristics of our time, our particular contemporaneity, and how does that of the Metabolists relate to this? By way of a conclusion, the following generalized observations offer a brief characterization of the temporal distance separating us.

The ambition and ideas of Metabolism were gestated in the context of postwar reconstruction and a resurgent sense of national mission. The Metabolists' proposals sought to address the conditions of rapid economic and population growth, industrialization, and the pressing urgencies of urban transformation. Powerful state agencies and major business enterprises supported their activities and engaged their services. The proliferation of audacious schemes for extending urban structures over the water and rising into the air was bolstered by a faith in technological capability, exemplified by dramatic advances in genetics, computing, and space exploration. While the Metabolists sought to offer an alternative conception of urban processes based on biological rather machinic metaphors, the unfolding of the movement extended rather than overturned modernity's grand narrative of historical progress based on purposive technocratic rationality.

The intervening period has seen the undermining or dissolution of all these enabling contexts. In the twenty-first century, depopulation is the pressing demographic challenge for Japan and for much of the developed world; economic growth has been largely flat since the collapse of the bubble economy at the end of the 1980s. The revalorization of the city as it actually exists, in all its intricate, polyphonic, self-organizing vitality, has replaced the dream of centrally planned and optimally configured urban utopias. The transformation of lived experience effected by expanded mobilities and ubiquitous global communications has engendered a combination of cosmopolitan fluency and cultural flattening, while the East-West cultural binary that proved so productive for the Metabolist generation has proliferated into innumerable atomized encounters across cultural and social difference.

Most consequential for the purposes of this discussion is that the configuration of temporality itself has appears to have shifted. With the specter of climate and extinction emergencies made tangible by devastating fires, floods, and storms, and given further apocalyptic overtones by a calamitous global epidemic, the contemporary moment involves both the sense of the loss of a positive future and a severing or tangling of the threads connecting us via a progressive unfolding to the recent past. This contemporary condition invites new temporal geometries: primitive futures,[33] folded palimpsests, and stillness.[34]

Buildings and cities are not just assemblages of spaces; they are collections of times. In reconsidering the work of the Metabolists today, 60 years after their sudden irruption into the global architectural consciousness, it is this temporal dimension that I suggest offers us the most provocative and poignant illumination on the predicament of our contemporary situation.

Notes

1 This chapter extends an analysis first presented in "Metabolist Time," in *Invisible Architecture: Italian and Japanese Architectural Movements of the 1960s and 1970s and Contemporary Debates*, eds. Rita Elvira Adamo, Cristiano Lippa and Federico Scaroni (Rome: Silvana Editoriale, 2017), 145–149.
2 Noboru Kawazoe, ed., *Metabolism 1960: The Proposals for New Urbanism* (Tokyo: Bijutsu Shuppansha, 1960), 5. Published on the occasion of the World Design Conference in Tokyo in 1960.
3 Ibid., 5.
4 Ibid., 13.
5 Ibid. 10.
6 Kiyonori Kikutake, "The Order of Things One Can See," in *Kiyonori Kikutake: Between Land and Sea*, ed Ken Tadashi Oshima (Zurich: Lars Müller, 2016), 107.
7 Kikutake, Kiyonori, *Megastructure: Atarashii Toshikankyo* (Tokyo: Waseda University Press, 1995).
8 Souhei Imamura, "The Theory of Kikutake Kiyonori: A City on the Ocean," in *Metabolism, the City of the Future* (Tokyo: Mori Art Museum, 2011), 252.
9 *Metabolism 1960*, 23.
10 Ibid., 34.
11 Ibid., 9.
12 From a magazine profile of Kisho Kurokawa in *Heibon Punch*, February 9, 1970. Quoted in Rem Koolhaas and Hans-Ulrich Obrist, *Project Japan, Metabolism Talks…*, ed. Kayoko Ota, James Westcott, and AMO (Cologne: Taschen, 2011), 456.
13 Kisho Kurokawa, "Will the Future Suddenly Arrive," trans, Nathan Elchert. First published in *The Design Review* no. 3 (1967), extracted in *Metabolism, the City of the Future*, 259.
14 Fumihiko Maki and Masato Ōtaka, "Towards Group Form," in *Metabolism 1960*, 52–69.
15 Ibid., 59.
16 Ibid.
17 Fumihiko Maki, *Investigations in Group Form* (Seattle: School of Architecture, Washington University, 1964).
18 Arata Isozaki, interview with Rem Koolhaas, in *Project Japan*, 37.
19 For details of this formative experience, see "Arata Isozaki in Conversation with Thomas Daniell," *AA Files*, no. 68 (July 2014): 22–42.
20 Arata Isozaki, *The Island Nation Aesthetic* (London: Academy Editions, 1996), 28.
21 Arata Isozaki, "Toshi hakaigyo KK", *Shinkenchiku* vol. 37, no. 9 (1962): 183–190; "City Demolition Industry, Inc.," trans. Richard Gage, in *Project Japan*, 52–54.
22 Arata Isozaki, "Yami no kukan" ["Space of Darkness"] (1964). Quoted in Arata Isozaki, *Japan-ness in Architecture* (Cambridge, MA: MIT Press, 2006), 89.
23 Quoted in Arata Isozaki, *Japan-ness in Architecture*, 87.
24 Ibid., 90.
25 Charles Jencks, *The Language of Post-modern Architecture* (New York: Rizzoli, 1977), 9.
26 For a recent account of this episode, see Thomas Daniell, "Arata Isozaki, Renaissance Man," in *An Anatomy of Influence* (London: Architectural Association, 2018), 56.
27 *Project Japan*.
28 *Metabolism, the City of the Future*.
29 Julian Worrall, "Metabolism: When the Future Was Still Ahead," *The Japan Times*, September 29, 2011, 17.
30 Koh Kitayama, Yoshiharu Tsukamoto and Ryue Nishizawa, *Tokyo Metabolizing* (Tokyo: TOTO Publishing, 2010).

31 This project was presented at the Venice Architecture Biennale of 2012, winning the Golden Lion for Best National Participation. See Toyo Ito, Kumiko Inui, Akihisa Hirata, and Naoya Hatakeyama, *Architecture: Possible Here? Home-for-All* (Tokyo: TOTO Publishing, 2013).

32 Toyo Ito, "Postscript," in *Project Japan*, 697.

33 This formulation co-opts the title of Sou Fujimoto's first monograph: Sou Fujimoto, *Primitive Future* (Tokyo: INAX, 2008).

34 For an elaboration of this idea, which has links to the "decroissance" movement, in the Japanese context, see the *Still City Project*, a research project led by Edwin Gardner and Christiaan Fruneaux that aimed "to find and make the images and stories we need to construct a post-growth urban society." This research was conducted in Tokyo in 2012, resulting the publication of *Tokyo Totem* (Tokyo: Flick Studio, 2015). See https://stillcity.org.

AFTERWORD

Gevork Hartoonian

I have been amusing myself with the idea that whenever architecture is in crisis in the Euro-American hemisphere, architects in Japan offer the way forward, which most often discloses a paradox. Central to any comprehensive assessment of the state of architecture in countries historically positioned external to the Western culture of Humanism and its culmination in the Enlightenment is the issue of modernization. Consider this: the early modernist advocacy for the International Style architecture was one thing; its dissemination to non-Western countries under the ideological rubric of the "international" was another. Regardless of the sociopolitical agendas of capitalism, the globalization that capitalism has been undergoing since the 1990s offers the opportunity to critically investigate the process of modernization, and its implications for the past and future of architecture anywhere, including in countries that during the 1970s were branded "developing" at best and "underdeveloped" at worst! At the heart of this brief observation is the singular notion of time in modernity, and its collusion with temporalities deeply rooted in religious myths, wars, and state ideologies that often overshadow class conflicts and group political interests in the name of nativism.

I contend that Japan's architecture of Metabolism is symptomatic of the process of modernization in Japan that has been unique and paradoxical at the same time. Flipping through the pages of the *Japan Architect* journal during the 1970s, even I, an architecture student educating in Iran, could not but associate the published images of buildings—mostly built-in concrete and occasionally covered by a hipped roof—with an aura of "Japan-ness." Interestingly enough, the widespread presumed filial relationship between architecture and Japanese culture was floated by Arata Isozaki, a member of the Metabolist group, who from the beginning maintained an ambivalent position compared to his colleagues' enthusiastic aspirations and those expressed by foreign experts. In *Japan-ness in Architecture,* Isozaki demonstrates the uneven temporalities permeating the islands' history, to the point that, once mediated by an external gaze, "*japonaiserie* provoked measures of response within Japan."[1] The reception of modernism in Japan, along with various architectural tendencies flourishing since architecture's encounter with capitalism after World War II, provided Japanese architects with an opportunity to establish a different rapport with modernity. In retrospect, and considering the global dissemination of capital and information today, the suggested difference speaks, on the one hand, for the *time* of a nation's entry to the processes of modernization. On the other hand, the decades following the war witnessed a commonality shared by both the winners and losers, which had significant implications for architecture emerging under the rubric of nation-building.

Japan entered the process of modernization during the decades between the two World Wars, expanding its industries thanks to the fact that the project of modernity had not yet been usurped by capitalism. Thus, we see the opportunity for aspects of Japanese traditional culture to exceed their historicity, commingling with the processes of cultural secularization. Isozaki writes that one of the reasons why Bruno Taut's aesthetic ideology was well received during his practice in Japan was that it sanctioned the "historical friction between imperial household and Tokugawa shogunate existing since the sixteenth century." Equally important is the coincidence between the periodic reconstruction of historical temples and the constant reproduction of the *new* essential for the longevity of modernity. Accordingly, there should be an obvious difference between the Japanese process of modernization and that of the Chinese, which is taking place at a time when the capitalist system has been globalized to the point that the Marxian separation between economy and culture is no longer sustainable, and commodity form has infused even the most rural settlements of China.

Before getting into the general state of postwar architecture, and the singular contribution of Metabolism, it is useful to reiterate the aforementioned paradox in modern Japanese architecture. The question concerns a particular vision of history, which, beyond the simplistic reduction of time to linear progress, sees the ongoing interaction of the pasts in the present. Such was the case with Japanese intellectual discourses unfolding after the war; in addition to the enemy out there, the debate also focused on the idea that, in lieu of the Meiji craze for *japonaiserie*, it was inevitable for romantic modernists to confront the historicity of the "sickness of Westernization." The tendency was not exclusive to Japan, but was shared by academics, artists, and architects practicing in non-Western nations, who would erroneously try to "overcome the modern," to recall the 1942 Kyoto Conference, discussed by a number of Japanese scholars, including Harry Harootunian.[2] Accordingly, the anxieties permeating postwar architecture concerned, among other issues, the revitalization of traditions that supposedly could have derailed the Western path to modernity, while also welcoming architectural tendencies from the West that critiqued the project of modernity. I am reminded of the turn to the historicist theorization of architecture in the late 1940s. This decade also witnessed the rise of an esteem for monumentality, the aestheticization of the techno-structural organization of utopic projects, and a post-Corbusian reformulation of architecture and the city.

Among these major architectural tendencies, Metabolism remained unique for several reasons. Written in the manifesto style of the historical avant-garde, Metabolism was penned by the architects Masato Otaka, Fumihiko Maki, and Noriaki Kurokawa and the critic Noboru Kawazoe, who were inspired by Kenzō Tange's groundbreaking design for the Hiroshima Peace Center (1949–1956). A stretched rectangular volume lifted on a Corbusian piloti, the main building allows the land to pass beneath, stretching to the point that the building's perceived monumentality remains congenial to the landscape. It was to Tange's credit that he brought forward the existential experience of the landscape even when he had to "bridge" the banks of Tokyo Bay, a project highlighted almost since its inception in every exhibition celebrating Metabolism and Japanese architecture. Even though Kikutake wrote in 1958 that the land is not the only means upon which to live, his Marine City shared the high-tech transformable prefabricated and replaceable component exemplified in Kisho Kurokawa's Nakagin Capsule Tower (1972). Beyond the group's techno-utopian proposals that tallied with those conceived by Archigram (England) and Superstudio (Italy), at the other end of the spectrum, Metabolist architects built considerable buildings with elementary tectonics—what Isozaki called flexible structure—perhaps in analogy to the Japanese modular wood structures. Along this line of consideration, the group's built-work recalls Louis I. Kahn's served-service space organization, as evident in Tange's Yamnashi Broadcasting and Press Center, Kofu (1966). Not only that, but his notion of expandable urban forms also recalls Kahn's Richard Laboratory (1957–1961); it also demonstrates Tange's design shift from Yayoi to Jomon style, the focus of Japanese architectural debates at that time. He wrote: "Jomon appeals to us with the flooding energy of the fundamental life of the people."[3] I want to push this analogy further and in reference to nineteenth-century German architect Gottfried Semper, who espoused the idea that most architectural motifs are drawn from applied art objects. Semper used the German word *Stoffwechsel* to connote a complicated process of transdisciplinary appropriation of motifs. Interestingly enough, Nishida Kitaro, a founder of the Kyoto School of Japanese philosophy, used the term to suggest a metabolic process of production.[4]

Accordingly, the ontological dimension of the architecture of Metabolism, its poises of production in conjunction with the heydays of Japanese capitalism were signaled in the World Design Conference held in May 1960 in Tokyo, and the 1970 Osaka Expo, designed by Tange's lab. The same design strategy can be traced in Tange's expansive urban projects designed for several Asian satellite islands.

The existential dimension of the best work of the Metabolist group contrasts with the abstract formal and historicist architecture of the USA of the 1970s, as Kenneth Frampton elaborates in a book titled *A New Wave of Japanese Architecture*. Frampton states that, bridging the old and the new generations of architects, Isozaki and Maki's influence remains above all their "capacity to synthesize form into an incisive and powerful gestalt."[5] Even though Frampton expands a comparative analysis of the work collected in the book with what was happening in American and European architecture, the diversity of the displayed work, from Tadao Ando to Toyo Ito, foretold the beginning of a post-Metabolist era in Japanese architecture. This is convincing considering the *A Constellation: Toyo Ito, SANNA, and Beyond* exhibition at MoMA, 2016. Ito's diagram drawing—a central circle connected with smaller ones—suggested that the baton had been passed from Isozaki to Ito and that, instead of megastructures, different sensibilities such as minimalism and landscape prevail in Japanese contemporary architecture. Should we extend the generational transformation today to Kengo Kuma's tectonic re-interpretation of the ancient Jomon traditions of timber construction, which is welcomed beyond the island's boundaries?

Notes

1 Arata Isozaki, *Japan-ness in Architecture* (Cambridge, MA: MIT Press, 2003).
2 Harry Harootunian, *Over Come by Modernity: History, Culture, and Community in Interwar Japan* (Princeton: Princeton University Press, 2001), ch. 2.
3 Rem Koolhaas and Hans Ulrich Obrist, *Project Japan: Metabolism Talk* (Cologne: Taschen, 2011), 119.
4 Nishida Kitaro, *Ontology of Production: Three Essays* (Durham, NC: Duke University Press, 2012),
5 *A New Wave of Japanese Architecture*, ed. with an introduction by Kenneth Frampton (New York: Institute for Architecture and Urban Studies, 1978).

BIBLIOGRAPHY

Adamo, Rita Elvira, et al., eds., *Invisible Architecture: Italian and Japanese Architectural Movements of the 1960s and 70s and Contemporary Debates*. Rome: Silvana Editoriale, 2017.

Allen, Stan, "Infrastructural Urbanism," in *Points+Lines: Diagrams and Projects for the City*. New York: Princeton Architectural Press, 1999.

Arellano, Mónica, "Archigram and the Dystopia of Small-Scale Living Spaces," *ArchDaily*, trans. Maggie Johnson, https://www.archdaily.com/948954/archigram-and-the-dystopia-of-small-scale-living-spaces.

Attenborough, David, *A Life on Our Planet: My Witness Statement and a Vision for the Future*. London: Witness Books.

Auge, Marc, *Non-places: Introduction to an Anthropology of Supermodernity*. New York: Verso, 1995.

Bakema, Jaap, "1960–2000," in *Post Box for the Development of the Habitat (B.P.H.)*, ed. Jaap Bakema (no. 5, 27 January 1961), Collection Het Nieuwe Instituut, Rotterdam, 4.

Bakema, Jaap, *Post Box*, no. 6 (12 May 1961), 1; no. 9 (1 June 1962).

Bakema, Jaap, "Bouwen voor de anonieme opdrachtgever," *Forum* 16, no. 2 (1962): 44.

Banham, Reyner, *Theory and Design during the First Machine Age*. Cambridge, MA: MIT Press, 1960.

Banham, Reyner, *A Clip-on Architecture*. Minneapolis: Walker Arts Centre, 1965.

Banham, Reyner, *Megastructure: Urban Futures of the Recent Past*. New York: Harper & Row, 1976.

Barles, Sabine, "Society, Energy and Materials: The Contribution of Urban Metabolism Studies to Sustainable Urban Development Issues," *Journal of Environmental Planning and Management* 53, no. 4 (2010).

Barnett, Jonathan, "The Way We Were, the Way We Are: The Theory and Practice of Designing Cities since 1956," *Harvard Design Magazine* 24 (2006).

Bellamy Foster, John, "Marx's Theory of Metabolic Rift: Classical Foundations for Environmental Sociology," *American Journal of Sociology* 105, no. 2 (1999).

Bellamy Foster, John, and Paul Burkett, "The Dialectic of Organic/Inorganic Relations: Marx and the Hegelian Philosophy of Nature," *Organization & Environment* 13, no. 4 (2000).

Bellamy Foster, John, and Paul Burkett, *Marx and the Earth: An Anti-critique*. Chicago: Haymarket Books, 2017.

Bellamy Foster, John, Brett Clark, and Richard York, *The Ecological Rift: Capitalism's War on the Earth*. New York: Monthly Review Press, 2010.

200 Bibliography

Benevolo, Leonardo, *History of Modern Architecture*. Cambridge, MA: MIT Press, 1971.

Bernstein, Fred A., "My Favorite Building," *Architectural Record*, https://www.architecturalrecord.com/articles/11875-my-favorite-building.

Bettinotti, Mario, ed., *Kenzo Tange 1946–1996*. Milan: Electa, 1996.

Bhatia, Neeraj, "Collective Form: Forming a Collective," *Log* (Summer 2020).

Bognar, Botond, *Contemporary Japanese Architecture: Its Development and Challenge*. New York: Van Nostrand Reinhold Company, 1985.

Bognar, Botond, *The New Japanese Architecture*. New York: Rizzoli International, 1990

Bognar, Botond, "Fumihiko Maki – Making an Urban Architecture", *Fumihiko Maki*. Special Japanese Issue of *World Architecture* No.16, London: 1992.

Bognar, Botond, "Toward Another (New Age) Modernism: Three Recent Large Scale Projects by Maki", *Fumihiko Maki 1987–1992*. Tokyo: Kajima Shuppan-sha 1994.

Bognar, Botond, ed., *World Cities: TOKYO*. London: Academy Editions, 1997.

Bognar, Botond, "What Goes Up, Must Come Down: Recent Urban Architecture in Japan", *Durability and Ephemerality – Harvard Design Magazine*. Cambridge, MA: Harvard University Graduate School of Design (Fall 1997).

Bognar, Botond, *Nikken Sekkei 1900–2000: Building Future Japan*. New York: Rizzoli International, 2000.

Bognar, Botond, Beyond the Bubble: *The New Japanese Architecture*. London: Phaidon Press Ltd., 2008.

Bognar, Botond, *Architectural Guide Japan*. Berlin: DOM Publishers, 2021.

Boudon, Philippe. *Lived-in Architecture: Le Corbusier's Pessac Revisited*. Cambridge, MA: MIT Press, 1979.

Boulding, Kenneth, 1966 "The Economics of the Coming Spaceship Earth," in Henry Jarrett (ed.), *Environmental Quality in a Growing Economy*. Baltimore: Resources for the Future/ Johns Hopkins University Press.

Boyd, Robin, *New Directions in Japanese Architecture*. New York: George Braziller, 1968.

Broto, Vanesa Castán, Adriana Allen, and Elizabeth Rapoport. "Interdisciplinary Perspectives on Urban Metabolism," *Journal of Industrial Ecology* 16, no. 6 (2012).

Brown, Azby, and Joseph Cali, *The Japanese Dream House. How Technology and Tradition are Shaping New Home Design*. Tokyo: Kodansha International, 2001.

Cho, Hyunjung, "Competing Futures: War Narratives in Postwar Japanese Architecture 1945–1970," Ph.D. dissertation, University of Southern California, 2011.

Cho, Hyunjung and Chunghoon Shin, "Metabolism and Cold War Architecture," *Journal of Architecture* 19, no. 5 (2014)

Clark, Brett and Richard York, "Carbon Metabolism: Climate Change, and the Biospheric Rift," *Theory and Society* 34, no. 4 (2005).

Coaldrake, William H., *Architecture and Authority in Japan*. London: Routledge, 1996.

Collins, George R., *Visionary Drawings of Architecture and Planning: 20th Century*. Cambridge, MA: MIT Press, 1979.

Croset, Pierre Alain, and Canclini, Andrea, "On the CIAM 7 Grid; From an Ideological to a Critical Tool," *Plan Journal* 5, no. 1 (2020).

Crosby, Theo, ed., *This is Tomorrow*. London: Whitechapel Art Gallery, 1956.

Crutzen, Paul J., "Albedo Enhancement by Stratospheric Sulfur Injections: A Contribution to Resolve a Policy Dilemma?", *Climate Change* 77, no. 3 (2006).

Cybriwsky, Roman, *Tokyo: The Changing Profile of an Urban Giant*. Boston, MA: G.K. Hall & Co., 1991.

Dahinden, Justus, *Urban Structures for the Future*, trans. Gerald Ohm. New York: Praeger, 1972.

Daniell, Thomas, "Arata Isozaki in Conversation with Thomas Daniell," *AA Files* 68 (2014).

Daniell, Thomas, *An Anatomy of Influence*. London: AA Publications, 2018.

Daniell, Thomas, "Arata Isozaki, Renaissance Man," in *An Anatomy of Influence*. London: AA Publications, 2018.

Davies, William Henry, "Leisure," in *Songs of Joy and Others*. London: A.C. Fifield, 1911.

Davis, Heather, *Plastics*. Durham, NC: Duke University Press, forthcoming, 2022.

Davis, Heather and Etienne Turpin, eds., *Art in the Anthropocene: Encounters among Aesthetics, Politics, Environments and Epistemologies*. London: Open Humanities Press, 2015.

Didero, Maria, "Toyo Ito: Re-building from Disaster," *Domus* (January 2012), https://www.domusweb.it/en/interviews/2012/01/26/toyo-ito-re-building-from-disaster.html.

Dijst, Martin et al., "Exploring Urban Metabolism: Towards an Interdisciplinary Perspective," *Resources, Conservation and Recycling* 132 (2018).

Drexler, Arthur, "Visionary Architecture," *Arts and Architecture* 78, no. 1 (1961).

Drexler, Arthur, "Visionary Architecture," *Kokusai Kenchiku* 30, no. 10 (1963).

Drexler, Arthur, Visionary Architecture: And Exhibition Prepared and Circulated by the Museum of Modern Art, New York, under the Auspices of the International Council (n.p. 1963).

Drew, Philip, "Japan Travel Diary, 17th June to 1st September 1967," unpublished manuscript, 1967.

Drew, Philip, "The Spirit of Japanese Architecture," unpublished manuscript, 1969.

Drew, Philip, *Third Generation: The Changing Meaning of Architecture*. English edn London: Pall Mall Press; Japanese edn Tokyo: Kajima Institute Pub. Co., 1972.

Drew, Philip, "Travel Diary: Japan, USA, Italy, Germany, Denmark, Netherlands, Belgium, UK, 11th June to 21st November 1978," unpublished manuscript, 1978.

Drew, Philip, *The Architecture of Arata Isozaki*. London: Granada, 1982.

Drew, Philip, *Arata Isozaki: The Museum of Modern Art, Gunma*. London: Phaidon, 1996

Ellis, Russell, and Dana Cuff (eds.), *Architects' People*. New York: Oxford University Press, 1989.

Fisher, Berenice, and Joan C. Tronto, "Toward a Feminist Theory of Care," in *Circles of Care: Work and Identity in Women's Lives*, ed. Emily K. Abel and Margaret K. Nelson. New York: State University of New York Press, 1990.

Fleming, James Rodger, Fixing the Sky: The Checkered History of Weather and Climate Control. New York: Columbia University Press, 2010.

Foster, John Bellamy, *Marx's Ecology: Materialism and Nature*. New York: Monthly Review Press, 2000.

Freuerstein, Günther, *Urban Fiction: Strolling through Ideal Cities from Antiquity to the Present Day*. Fellbach: Edition Ariel Menges, 2006.

Friedman, Yona, *Prodomo*. Barcelona: Aktar Publishing, 2006.

Fujisaki Keiichiro, "Kikutake sensei, ano yoru, kahn to nani ga attandesuka?" [Kikutake-sensei, what happened on that night with Kahn?], *Casa Brutus* (July 2004).

Fujimoto, Sou. *Primitive Future*. Tokyo: INAX, 2008.

Fujimori, Terunobu, and Kenzo Tange, *Kenzo Tange*. Tokyo: Shinkenchiku-sha, 2002.

Fujita, Kuniko, and Richard Hill, *Japanese Cities in the World Economy*. Philadelphia: Temple University Press, 1993.

Fukusawa, Keita, "Hand Man: Kikutake Kiyonori," *Numéro*, 53, no. 186 (2012).

Furuhata, Yuriko, *Climatic Media: Transpacific Experiments in Atmospheric Control*. Durham, NC: Duke University Press, forthcoming, 2022.

Gans, Herbert, *The Urban Villagers: Group and Class Structure in the Life of Italian Americas*. New York: The Free Press, 1962.

Gardner, Edwin, and Christiaan Fruneaux, eds., *Tokyo Totem*. Tokyo: Flick Studio, 2015.

Gardner, William O., *The Metabolist Imagination*. Minneapolis, University of Minnesota Press, 2020.

Glickman, Norman, *The Management of the Japanese Urban System: Regional Development and Regional Planning in Postwar Japan*. New York: Academic Press, 1979.

202 Bibliography

Ginzburg, Moisei, *Style and Epoch*, trans. Anatole Senkevitch. Cambridge, MA: MIT Press, 1982.

Gottmann, Jean, *The Urbanized Northeastern Seaboard of the United States.* New York: Twentieth Century Fund, 1961.

Gravagnuolo, Benedetto, *La Progettazione Urbana in Europa.* Milan: Edizioni Laterza, 1991.

Habraken, N. John, *Supports: An Alternative to Mass Housing.* London: Architectural Press, 1972.

Hamilton, Clive, *Earthmasters: The Dawn of the Age of Climate Engineering.* New Haven: Yale University Press, 2013.

Harada, Masazumi, "Minamata Disease: Methylmercury Poisoning in Japan Caused by Environmental Pollution," *Critical Reviews in Toxicology* 25, no. 1 (1995).

Hauser, Arnold, 1965, *Mannerism.* London: Routledge & Kegan.

Heiesinger, Kathryn B., and Felice Fisher, *Japanese Design. A Survey since 1900.* New York: Harry Abrams Inc., 1995.

HEXA Architects and Planners, "Tojuso Tokui-Cho Apartments." *Japan Architect* 58, no. 8 (1983).

Hirose, Mami, et al., eds., *Metabolism—The City of the Future: Dreams and Visions of Reconstruction in Postwar and Present-Day Japan.* Tokyo: Mori Art Museum, 2011.

Hofmann, Werner, and Udo Kultermann, *Modern Architecture in Colour.* London: Thames & Hudson, 1970.

Huxtable, Ada Louise, "The Architect as a Prophet," *New York Times*, October 2, 1961.

Igarashi, Tarō, and Ryō Yamazaki, *3.11 iko no kenchiku: shakai to kenchika no atarashii kankei* [Architecture after 3.11: New Relationship between Society and Architecture]. Tokyo: Gakuei Shuppan, 2014.

Inabe, Kazuya, and Shigenobu Nakayama, *Japanese Homes and Lifestyles: An Illustrated Journey through the History.* Tokyo: Kodansha International, 2000.

Imakiire, Tetsuro and Koarai, Mamoru, "Wide-Area Land Subsidence Caused by "the 2011 off the Pacific Coast of Tohoku Earthquake,'" *Soils and Foundations* 52, no. 5 (2012).

Ishii, Kazuhiro and Hiroyuki Suzuki, "Post-Metabolism," *Japan Architect*, 247 (October–November 1977).

Iso, Tatsuo, "Kikutake Yuki shi ni kiku" [Interview with Kikutake Yuki], in *Kikutake Kiyonori jun rei.* Tokyo: Nikkei BP, 2012.

Isozaki, Arata, *The Island Nation Aesthetic*, London: Academy Editions, 1996.

Isozaki, Arata, *Japan-ness in Architecture.* Cambridge, MA: MIT Press, 2006.

Ishiyama, Osamu, "Messages from the Next Generation," in *Takamasa Yosizaka as a Labyrinth*, ed. Takamasa Yosizaka Exhibition Executive Committee. Tokyo: TOTO Publishing, 2005.

"Itō Toyoo shi ga 'gashō zukuri' no shūgō jutaku! Kamaishi shi no fukkoukeikaku ni teaian," *Kensetsu tsūshin shinbun*, March 5, 2012.

Itoh, Teiji, *Traditional Domestic Architecture of Japan.* New York and Tokyo: Weatherhill/Heibonsha, 1972.

Ito, Toyo, Kumiko Inui, Akihisa Hirata, and Naoya Hatakeyama, *Architecture: Possible Here? Home-for-All.* Tokyo: TOTO Publishing, 2013.

Izumi, Kiyo, 1968, "Some Psycho-social Considerations of Environmental Design" (mimeograph).

The Japanese House: Architecture and Life after 1945. Special issue. Tokyo: Shinkenchiku-sha Co. Ltd., 2017.

Jencks, Charles, *The Language of Post-modern Architecture.* New York: Rizzoli, 1977.

Jeska, Simone, *Transparent Plastics: Design and Technology.* Basel: Birkhäuser, 2008.

Kahn, Louis, "Order and Form," *Perspecta* 3 (1955).

Kahn, Louis, "Architecture is the Thoughtful Making of Spaces," *Perspecta* 4 (1957).

Kahn, Louis, "Law and Rule in Architecture," in *Louis Kahn: Essential Texts,* ed. Robert Twombly. New York: W.W. Norton, 2003.

Kamiya, Koji, "Ōyane," *Shinkenchiku* 45, no. 5 (1970).

Karan P. Prasad, and Kristin Stapleton, *The Japanese City*. Lexington: University Press of Kentucky, 1997.

Kawazoe, Noboru, "Modern Japanese Architecture Confronts Functionalism," *Zodiac* no. 3 (1958).

Kawazoe, Noboru, *Kenchiku no metsubō* [*The Death of Architecture*]. Tokyo: Gendai shichō-sha, 1960.

Kawazoe, Noboru, "Afterword," in *This is Design*. Tokyo: Kadokawa Publishing, 1961.

Kawazoe, Noboru, *Architects: Person and Works*. Tokyo: Inoue-shoin, 1968.

Kawazoe, Noboru, "The City of the Future," *Zodiac* no. 9 (1961).

Kawazoe, Noboru, "Dai Tōkyō saigō no hi [The Last Day of Tokyo]." *Kenchiku bunka* 16, no. 171 (January 1961).

Kawazoe, Noboru, "Fuller's Concept," *Yomiuri Shimbun*, March 3, 1961.

Kawazoe, Noboru, "Interview with Kisho Kurokawa," *Bijutsu Techo* no. 186 (1961).

Kawazoe, Noboru, "A New Tokyo: In, on, or above the Sea?" *This is Japan* no. 9 (1962).

Kawazoe, Noboru, *Contemporary Japanese Architecture*. Tokyo: Kokusai Bunka Shinkokai, 1968.

Kawazoe, Noboru, "Metaborisuto Tachi to Mananda Toki to Ima," in *Metaborizumu to Metaborisuto Tachi*, ed. Ōtaka Masato and Kawazoe Noboru. Tokyo: Bijutsu Shuppansha, 2005.

Kawazoe, Noboru, et al., *Metabolism 1960: The Proposals for New Urbanism*. Tokyo: Bijutsu Shuppansha, 1960.

Kendall, Stephen, and Jonathan Teicher, *Residential Open Building*. London: E & FN Spon, 2000.

Kennedy, Christopher, John Cuddihy, and Joshua Engel-Yan. 2007. "The Changing Metabolism of Cities," *Journal of Industrial Ecology* 11, no. 2 (2007).

Kikutake, Kiyonori, and Maurizio Vitta. *Kiyonori Kikutake: From Tradition to Utopia*. Milan: L'Arca Edizioni, 1997.

Kikutake, Kiyonori, "Sky House," *Japan Architect* 34 (1959).

Kikutake, Kiyonori, "Tower-Shape Community," *Kokusai kenchiku* 26, no. 1 (1959).

Kikutake, Kiyonori, "Marine City," *Kokusai kenchiku* 26, no. 2 (1959).

Kikutake, Kiyonori, "Design Hypothesis," *Kenchiku* no. 15 (1961).

Kikutake, Kiyonori, "New Form and Old Tradition," *Arts & Architecture*, December 1964.

Kikutake, Kiyonori, "Bath Movenet," *Kenchiku*, April 1965.

Kikutake, Kiyonori, "The Great Shrine of Izumo." Originally published in English in *World Architecture* 2 (1965); revised complete version published as *Taisha kenchikuron ka kata katachi*. Tokyo: Shōkokusha, 1969).

Kikutake, Kiyonori, "The Order of Things One Can See: Floors and Columns," in *Taishak-enchikuron ka kata katachi*. Tokyo: Shōkokusha, 1969.

Kikutake, Kiyonori, *Kaijō toshi SD84*. Tokyo: Kajima Shuppankai, 1973.

Kikutake, Kiyonori, *Kaijōtoshi no hanashi (Discussions on the Marine City)*. Tokyo: NHK Books, 1975.

Kikutake, Kiyonori, *Metabolist Kiyonori Kikutake*, Special issue of *Space Design* 193 (1980).

Kikutake, Kiyonori, *Megastructure: Atarashii Toshikankyo*. Tokyo: Waseda University Press, 1995.

Kikutake, Kiyonori, "Kenchiku to mizu," *GA Japan* 70 (2004).

Kikutake, Kiyonori, "Interview: When Metabolism was Born of Renovation/Skyhouse," *Japan Architect* 73 (2009).

Motoyoshi Isao, "Kiyomizu dera," *Shinkenchiku* 31 (1956).

Kikutake, Kiyonori, and Norie Kikutake, "Sky House," *Kenchiku bunka* (December 1957).

Kikutake, Kiyonori, and Yukio Futagawa, "Sky House, its Background and Significance: Interview with Kikutake Kiyonori," *GA Houses* 100 (2007).

Kitayama, Koh, Yoshiharu Tsukamoto, and Ryue Nishizawa. *Tokyo Metabolizing*. Tokyo: TOTO Publishing. 2010.

Knabe, Christopher, and Rainer Noennig Joerg, eds., *Shaking the Foundations: Japanese Architects in Dialogue*. Munich: Prestel Verlag, 1999.

Kōmatsu, Sakyō, *Japan Sinks*. New York: Dover Publications, 1973.

Kōmatsu, Sakyō, and Tani Koshu, *Japan Sinks: Part II*. Tokyo: Shogakukan, 2007.

204 Bibliography

Koolhaas, Rem and Mau, Bruce, eds., *S, M, L, XL*. Rotterdam: 010 Publishers, 1995.

Koolhaas, Rem, and Hans Ulrich Obrist, *Project Japan: Metabolism Talks*. Cologne: Taschen, 2011.

Kuan, Seng, ed., "Drawings from the Kenzo Tange Archive: National Gymnasium for Tokyo Olympics," *Architecture and Urbanism (A+U)*, 10, no 580 (2019).

Kurokawa, Kisho, "Oh! Saibogu no Okite" ("Oh! The Code of the Cyborg"), *SD – Space Design* 3 (1969).

Kurokawa, Kisho, ed., *After CIAM*. Tokyo: Shokoku-sha, 1971.

Kurokawa, Noriaki (Kisho), "Deux Propositions de Tours Hélicoidales," *L'Architecture d'Aujourd'hui* no. 101 (1962).

Kurokawa, Noriaki (Kisho), "Metabolism: The Pursuit of Open Form," in *World Architecture One*, ed. John Donat. London: Studio Vista, 1964.

Kurokawa, Noriaki (Kisho), "Challenge to the Capsule: Nakagin Capsule Tower Building," *Japan Architect* 47 (October 1972).

Kurokawa, Noriaki (Kisho), *Metabolism in Architecture*. London: Studio Vista, 1977.

Kurokawa, Noriaki (Kisho), *From Metabolism to Symbiosis*. New York: St. Martin's Press, 1992.

Kurokawa, Noriaki (Kisho), *Shin kyōsei no shis*. Tokyo: Tokuma shoten, 1996.

Kornhauser, David, *Urban Japan: Its Foundation and Growth*. London: Longman Group Ltd., 1976.

Krasny, Elke, "Architecture and Care," in *Critical Care: Architecture and Urbanism for a Broken Planet*, ed. Angelika Fitz and Elke Krasny. Cambridge, MA: MIT Press, 2019.

Kultermann, Udo, *Kenzo Tange. Works and Projects*, ed. Gustavo Gill. Barcelona: Editorial Gustavo Gili, 1989.

Lampugnani, Vittorio Magnago, *Architecture and Planning in the Twentieth Century*. New York: Van Nostrand Reinhold Company, 1985.

Lang, Jon, *The Routledge Companion to Twentieth and Early Twenty-First Century Urban Design*. New York: Routledge, 1968.

Lang, Jon, 2005. *Urban Design: A Typology of Procedures and Products*. Burlington, MA: Elsevier/Architectural Press.

Le Corbusier, *The Four Routes*, trans. Dorothy Dodd. Paris: Gallimard and Architectural Press, 1947.

Le Corbusier, *The Radiant City*, trans. Eleanor Levieux et al. New York: Orion Press, 1967.

Lefaivre, Liane, "Space, Place and Play," in *Aldo Van Eyck: The Playgrounds and the City*, ed. Ingeborg de Roode and Liane Lefaivre. Rotterdam: NAI Publishers, 2002.

Leslie, Thomas, "Just What is it That Makes Capsule Homes So Different, So Appealing? Domesticity and the Technological Sublime, 1945 to 1975," *Space and Culture* 9, no. 2 (2006).

Lin, Zhongjie, *Kenzo Tange and the Metabolist Movement: Urban Utopias of Modern Japan*. (Abingdon: Routledge, 2010).

Mack, Casey, *Digesting Metabolism: Artificial Land in Japan 1954–2202*. Berlin: Hatje Cantz Verlag, 2022.

Maki, Fumihiko, "Attending the Team-X Meeting in 1960," *Shinkenchiku* (February 1961).

Maki, Fumihiko, *Investigations in Group Form*, Seattle: School of Architecture, St. Louis, Washington University, 1964.

Maki, Fumihiko, "Shugotai-Yottsuno Study," *Kenchiku Bunka* (June 1967).

Maki, Fumihiko, *Investigations in Collective Form*. St. Louis: Washington University, School of Architecture.

Maki, Fumihiko, "Tooku kara mita 'Daikanyama syugo jutaku keikaku,' " *Shin Kenchiku* (April 1978).

Maki, Fumihiko, "Modernism tono deai," *Shinkenchiku* (January 1991).

Maki, Fumihiko, "Notes on Collective Form." *Japan Architext* 4 (1994).

Maki, Fumihiko, *Another Utopia: Thinking of a City from an Open Space*. Tokyo: NTT Publisher.

Maki, Fumihiko, ed., *Hillside Terrace + West no sekai*. Tokyo: Kashima Publisher, 2006.

Maki, Fumihiko, and Mark Mulligan, *Nurturing Dreams: Collected Essays on Architecture and the City*. Cambridge, MA: MIT Press, 2008.

Maki, Fumihiko and Masato Ōtaka, "Collective Form: Three Paradigms," in *Investigations in Collective Form*. St. Louis: University of Washington Press, 1964.

Maki, Fumihiko, et al., *City with a Hidden Past*. Tokyo: Kashima Institute Publishing, 2018.

Marchi, Leonardo, *The Heart of the City: Legacy and Complexity of a Modern Design Idea*. New York: Routledge, 2017.

Marx, Karl, *Capital: Volume III*, trans. David Fernbach. London: Penguin, 1991.

Masai, Yasuo, "Metropolitization in Densely Populated Asia: The Case of Tokyo," in *The Asian City: Processes of Development, Characteristics, and Planning*, ed. Ashok Dutt, Frank Costa, and Allen Noble. Dordrecht: Kluwer Academic Publishers, 1994.

McCoy, Esther, *Case Study Houses 1945–1962*, 2nd edn. Santa Monica: Hennessey+Ingalls, 1977.

McKinsey & Company, "The Next Normal in Construction: How Disruption is Reshaping the World's Largest Ecosystem" (June 2020), https://www.mckinsey.com/business-functions/operations/our-insights/the-next-normal-in-construction-how-disruption-is-reshaping-the-worlds-largest-ecosystem.

McLuhan, Marshall, *Understanding Media: The Extensions of Man*. New York: McGraw-Hill, 1964.

Minohara, Kei et al., eds., *Kenchikuka Ohtaka Masato no Shigoto*. Tokyo: Ex-Knowledge, 2014.

Motoyoshi, Isao, "Kiyomizu dera," *Shinkenchiku* 31 (1956).

Musango, Kaviti Josephine et al., *Urban Metabolism for Resource-Efficient Cities: From Theory to Implementation*. Paris: UN Environment, 2017.

Nakawada, Minami and Atmosphere Ltd., *Expo' 70: Kyōgaku Osaka Hakurankai no Subete*. Tokyo: Daiyamondo Sha, 2005.

Napier, Susan, "Panic Sites: The Japanese Imagination of Disaster from Godzilla to Akira," *Journal of Japanese Studies* 19, no. 2 (1993).

'Nature, Space and Japanese Architectural Style', *Japan Architect* (June 1964).

Nishizawa, Ryue, "Kikutake Kiyonori," *Shinkenchiku* (May 2012).

Nitschke, Gunter, "The Metabolists of Japan," *Architectural Design* 34 (1964).

Nitschke, Gunter, "Akira Shibuya-City Center Project," *Architectural Design* (April 1967).

Nitschke, Gunter, "The Metabolists," *Architectural Design* (May 1967).

Ogimachi, Ichiro, "Current Criticism on the Proposals of Artificial Land on the Sea," *Kokusai Kenchiku* (February 1959).

Osaka Gas Experimental Housing: NEXT21. Osaka: Osaka Gas Co., 2007.

Oshima, Ken Tadashi, "Metabolist Trajectories," *Log* (Winter/Spring 2012).

Oshima, Ken Tadashi, ed., *Kiyonori Kikutake: Between Land and Sea*. Cambridge, MA/Zurich: Harvard GSD/Lars Müller, 2016.

"'Pandemic Urbanism': Game Changer for Urban Resilience and Sustainability?" Special issue of the open access e-journal *Sustainability* (2021). https://www.mdpi.com/journal/sustainability/special_issues/Aligning_Urban_Resilience#info.

Pearce, Fred, "Geoengineering the Planet? More Scientists Now Say it Must Be an Option," *Yale Environment 360* (May 29, 2019), https://e360.yale.edu/features/geoengineer-the-planet-more-scientists-now-say-it-must-be-an-option.

Pernice, Raffaele, "Metabolism Reconsidered. Its Role in the Architectural Context of the World," *Journal of Asian Architecture and Building Engineering* 3, no. 2 (2004).

Pernice, Raffaele, "The Transformation of Tokyo during the 1950s and the Early 1960s. Projects between City Planning and Urban Utopia," *Journal of Asian Architecture and Building Engineering* 5, no. 2 (2006).

Pernice, Raffaele, "The Issue of Tokyo Bay's Reclaimed Lands as the Origin of Urban Utopias in Modern Japanese Architecture," *Journal of Architecture and Planning (Transactions of AIJ)* (March 2007).

Power, Emma R., and Kathleen J. Mee, "Housing: An Infrastructure of Care," *Housing Studies* 35, no. 3 (2020).

Richards, J.M., et al., "The Functional Tradition," *Architectural Review* 107, no. 637 (1950).

Risselada, Max, and Dirk van den Heuvel, eds., *Team 10 in Search of a Utopia of the Present*. Rotterdam: NAI Publishers, 2006.

Rykwert, Joseph, *The Dancing Column: On Order in Architecture*. Cambridge, MA: MIT Press, 1996.

Schalk, Meike, "The Architecture of Metabolism. Inventing a Culture of Resilience," *Arts (Basel)* 3, no. 2 (2014).

Schnellächer, Thomas, "Has the Empire Sunk Yet? The Pacific in Japanese Science Fiction," *Science Fiction Studies* 29 (2002).

Schwarz, Michiel, and Joost Elffers, *Sustainism is the New Modernism: A Cultural Manifesto for the Sustainist Era*. New York: Distributed Art Publishers, 2010.

Schwartz, Claire, "June Jordan and Buckminster Fuller Tried to Redesign Harlem," *New Yorker* (August 22, 2020), https://www.newyorker.com/culture/culture-desk/when-june-jordan-and-buckminster-fuller-tried-to-redesign-harlem.

Scott, Robert, *Kenneth Boulding: A Voice Crying in the Wilderness*. New York: Palgrave Macmillan, 2014.

Scott Brown, Denise, "The Redefinition of Function," in *Architecture as Signs and Systems for a Mannerist Time*. Cambridge, MA: MIT Press, 2004.

Šenk, Peter, "The Plug-in Concept: Technology and Aesthetics of Change." *Arhitektura, Raziskave* 1 (2013).

Šenk, Peter, *Capsules: Typology of Other Architecture*. New York: Routledge, 2018.

Šenk, Peter, "Arhitektura, infrastruktura," *Architect's Bulletin* 223 (2020)

Sert, José Luis, and Congrès Internationaux d'Architecture Moderne (CIAM), *Can Our Cities Survive? An ABC of Urban Problems, Their Analysis, Their Solutions*. Cambridge, MA: Harvard University Press, 1942.

Siniawer, Eiko Maruko. *Waste: Consuming Postwar Japan*. Ithaca, NY: Cornell University Press, 2018.

Smithson, Alison Margaret, ed., *Team 10 Primer*. Cambridge, MA: MIT Press, 1974.

Soleri, Paolo, *Arcology: The City in the Image of Man*. Cambridge, MA: MIT Press, 1969.

Sorensen, Andre, *The Making of Urban Japan: Cities and Planning from Edo to the Twenty-First Century*. New York: Routledge, 2002.

Stewart, David B., *The Making of a Modern Japanese Architecture 1868 to the Present*. New York: Kodansha International, 1987.

Strauven, Francis, *Aldo van Eyck: The Shape of Reality*. Amsterdam: Architectura & Natura Press, 1998.

"Tadayou Modernism," *Shin-Kenchiku* (September 2012).

Tafuri, Manfredo, *Architettura Moderna in Giappone*. Bologna: Cappelli Editore, 1964.

Tafuri, Manfredo and Francesco Dal Co, *Modern Architecture*, 2nd edn. Milan: Electa, 1986.

Takegawa, Shogo, "The Development of Regional Social Planning in Postwar Japan," *Journal of the Faculty of Literature, Chuo University* CLXXIX (1999).

Tange, Kenzo, "A Building and a Project," *Japan Architect* (October 1960).

Tange, Kenzo et al., "About Metabolism," *Kindai Kenchiku* 14, no. 11 (1960).

Tange, Kenzo, "A Plan for Tokyo, 1960." *Ekistics* 12, no. 69 (July 1961).

Tange, Kenzo, *Space Design-SD* 8001, N. 184 (January 1980). Special Feature Kenzo Tange & URTEC (English and Japanese Edition).

Tange, Kenzo, "Yamanashi Press and Broadcasting Centre," *Works of Kenzo Tange and URTEC*, special issue of *SD – Space Design* 1 (1980).

Tange, Kenzo, "Recollections, Architect Kenzo Tange, no. 7," *Japan Architect* (October 1985).

Tange, Kenzo, *Ippon no enpitsu kara. Tokyo:* Nihon tosho sentā, 1997.

Tange, Kenzo, and Noboru Kawazoe, *Ise: Prototype of Japanese Architecture*. Cambridge, MA: MIT Press, 1965.

Tatsumi, Kazuo and Mitsuo Takada, "Two Step Housing System," *Open House International* 12, no. 2 (1987).

Taut, Bruno, *Houses and People of Japan*, 2nd edn. Tokyo: Sanseido Co., Ltd., 1958.

"*This is Your City: Urban Planning and Urban Life* Exhibition," *Kindai Kenchiku* 16, no. 11 (1962).

Tsuji, Yasutaka, "Too Far East is West: The *Visionary Architecture* Exhibition as a Background to Metabolism," in *East Asian Architectural History Conference 2015 Proceedings.* Seoul: EAAC 2015 Organizing Committee, October 2015.

Tsuji, Yasutaka, "From Design to Environment: 'Art and Technology' in Two 1966 Exhibitions at the Matsuya Department Store," *Review of Japanese Culture and Society* 28 (2016).

Utida, Yositika, "NEXT21," *Japan Architect* 73 (2009).

Van den Heuvel, Dirk, ed., *Jaap Bakema and the Open Society*. Amsterdam: Archis Publishers, 2015.

Van Eyck, Aldo, "Step towards a Configurative Discipline," *Forum* (August 1962).

Van Eyck, Aldo, *Aldo Van Eyck Writings: The Child, the City, and the Artist*, vol. 1. Sun Publisher, 2006.

Van Eyck, Aldo, *Aldo Van Eyck Writings: The Child, the City, and the Artist*, vol. 2. Amsterdam: Sun Publisher, 2006.

Van Eyck, Aldo, *Collected Articles and Other Writings 1947–1998*. Amsterdam: Sun Publisher, 2008.

"Visionary Architecture," *Mainichi Shinbun* (January 10, 1964).

Vos, Martijn, "The Foundation for Architects' Research (SAR) in Good Times and Bad," in *Housing for the Millions: John Habraken and the SAR (1960–2000)*, ed. Koos Bosma et al. Rotterdam: NAI Publishers, 2000.

Walker, Brett L., *Toxic Archipelago: A History of Industrial Disease in Japan*. Seattle: University of Washington Press, 2010.

Waswo, Ann, *Housing in Postwar Japan: A Social History*. London: Curzon Press, 2002.

Watanabe, Hiroshi, *The Architecture of Tokyo*. Stuttgart/London: Edition Axel Menges, 2001.

Wendelken, Cherie, "Putting Metabolism Back in Place," in *Anxious Modernisms: Experimentation in Postwar Architecture Culture*, ed. Sarah Williams Goldhagen and Réjean Legault. Cambridge, MA: MIT Press, 2000.

White, Morton, and Lucia White, *The Intellectual versus the City from Thomas Jefferson to Frank Lloyd Wright*. New York: New American Library, 1964.

Wolman, Abel, "The Metabolism of Cities," *Scientific American* 213, no. 3 (1965).

Worrall, Julian, "Metabolism: When the Future was Still Ahead," *The Japan Times* (September 29, 2011).

Worrall, Julian, "Metabolist Time," in *Invisible Architecture: Italian and Japanese Architectural Movements of the 1960s and 70s and Contemporary Debates*, ed. Rita Elvira Adamo, Cristiano Lippa, and Federico Scaroni. Rome: Silvana Editoriale, 2017.

Wright, Frank Lloyd, *Skyscraper Regulation, 1926*. Scottsdale: Frank Lloyd Wright Foundation, 1969.

Yatsuka, Hajime, "Architecture in the Urban Desert: A Critical Introduction to Japanese Architecture after Modernism," in *Oppositions Reader: Selected Readings from a Journal for Ideas and Criticism in Architecture, 1973–1984*, ed. K. Michael Hays. New York: Princeton Architectural Press, 1981.

Yatsuka, Hajime, "Between West and East-Japan: The State of the Architecture," *Telescope* III (1992).

Yatsuka, Hajime, *Metabolism Nexus*. Tokyo: Ohmsha, 2011.

Yatsuka, Hajime, "The Structure of This Exhibition: Metabolism Nexus' Role in Overcoming Modernity," in *Metabolism: The City of the Future*. Tokyo: Mori Art Museum, 2011.

208 Bibliography

Yatsuka, Hajime, and Hideki Yoshimatsu, *Metaborizumu: 1960 nendai nihon no kenchiku avuangiyarudo*. Tokyo: INAX Publisher, 1997.

Yosizaka, Takamasa, "Jukyo wa Ko to Shudan no Rieki no Kyokaisen," *Kokusai Kenchiku* 21, no. 1 (1954).

Yosizaka, Takamasa, *Aru Jukyo: Hitotsu no Kokoromi*. Tokyo: Sagami Shobo, 1960.

Zaera, Alejandro, "Finding Freedoms: Conversations with Rem Koolhaas," in *El Croquis 53: OMA/Rem Koolhaas 1987–1993*, ed. Alejandro Zaera. Barcelona: El Croquis Editorial, 1994.

INDEX

Note: Figures indexed in *italic* page numbering.

Acts and Regulations: *Agricultural Land Reform Law 1947* 9; *Amendments to Building Standards Law 1970* 53; *City Planning Law 1919* 53; *Height Building Law 1963* 53; *Land Reform Act 1947* 116; *New City Planning Law 1968* 53; *Occupation Army Agricultural Land Reform Law 1947* 9, 11; *Urban Building Law 1919* 53
affordable housing 74
Agricultural City project 3, 11, *13*, 14, 163, *164*
Agricultural Land Reform Law 1947 9
Aida, Takefumi 148
AIJ *see* Architectural Institute of Japan (AIJ)
air pollution 68, 74, 180; *see also* pollution
air raids *47*
Amendments to Building Standards Law 1970 53
amusement parks 41
Aquapolis floating platform 11, 58, 124, 126, *136*
Archigram group 63–4, 67, 76, 101, 154–5, 164, 187, 197
architects 2–3, 5, 22–3, 33, 41, 134, 175–7, 179, 184, 197; Buckminster Fuller 4, 63, 65–6, 69, 71, 76, 161; ethnographic 120; foreign 55, 166; Hugh Ferriss 61, 161; Kiyonori Kikutake 2, *11, 23, 26, 28*, 54, *56, 58*, 74, 76–7, *92*, 160–1, 163, 169–70; Konrad Wachsmann 3; Louis Kahn 3, 19–20, 77, 124, 148, 161, 197; Maki Fumihiko 2, 74, 77, 104, 110–11, 114, 121, 136, 139, 187, 196; Masato Otaka 2, 17–18, 27, 29, 41, 55, 89, 95, 114, 196; metabolist movement 1–3,

5–6, 8–9, 16, 22–3, 33, 41–2, 45–6, 53–4, 61–3, 66–8, 70–1, 84–6, 91, 95, 133–5, 138, 166–71, 174–7, 195–7; Murano Togo 118; Noriaki "Kisho" Kurokawa 2–3, 11, *13, 14, 35, 36, 39*, 54–5, *57*, 74, 76–9, 150–1, 154–6, 163, *164*, 165–6, 173–4, 176–7, *178*, 179, 186–9; pioneer 50; progressive 54, 103; Zaha Hadid 70, 138
architectural 50, 55, 78; designs 1, 5, 169, 173; ideas 4, 71; language 1, 15, 54; programs 70; projects 1–3, 8–9, 11, 13–19, 54–5, 73–4, 77, 91, 95, 102, 163–6, 174, 177, 185, 187–90; proposals 55; spaces 53, 55, 135, 143, 189; theories 46, 48; works 5, 163, 170
Architectural Design 75, 170
Architectural Institute of Japan (AIJ) 95
architecture 2, 4–6, 20, 27, 29–30, 33, 41–2, 76–82, 86, 101–2, 104, 116–18, 121, 132–3, 138–9, 150–1, 161, 163–4, 170–1, 195–6; capsule 6, 33, 35–6, 54, 78, 173–4, 177, 179; of change and continuity 118; and cities 42, 184; cyborg 80, 135–6; infrastructural 78, 81; of structural dexterity 68; time-based 84; and urban planning 5, 169, 171; and urbanism 2, 46, 77, 131, 170–1
Architecture without Architects 19, 138
Arcosanti *65*
artificial land 9, 11, 17, 19, 73, 75, 77–81, 84–7, 91, 93–5, 98, 102, 134–6, 185–6; A-frame structure of 91; architectural concepts of 81; concept of 91; and group-form theory 19; house, Shinjuku, Tokyo *87*; house frame *89*; layers of 185; Le Corbusier's

210 Index

declaration of 87; of Masato Ōdaka 166; megastructures 14; platform of 11; platforms 14; with program (capsule) units *79*; sketch, 1954 *85*; spatial flexibility 89, 98; Yosizaka's model of 94
Artificial Land Committee 1962 95
Asada, Kawazoe 16–17, 142
Asada, Takashi 16, 191
Association of People Who Wish to Create Their Own Urban Apartment Buildings 98
astronauts 135, 177, 179, 186
atomic bomb 16, 154
Attenborough, David 156–7
Awazu, Kiyoshi 2, 74, *75*, 160, 169–70

Bakema, Jaap 101, 103–5, 107
barracks *88*
biogenic environment 70
"Blissful Mountain" *157*
Blom, Piet 107, *109*
Bognar, Botond 22–43
bomb damage, Tokyo 1945 *47*
Boston Bay 15–16, 91
Boulding, Kenneth 179
Boyd, Robin 1, 41, 142
Buddhism 3, 13, 116, 143, 189
buildings 29, 33, 41–3, 51, 61, 77–8, 102–3, 108–10, 121, 134–5, 137–8, 142–3, 161–3, 174–7, 187–9, 197; early 155; Hammer and Sickle 61–2; high-rise 126; Hotel Tōkōen 25, *28*, 30, *123*; independent 109; individual 19, 138, 168; Kagawa Prefectural Building 119; megascale 138; Metabolist 25, 27, 33; multi-purpose 43; Nakagin Capsule Tower, Tokyo 27, 35–6, *39*, 76, *86*, 91, 174; new 146, 161; Peace Memorial Park 16; projects 150; public 43; residential 43, 50, 139; self-supporting 134; Shrine Office Building 25; Tange Kagawa Prefectural Government Office 154; Tochigi Prefectural Conference Center 27; Yamanashi Press and Broadcasting Headquarters, Kofu 29

Can Our Cities Survive 52
capitalism 175, 179–80, 195–6
capsular living units 75, 77
Capsule Declaration 76, 79, 135, *178*
"Capsule for Living", Osaka Expo, 1970 *36*
Capsule House (Theme Pavilion) project 76, 160, 174, *178*
capsules 4, 8, 11, 15, 33, 35–6, 73–82, 84, 135–6, 174–5, 177, 179, 186–8; architectural 6, 33, 35–6, 54, 78–9, 173–4, 177, 179; designing 180; developing luxury 177; enclosed 179–80; extraterrestrial 179; group's use of 175; housing 91, 174; iconic makers of 11, 176; plastic ski lodge *137*; plug-in 67, 78; polyester 174; prefabricated

apartment 3; space 51, 136, 177, 179, 186; theorists 76; toilet 155
Case Study Houses projects 51–2
catastrophes 132–4, 189
Central Alps, Honshu *151*
Cerda, Ildefons *63*
chart showing urban immigration, Tokyo, Osaka, Nagoya *49*, 55
chemical plants 49
Chernikov, Iakov 61, *62*
Chikugo River, Kurume 116, *117*, 135, 185
The Child, the City and the Artists 104, 106–7, 176
children 9, 71, 106, 110
Chisso Corporation 176
Cho, Hyunjung 131–40
CIAM *see* Congrès Internationaux d'Architecture Moderne (CIAM)
cities 1–3, 5, 19–20, 22–4, 41–3, 48–53, 61–4, 66–71, 77–8, 80–1, 93, 103–4, 106–7, 109–10, 131–4, 154–5, 160–71, 174–7, 184–5, 187–93; amorphous 2; capital 9; compact 4, 69; comprehensive 107; contemporary 5–6, 73–4, 81, 103, 116; destroyed 46; existing 62, 64, 68, 71, 185, 187–8; feudal 116; fire-bombed 66, 189; floating 10, 124, 134–5; healthier 68; helicoidal 54; large 48, 50, 52–3; marine 4, 6, 54, 121, 126, 128; metabolic 121; metropolitan 77, 133; modern 3, 106; multi-layered 61, 63; new 23, 163; planning 3, 5, 52, 93; post-industrial 5; ruined 133; segmented 79; self-regulating 53; skyscraper 61; spiraling 54; underwater 133
"The City Plan for Ikebukuro" 166
City Planning Law 1919 53
City with a Hidden Past 106
collaborators 19, 114, 166
collective form (three paradigms) *104*
"collective housing" projects 50, 84
Collins, George R. 150
community 9, 16–17, 19, 50–1, 54, 76, 80, 91, 95, 102, 110, 116; and architecture 80; buildings 81, 139, 191; crafts-making 69; facilities 64; infrastructure 13; residential 51; rural 17, 134; services 73; traditional 13; urban 42, 50
configurative discipline 106–7, 109
Congrès Internationaux d'Architecture Moderne (CIAM) 46, 50, 53, 62–3, 68, 86, 101–4, 110, 120, 122, 168
Constructivist City: Hammer and Sickle, 1933 62
COVID-19 pandemic 1, 126, 156, 184
Crutzen, Paul 180
cycles 4, 45, 54, 77, 128, 143, 185–6; industrial metabolism capitalist 176; long-term 89, 134; metabolic 133, 174, 176, 180; short-term 134

Dahinden, Justus 76
Daikanyama *111*, 188
Davis, Heather 174
Deleuze, Gilles 137
demolition 126, 155, 190
density 4, 17, 52; extreme 108; high 19; horizontal 88; low 110; urban 15
design models 4, 45
designers 1, 6, 15, 45–6, 64, 114, 133, 137
designs 4–5, 14–15, 18–20, 52, 54–5, 63, 67–9, 71, 85, 95, 106–8, 114, 119–20, 124, 180; of artificial land megastructures 14; compact 176; concrete 114, 116; experimental 58; futuristic 14; generic 71; geodesic dome 65; large-scale 51; minimalist 54; pop 76; schematic 58; skillful 35; sustainable 173
development 19–20, 50, 53, 66, 69, 73, 75–6, 78, 93, 104, 176, 185, 188; active metabolic 41, 114; industrial capitalism's 2, 175; infrastructure 45, 49; marine 116; of modern infrastructural-megastructural platforms 75; of petrochemical and chemical industries 176; of petrochemical and chemical industries in Japan 176; technological 73, 142; urban 2, 45–6, 48, 50, 58, 65, 78, 106, 110
dining-kitchen unit (DK) 47
disasters 8, 14, 42, 54, 77, 116, 133, 138, 191–2; human 131, 133; nuclear 190; prevention 6, 135; recurring 11; triple 190–1; urban 43
disciplines 4, 80, 106–7, 109; of architecture 77; configurative 106–7, 109; new 52; scientific 45
DK *see* dining-kitchen unit (DK)
Drew, Philip 142–57
Drexler, Arthur 8, 15, 161, 163, 165–6, 170
dwellings 9, 53, 84, 88, 94, 106, 185–6; accommodating 89; building their own 93; individual 106; minimum 86; working-class 54

earthquakes *88*, 119, 134, 138, 143–4, 190
economic growth 6, 46, 48, 58, 131, 160, 192; accelerated 2, 22; high 168; progressive 48; rapid 49; strong 2
Eco-urban Design, and City Regeneration 5
Eifukuji Kindergarten, Kurume 118, *119*
Eixample 63
Elffers, Joost 75
Endless House *162*
energy 6, 42, 73, 173, 185–6; concentrated urban 188; consumption 68; efficient construction 4; embodied 71; and growth 185; potential 93; renewable 42–3; systems 95
environment 19, 22, 41–3, 49–50, 52, 64, 66, 68–9, 71, 78, 81, 84, 133, 135–6; artificial 67, 82, 186; biogenic 70; city 81;

climate-controlled 65; controlled 135–6, 179; enclosed 179; natural 4, 68, 116; social 76; socioeconomic 3; sustainable 126; technological 77; urban 6, 25, 51, 73–4, 81, 121, 128
ethnographic architects 120
exhibitions 131, 138, 161–6, 168–71, 190–1, 197; *Architecture without Architects* 19, 138; celebrating Metabolism and Japanese architecture 197; "Metabolism: The City of the Future" 160; at the Museum of Modern Art, New York 3; "Tectonic Visions between Land and Sea: Works of Kiyonori Kikutake" 160; *This is Your City* 161, 166, *167*, *168*, 169–71; *Visionary Architecture* 3, 8, 161, 163–6, 170–1; "Void Metabolism" 139, 191
experimental housing 124
experiments 15, 18, 88, 154, 163, 171, 173–4; architectural 174; bold 17; career-long 187; resident participation 95; social engineering 50; structural 18
Expo 1970 33, 36, 41, 65, 84, 126, 154, 174, 190
Expo Tower, Osaka *56*
extension 19–20, 29–30, 32–3, 53, 163, 174; of concept and scale 19; and growth 53; horizontal 33; spatial 186; urban 184
exterior 39, 108, 125, 163; cone-shaped 108; interior spatial correlation 108, 110; interiorized 108; landscape 143
extraction, fossil fuel 174, 176–7

factories 4, 48, 91, 93, 150, 176; industrial 50; integrated 50; manufacturing 50; new 52; small 9
families 9, 51, 69, 104, 114, 120, 125, 186
Ferriss, Hugh 61, 161
Fiera District Redevelopment project 30, *32*
flexibility 25, 33, 42–3, 50, 76, 95, 136, 143, 186; of architecture 42; maximizing 134; of metabolism 149; replacement 119; spatial 89, 98
flooding 54, 128, 134–5; annual 135; catastrophic 54; energy 197; frequent 116; periodic 135
floods 8–11, 55, 124, 133, 185, 192; in South Japan 55; stone structures withstanding *116*; withstanding 116
floor plans 36, 39
floors 15, 19, 25, 30, 55, 117, 134, 148, 162–3, 186
"formal vertical artificial ground" 75
formalism of change 22–43
Forum 104, 107
fossil fuel extraction 174, 176–7
Foster, John Bellamy 93, 175
Frampton, Kenneth 170, 197

212 Index

Freie Universität Berlin project 13
Friedman, Yona 63, *64*, 71, 101
Fuller, Buckminster 4, 63, 65–6, 69, 71, 76, 161
functionalism 68, 76, 162, 167–8
functions 50, 53, 66, 68, 71, 77, 80, 103, 110, 133–4, 138, 162–3; basic 80; instrumental 63; organic 78; singular 162; urban 50, 55, 134

Geddes, Peter 53
geoengineering 173–4, 180
GHLC *see* Government Housing Loan Corporation (GHLC)
globalization 41–2, 195
Goldberg, Jerry 107
Golden Lane project 16
Gottmann, Jean 53
Government Housing Loan Corporation (GHLC) 87–8
Graham Foundation of Chicago 101, 138
Great Kanto earthquake, 1923 *88*
Gropius, Walter 52, 103
group form 78, 101, 103–4, 106–9, 112, 134, 136–8, 150, 154, 188; and configurative discipline 109; core of 188; developments on 104; and horizontal megastructure 80; idea of 137; and linkage 109; Maki's proposal for 106–7, 136; and megastructure 134, 137; Ōtaka proposal for 104, 136; proposal for 138; theory 19
growth 27, 33, 35, 53, 55, 73–4, 81, 134, 139, 173, 175, 185–6, 189; horizontal 30, 33; and maximum individuality 102; population 6, 134, 192; potential 50; sustainable 177; uncontrolled 3, 185; urban 1, 51, 55, 67, 70, 185
Guattari, Felix 137

Habraken, John 50, 93
hadaka-gashi ("bare rental") 94
Hadid, Zaha 70, 138
Hammer and Sickle building 61–2
Harlem 65–6, 69
Harootunian, Harry 196
Harumi Apartments project 15–16, *89*, *90*
Harumi *minka* inspiration, 1957 *90*
Harvard University 19–20, 52, 63, 104
Hashima Island 50
Height Building Law 1963 53
Herron, Ron 64
Hill, Richard C. 49
Hillside Terrace buildings 108, 110, *111*, 138, *139*, 187–8
Hirose, Kenji 46
Hiroshima 16–17, 66, 118, 126, 133
horizontal growth 30, 33
Hotel Tokoen, Yonago project 25, *28*, 30, *123*

housing 16–18, 69, 73–4, 76, 84, 86–7, 89, 91–2, 94, 107–8, 124, 126, 128; affordable 74; capsule-type 91, 174; collective 50, 84, 98; crisis 47, 50, 55, 86; experimental 124; and infrastructure 53, 73, 77; initiatives 84; and landscape elements 128; low-cost 46; low-rise private 77; mass 50, 53, 91; mobile 81; modern 86; Motomachi 16; Pasadena 150; pop designs for 76; in postwar Japan 120; prefab 93; regional 94; sustainable 95; terraced 124; units 107, 110, 124, 185
Hydra, Greece (town) *102*
hyperbolic paraboloid 119

"Ideas for the Reorganization of Tokyo City, Kikutake Kiyonori" *122*
Ikebe, Kiyoshi 46
inaka-ma system based on a module set 94
industrial capitalism 175
industrial cities 5, 48–9, 52, 54
industrial plants 50
industrial pollution 176
industries 4, 41, 46, 51, 92, 124, 143, 156, 168–9, 176; capital-intensive 93; fishing 176; local 17, 55; manufacturing 2; petrochemical 173–7; prefabricated house 91–2; tourist 177
infrastructure 2, 50, 53, 58, 67, 73, 79–82, 92, 107, 116, 139; of care 73–5, 77, 79, 81; civic 78; communal 98; complex 74; developments 45, 49; flexible 135; horizontal 78; megascale 131; megastructural 78; metabolic 79–80; and private prefabricated housing 73; public 50, 77, 128; social 22; urban-scale 103; vertical 77
Inland Sea 155
international events 2, 4, 9, 11, 15, 46, 50, 77–8, 81, 101–2, 126, 133, 135; Olympic Games (Tokyo 1964) 2–3, 33, 54, 138, 142, 160; World Design Conference, Tokyo (1960) 1–4, 8, 16, 19, 22, 53, 73–4, 102, 121, 124, 160, 163, 165–8; World Expo (Okinawa 1975) 58; World Expo (Osaka 1970) 2, 4, *56*, *57*, 76
Investigations in Collective Form 19
Ise Bay typhoon 1959 11, 116, 134, 163
Isozaki, Arata 23, *25*, 76, 148, 150, 154, *155*, 156, 188–90, 195, 197; contribution to the visual and urban repertoire associated with metabolism 189; curation of the Japan Pavilion at the 1996 Venice Architecture Biennale 190; figuration of time 189; and Greek columns superimposed on a ruined Hiroshima after the atomic bomb 154; visionary projects 29
Ito, Toyo *26*, 192, 197
Itsukushima Shrine, Hiroshima 117, *118*, 124
Izumo Administration Building project 121, 124

Japan 2–4, 8, 13–16, 22, 42, 45–6, 48–9, 76, 102–3, 116, 131–4, 142–3, 145–8, 160, 164–7, 169–71, 176–7, 195–6; "bubble-era" (Rem Koolhaas) 95; massive industrialization of 2; and metabolism representing an era of economic growth 131; overemphasizing of wartime devastation 132; postwar 45–6, 53, 77, 91, 93, 120–1, 132–3, 164–5, 168; reshaping from the ruins of defeat 46; transforming into a huge industrial archipelago 2; unstable and earthquake prone 143
Japan Architect 16, 142, 148, *150*, 156
Japan Design Committee 169
Japan Housing Corporation (JHC) 47
Japan Loan Corporation (JLC) 47
Japanese 3, 15, 143, 148, 197; agricultural community 9; architects 1, 3, 22, 33, 35, 42, 63, 66, 165–6, 171, 179; architectural canons 143; architectural community 19; architectural tradition 4; capitalism 197; crests *75*; cultural diplomacy 165; cultural traditions 3; culture 142–3, 195; democracy 9; design 74; economic miracle 22; governments 3, 48, 133; industrialization 59, 160; legacy 95; people 8, 16, 84; postwar housing crisis 84; pro-democracy slogan 86; process of modernization 196; society 22, 138; traditions 75, 81, 132, 145, 196
Japanese architecture 20, 33, 93, 128, 139, 142–4, 156, 195, 197; ancient 3; modern 4–5, 8, 54, 142–3, 156, 196; a post-and-beam carpentry tradition *144*; post-Metabolist era in 197; and urbanism 5
"Japanese Calligraphy" 165
Japanese cities 22–3, 41–2, 47, 49, 58, 88, 133; contemporary 54, 185; destruction of 133; horizontal density of 88; increasing congestion in 23, 53; and society 42
Japanese Pavilion Exhibition 1975 58, 139, 145
Jencks, Charles 190
JHC *see* Japan Housing Corporation (JHC)
JLC *see* Japan Loan Corporation (JLC)
Johnson, Philip 154
joint core systems 4, 24, *25*

Kahn, Louis 3, 19–20, 77, 124, 148, 161, 197
Kaijō toshi no hanashi 127
Kasamori Temple 117, 119, 124
Kasumigaura Lake project *14*
Katsura Imperial Villa project 54, 147
Kawazoe, Noboru 16, 74, 76, 84, 87, 91–4, 114, 119, 121, 132–5, 166–8, 170, 174; anxiety and fear of impending catastrophe 132; critic 2, 16, 74, 132–3, 142, 196; description of components with "standardized systems and joints"

wielded by resident-builders 93; freedom of expression 93; journalist 121; optimism resides in his faith in the endless process of metabolism 133
Kenchiku Bunka 119, 133
Kenji, Ekuan 76, *137*
Kenzo Tange Laboratory 101; *see also* Tokyo University
Kiesler, Frederick 161, *162*, 163, 166
Kikutake, Kiyonori 9, *10*, *11*, *12*, *23*, 25, *26*, *28*, 54–5, *56*, *58*, 76–7, *92*, 114–19, *120*, 121, *122*, 123–6, *127*, 128, 134–5, *136*, 146–8, 150, 163–6, 185–6; A-Frame Stratiform Structure System 128; Capsule Tower project 154; designs 124, 126; family landholdings 116; household 116; interest in architecture and biology 121; interest in prefabrication and housing 124; Marine City project 12, 58, 125; and Noriaki "Kisho" Kurokawa 54, 78, 151, 164, 166, 170, 187, 189; pursuit of metabolism 121; Sky House project 9–10, 25–6, 85, 119–21, 124–5, 128, 186; Stratiform Structure Module 91; Tree-Shaped House 74
Kiomizu-dera Temple, Kyoto *153*
Kitakyushu Art Museum 155
Kiyomizu Temple 117
Kobo, Abe 133
Kon, Wajiro 85, *88*
Koolhaas, Rem 2, 9, 22, 27, 92, 95, 114, 116, 131–2, 190, *191*
Korean War 48, 143
Koto Ward project 9, *11*
Kuragaike Commemorative Hall project 154
Kurokawa, Noriaki "Kisho" 2–3, 11, *13*, *14*, *35*, *36*, *39*, 54–5, *57*, 74, 76–9, 150–1, 154–6, 163, *164*, 165–6, 173–4, 176–7, *178*, 179, 186–9; capsule architecture 33; capsule design principle 177; "Capsule for Living in the Space Frame" *36*; conceptualization of architectural metabolism 173, 179; ecological vision 175; holistic vision of metabolism 174; Kasumigaura Lake project 14; and Kiyonori Kikutake's pursuit of metabolism 54, 78, 151, 164, 166, 170, 187, 189; Nakagin Capsule Tower 84, 187; theory of metabolism 179, 186
Kurume 116–17, 119, 135, 186
kyo-ma (interpost measurement system) 93–4, 98
Kyoto 117, *153*
Kyoto International Conference Centre project 147
Kyūshū 116, 126, 135, 155, 176, 186

land 46–9, 86–7, 111, 117, 121, 124, 128, 175, 179, 185, 197; agricultural 64; coastal

214 Index

128; cultivated 116; floating 121; layered 87–8; reclaimed 185; and sea 124, 128, 160; shortages 23; subsidence 128; of technological innovation and futuristic cities 2; terraced 128

Land Reform Act 1947 116

landlords 94, 111, 116

landscape 2, 48, 54, 197; architecture 52; dispersed suburban 48; natural waterfront 49; provincial 14; sacred 154; sonic 68; surrounding 55, 124; *see also* urban landscape

Lang, Jon 61–71

Le Corbusier 15, 53, 61–2, 75, 85–6, *87*, 89, *145*, 148; City in a Park 66; Paris studio (Sakakura) 145, 148; unbuilt design for Fort l'Empereur, Algiers 85

Lissitzky, El 61, 161

living 3, 6, 15–16, 35–6, 65, 68–9, 71, 84, 87, 104, 107, 117, 119, 121, 139; organisms 6, 25, 67, 133, 140, 174–7; spaces 47, 95, 119–20

living units 75, 77, 121, 186; capsular 75, 77; embedded 80; human-scale 120; prefabricated 135; standard individual 15

Lloyd Wright, Frank 61, 161

Lucas, George 147

Lynch, Kevin 20, 103

Mack, Casey 84, 84–98

Maekawa, Kunio 15–16, 46, 89, *90*, 102, 145, 148

magazines 16, 51, 75, 104, 133, 142; architectural 133; *Architectural Design 75*, 170; *Forum* 104, 107; *Japan Architect* 16, 142, 148, *150*, 156; *Kenchiku Bunka* 119, 133; popular science 61

Maki, Fumihiko 18–20, 74, 77–8, 101–11, 114, 116, 121, 136, 138, *139*, 142, 146, 148, 150–1, 187–8; and the concept of "Group Form" 20, 188; conceptualization of urban spatial formations 78; entry proposal for PREVI experimental housing project competition in Lima 55; and the *Golgi* structures 20, 74; Hillside Terrace 138; influence of 197; interest in urban form 187; and the *Investigations in Collective Form* 19, 78, 101–4, 106–9, 136; Kuragaike Commemorative Hall project 154; quoted as not denying megaform 107; works with Aldo van Eyck using megaform to design a comprehensive city while allowing for expansibility and diversity 107; works with Masato Otaka on the 1962 Artificial Land Committee 137–8, 188

Manabe, Hiroshi *169*, 170

Marine City project 3, 10–11, *12*, *23*, *58*, 116, 121, 125–6, 128, 135, 163–4

Marine Expo, Okinawa 1975 11

Martin, Frank 142, *145*

Marx, Karl 92–3, 173, 175

mass housing 50, 53, 91

Massachusetts Institute of Technology Media Lab 140

Matsushita, Kiwa 101–12

measurement systems, comparison of *kyo-ma* and *inaka-ma 94*

megaform 77, 104, 107, 112; *see also* megastructures

megastructures 2, 4, 15–16, 20, 23, 25, 46, 63–4, 77–9, 107, 131, 134–8, 153, 156; formless 112; and group form 134, 137; projects 15, 177; proponents 64, 68–9; proposals 68–9, 71

metabolic infrastructure *79*, *80*

metabolic processes 41, 93, 114, 197

"metabolic rift" (John Bellamy) 93, 133, 173, 175–6, 180

metabolism 1–2, 4–5, 8–9, 19–20, 41–2, 74–5, 84–5, 89, 91–3, 101–3, 114–16, 120–1, 131–43, 156, 160–1, 164–71, 173–7, 184–5, 187–92, 195–7; analysis of 177; architectural 179; capsule architecture 173; concept 175–6; defined 92; design proposals 46; emergence of 156; enlightened 92; environmental 179; fundamental concept of 55; funding 6; group members 102; historical examinations of 160, 169; history of 160; idea of 9, 101, 173, 192; intelligent 94; legacy of 139; lessons of 5, 20; members 11, 13–14, 101, 166, 169–70; movement 1; process of 2, 133; proposals of 171; symbols *75*

Metabolism 1960: The Proposals for New Urbanism 1–2, 41, 46, 53–4, 61, 71, 74, 76, 114, 132, 136

"Metabolism against Kenzo Tange" (discussion) 167

Metabolism and the Future of the City 5, *115*, *160*

Metabolism Lessons in the Age of Climate Change 5

metabolist 63, 150, 197; architects 2–3, 5, 22–3, 33, 41, 134, 175–7, 179, 184, 197; buildings 25, 27, 33; designs 5, 186; groups 1, 4, 14–16, 53, 73, 76, 132–3, 161, 187, 195, 197; ideas 5, 73; infrastructure 75; legacy 190–1; megastructures 15; methodology 4; structures 29, 191; theories 8, 29, 41, 173; visions of capsule architecture 5, 17, 23, 153, 179, 184

metabolist architecture 4, 27, 30, 33, 36, 41, 73, 80, 173–4, 176, 180; contradictory relations to ecology 174; and ecology 174; reliance on plastics and oil 176; shares an ecological-economic perspective 179; working through the lens of contemporary Marxist theories of anthropogenic ecological crisis 173

Metabolist Manifesto: The Proposals for New Urbanism 4, 45, 54, 121, 150, 184–5, 187, 191

metabolist movement 6, 22, 36, 41–2, 126, 131, 138; historical 139; mainstream 138

metabolist projects 2–3, 46, 74, 76, 82, 177; characterized by a spirit of innovation 6; iconic 54; influence of 2; and Kawazoe 133; and Kenzo Tange 177

metabolists 3–6, 19–20, 27, 41–3, 53, 61–71, 73–4, 80–1, 84–5, 91–2, 131–2, 138–9, 142–3, 146, 173, 184–5, 187–8, 190–3; appearing radical by today's standards projects 6; concepts 73–4; designs and theories of 8, 68, 71; ecological dilemma of 180; goals of change 41; holistic vision of organic growth 176; projects 3, 6, 8, 58; proposals 77, 192; repertoire of imaginative urban forms and dynamic architectural prototypes 59, 185; sense of temporality 188; technocratic vision 139; visionary urban forms and advanced technological architectures 45

Milan Triennale 1968 189–90

Minamata disease 176

minka (houses) 9, 85, 89–90, 128, 148, 151

MIT proposal (community for 25,000 people over Boston Bay) *91*

mobile housing 81

models 68, 71, 78, 108, 110, 132, 136, 143, 161–3, 166, 171; advanced 47; alternative 139; balsa 148; conceptual 108; design 4, 45; ecosystemic 180; expansionist 179; holistic 179; mass housing 5; massive 166; representative 46; standardized 50; urban 45, 51; Western 143

modern Japanese architecture 4–5, 8, 54, 142–3, 156, 196

MoMA *see* Museum of Modern Art (MoMA)

Monroe, Marilyn 154

monumental masonry *144*

Mori Art Museum *115*, 131, 160, 190

Motomachi Apartments project, Hiroshima 16, *17*

movies 2, 104, 126; *Solaris* 2

movies, *Star Wars* 147

Mujica, Francisco 61

Mumford, Lewis 160

Municipal Orphanage project 103, 106

Museum of Modern Art (MoMA), New York 3, 8, 15, 62, 138, 148, 161–2, 164–6, 169–70, 197

Nagoya 11, 49, 134, 142, 146, 154

Nakagin Capsule Tower project 27, 35–6, *39*, 76, *86*, 91, 174

Nakamura, Toshio 148, 151

National Olympic Gymnasium No. 2 (Basketball), Yoyogi, Tokyo, 1964 *146*

natural disasters 8, 14, 42, 54, 77, 116, 133, 138, 191–2; *see also* disasters

networks 3, 20, 48, 78, 103, 110, 132, 191; architectural business 177; effective mobility 48; existing social 69; interconnected urban 52; railway 48, 50; showroom 92; three-dimensional space 29–30

New City Planning Law 1968 53

New Directions in Japanese Architecture 142

"New Metabolism" project 139

New York 3, 8, 19, 52, 61, 65, 67, 75, 161, 163–5, 170

New York World Fair 1939 51, 148

Newman, Oscar *120*, *122*

NEXT21 Experimental Housing, Osaka, 1993 *96*

nutrients 175

Occupation Army Agricultural Land Reform Law 1947 9, 11

Odakyu Drive-in Restaurant, project 33, *35*

Office Building of Izumo Shrine, Izumo *28*

offices 18, 95, 108, 118, 126, 147–8, 150; groups of 102; local 177; post 126; school's publishing 19

oil economy 11, 49, 173, 175–7, 180, 190

Oita Prefectural Library, Oita, Kyushu *155*

Okinawa Ocean Expo 1975 *136*

Olympic Games (Tokyo 1964) 2–3, 33, 54, 138, 142, 160

open spaces 27, 29–30, 103, 108–10, 112, 138; ephemerality of 110; and footpaths 110; impenetrable public 109; interlaced 188; intertwining small 110; sequential 108; shared 17; urban 188

Osaka Expo 1970 29, 33, 35–6, 41, 49, 51, 55–7, 95–6, 154, 160, 190, 197

Oshima, Ken Tadashi 114–28

Otaka, Masato 2, *17*, *18*, 27, *29*, 41, 89, 95, 114, 196; and Fumihiko Maki's idea of Collective Form 101; obsession with the idea of the artificial ground 17; proposes a contextual approach paying attention to the surrounding landscape and mobility issues 55; Tochigi Prefectural Conference Center, Utsunomiya 27, *29*

Otaka Motomachi Apartments project 17

Otani, Sachio 147

Otto, Frei 65

pandemic 1, 42–3

para-metabolists 84

Paris 52–3, 85, 190

Paris Exhibition 1957 145, 148

Park, Robert E. 67

parks 53, 66; *see also* amusement parks

216 Index

Pasadena Heights, Shizuoka Prefecture 124, *125*, 150, 185

pavilions 33, 35, 41, 65, 147

Peace Memorial Park project 16

Pernice, Raffaele 45–59

petrochemicals 2, 174–7

Piranesi, Giovanni Battista 161

Plan for Tokyo: Towards a Structural Reorganization 166

planners 1, 5, 9, 45–6, 54, 69, 142

planning 6, 9, 42, 53, 110, 112, 150, 167; activities 53; formal 103; laws 53; master 137; physical 77; policies 69

plans 3, 5, 17–18, 20, 23–4, 52, 54, 62, 67, 79–80, 161, 163, 165–8; 10-square-meter 120; ambitious 48; concrete 166; floor 36, 39; housing 55

plants 4, 17, 50, 67; chemical 49; industrial 50; new production 2; productive 49; water purification 136

plastic ski lodge capsule *137*

plastics 77, 173–7, 179; cheap 174; material and financial reliance on 175, 177; material history in Japan 173; material history of 173; materiality of 176; popularity of 174; production of 176; use of 173

pollution 42, 93, 174, 179–80, 185; air 68, 74, 180; environmental 22, 173–4, 176–7; industrial 176; related diseases 176; water 68

postwar 9, 51, 58, 119, 128, 131, 133, 190; cities 50; conditions 131–2; Japan 45–6, 53, 77, 91, 93, 120–1, 132–3, 164–5, 168

Postwar Japan as Dullness: A History of Art Movements and Exhibition Installations 164

Prix de Rome *109*

problems 3, 9, 15, 19, 42, 62, 64, 102–4, 106, 131, 138, 176, 180; city infrastructure 73; early twenty-first-century 171; growing 22; mass-housing 45, 107; politico-economic 176; social 65, 69; sociological 51

programs 51–2, 71, 73, 78–81, 95; behavioral 70; compacted 78; fixed 95, 98; manned space 135, 186; prioritized national industrial 58; privileged 41

Project Japan. Metabolism Talks 9, 22, *51*, 92, 114, 131, 190, *191*, 192

projects 2–3, 8–9, 11, 13–19, 54–5, 89, 91, 95, 102, 133, 163–6, 174, 177, 185, 187–90; Agricultural City 3, 11, 13–14, 163, *164*; ambitious 2; architectural 1–3, 8–9, 11, 13–19, 54–5, 73–4, 77, 91, 95, 102, 163–6, 174, 177, 185, 187–90; Broadcasting Centre 149, 151, 153–4; Case Study Houses 51–2; city 133; of contemporary European radical architects 14; current 148; early 53, 118; Fiera District Redevelopment 30, 32; Freie Universität Berlin 13; Fumihiko Maki 20,

107; Harumi Apartments 15–16, *89*, *90*; innovative 6; Izumo Administration Building 121, 124; by Kikutake 13; Koto Ward 9, *11*; large construction 41; large-scale 50; lifelong 185; marine city 54; Marine City 10–11, *12*, 23, *58*, 116, 121, 125–6, 128, 135, 163–4, 185; megastructural 19; megastructures 15, 177; metabolist 2–3, 46, 74, 76, 82, 177; by Metabolist architects 2; Municipal Orphanage 103, 106; "New Metabolism" 139; newest 148; by Noriki "Kisho" Kurokawa 13; recent 154; Shikoku Island 17, *18*; Shinjuku Redevelopment 19, 55, 85, 87, 102, 167, 187–8; Shizuoka Press and Broadcasting Centre *149*, 151; Tange Kagawa Prefectural Government Office 154; Tatebayashi City Hall 124; Tochigi Prefectural Conference Center 27, *29*; Tokuunji 124; Tortoise House 74; Tower-Shaped Community 9–11, 77, 121, 163; Trans World Airlines Flight Center 161; Ura House 85; urban 4, 51, 70, 177, 197; utopic 196; visionary 6; Yadokari Hermit Crab Capsule Lodge 174; Yamanashi Press and Broadcasting Centre *153*, 154; Yoshijima House, Takayama *152*; Yosizaka House 85, 98

public housing 16, 86; estates 50; ideology 86; low-cost 47; rental 88

public spaces 73–4, 110, 138

publications 1, 4, 53–4, 114, 116, 119, 121, 131, 136, 167, 169, 190–1; *CIAM '59 in Otterlo 122*; *Eco-urban Design, and City Regeneration* 5; *Eixample 63*; *Metabolism Lessons in the Age of Climate Change* 5; *Metabolist Manifesto, The Proposals for New Urbanism* 1, 4, 45, 54, 121, 150, 184–5, 187, 191; *Postwar Japan as Dullness: A History of Art Movements and Exhibition Installations* 164; *Project Japan Metabolism Talks* 114

qualities 3, 25, 27, 30, 49, 54, 62, 64, 70–1, 147; architectural 69; high design 52; of housing in postwar Japan 120; neighborhood 69; reciprocal 106; regional 107; spatial 27; strong visual 27

The Radiant City 87

rationalists 3, 61–2

recession 138–9

recycling 4–5, 43, 94, 179

Red Cross building 151

regionalism 107, 160, 166

replaceability 25, 33, 45, 54, 118, 121, 125; of metabolism 15; periodic 174; system of 118; technological 53

research 5, 19, 54, 81, 91, 114; conducting 148; on metabolism 5

residences 14, 17, 25, 95, 107, 126
residential units 16, 25, 54–5, 166, 174
residents 51, 54, 65, 69, 71, 84, 91, 93, 107, 110, 125–6
Richard Laboratory (Kahn) 197
Richards, James Maude 167
Rublyovo-Arkangelskoye, near Moscow *70*

Sadao, Shoji *66*
Sakaide *18*
Sakaide Housing project, Shikoku Island 17
Salzburg Superpolis, 1965–1967 *67*
schemes 2, 5, 46, 54, 62, 67, 69, 121, 124, 185; central spine 54; circular tower 125; city 5; hyper-modernist 70; hypothetical 64; land-based 125; metabolism 46, 187; multi-functional 62; provocative futurist 136; urban 24, 46; visionary 132
Schwarz, Michiel 75
scientists 16, 61, 114, 125, 174, 180
Scott Brown, Denise 68
sculpture 161, 163
sea 4–6, 8–9, 13–14, 18–20, 50, 52–4, 58–9, 102–3, 106, 114, 116–17, 120–1, 124–6, 128, 133–5, 145–6, 154–5, 176–7, 179–80, 184–6; and artificial land 116; planes 126; plants 135; *see also* water
Seibu Department Store, Ikebukuro 161, 166, *167*, *168*, 170
Šenk, Peter 73–82
Sert, José Luis 52, 62, *63*
Shikoku Island project 17, *18*
shinchintaisha (renewal) 118
Shinjuku Redevelopment project 19, 55, 85, 87, 102, 167, 187–8
Shizuoka Press and Broadcasting Centre project *149*, 151
shops 17–18, 48, 66, 126
Shrine of Ise 143, 154, 186–7
Shrine Office Building project 25
shrines 4, 13, 25, 28, 116–18, 124, 126, 143, 152, 154, 186–7
Shu-Koh-Sha Architecture and Urban Design Studio *97*
Sky House, Tokyo 9, *10*, 25, *26*, 85, 119, *120*, 121, 124–5, 128, 186
Sky Mile, Tokyo *70*
"Skyrise for Harlem" *66*
Smithson, Peter 16, 76, 102–3, 124, 167–8
social spaces 76, 78–9
society 1, 5, 41–2, 78, 104, 109–10, 114, 161, 168, 175, 179, 185, 188; advanced 64; aging 6; changed 162; collaborative 104; consumer-oriented 41; contemporary 136; democratic 78; human 114, 184; shifting 95; shrinking 139; surveillance 171; urban 5
soil 135, 174–6

Solaris 2
Soleri, Paolo 63–4
space 3, 5, 9, 17, 19, 47–8, 51, 73, 75–8, 124, 135, 186–9, 192–3; capsules 51, 136, 177, 179, 186; civic 74, 78; collective 103; communal 20, 76; empty 29; exploration 69, 192; exterior 20, 78, 108; external 19, 55; floating 124; floor 166; interiorized 20; interstitial 29–30; media 78; residential 187; self-organized 76; served 19, 77; service 147
space frame 33, 35–6, 65; cubical 35; gigantic 35; tubular steel 33
spaceship 135–6, 177, 179–80
'Spatial City' concept *64*
Star Wars 147
Stirling, James 124
Stratiform Structure System 91, *92*, 124, 185
Strauven, Francis 106
structural systems 17, 25, 29, 35, 42, 125
structures 3, 6, 14, 16, 20, 23, 25, 29–30, 33, 43, 61, 63–5, 67–8, 125–6, 186–8; bridge 24; cylindrical 10; economic 5; flexible 197; horizontal 137; mass-housing 47; mobile 64; modern 148; parking 20; permanent 75–6; primary 126; regional 103; reinforced-concrete 118; rice-paddy 128; single 63; small 33; supporting 9; suspended 117; terraced 185; topographic 128; towering 67
Sumida River *47*
superstructures 17, 156
Suzuki, Makoto 148
Sydney Opera House 161
system 25, 29, 33, 35, 92–4, 101, 103, 105, 107–9, 134, 136; ancient social 9; capitalist 196; changing urban 74; closed 179; complex layering 20; dialectic 15; expanding transportation 48; flexible urban 132, 134, 138; hierarchical 101, 107; interchangeable architectural 120–1; interpost measurement 94; linear 23; measurement 94; megastructural spaceframe 124; modern 137; network 77; non-repressive participatory 76; prewar 9; quasi-megastructural 25; standardized 93; transportation 135; urban 81

Tafuri, Manfredo 1
Takara Group Beautilion Pavilion 35, *57*, 76
Takenaka Construction Company 118
Tanaka, Kakuei (Prime Minister) 11
Tange Kagawa Prefectural Government Office project 154
Tange, Kenzo 2–3, 14–16, 23, 24, 29, 30, 32–3, 34, 54, 91; airy space-frame roof of the Capsule Tower 33, 154; carpentry stylization of modernism 143; design shift from Yayoi to Jomon style 197; iconic

218 Index

architect 53; Kagawa Prefectural Building 119; keynote speech at the 1960 World Design Conference (WoDeCo) in Tokyo 89; leadership of 33; megastructure project on Boston Bay 15; and Metabolist projects 177; Peace Memorial Park 16; *Plan for Tokyo: Towards a Structural Reorganization* 166; Yamanashi Press and Broadcasting Headquarters, Kofu 29
Tange Lab architects 174, 177
Tanmiura, Tomaki *65*
Taoist yin and yang *75*
Tarkovsky, Andrei 2
Tatebayashi City Hall project 124
Taut, Bruno 161, 196
technological 15, 76, 117, 143; changes 134, 143; developments 73, 142; fix for climate change 174; progress 45, 51, 82; solutions 41, 82; transfer and financial aid 48
technology 41–3, 74, 76–7, 80, 103, 107, 114, 120, 126, 151, 156, 189, 192; alternative 6; and architecture 151; changing 156; concrete piling 116; constructional 27; current 124; cutting-edge 6; developing 116; emerging communications 70; futuristic 3; industrial 41; information 69; modern 81, 87; transportation 51
"Tectonic Visions between Land and Sea: Works of Kiyonori Kikutake" 160
This is Your City (exhibition) 161, 166, *167, 168*, 169–71
Thompson, Fred 128
Tochigi Prefectural Conference Center project 27, *29*
Togo, Murano 118
Tokuunji project 124
Tokyo 1–3, 14, 18–19, 22–6, 47–9, 53–5, 85–7, 89–90, 101–2, 106–7, 118–19, 121–2, 132–3, 135–8, 145–6, 148–51, 164–6, 168–70, 187–8, 190–1; bomb damage 1945 *47*; lowland area 135; preparing for the 1964 Olympic Games 3
Tokyo Bay Plan 14, 16, 23, *24*, 49, 54, 70, 98, 107, 116, 150–1
Tokyo Exhibition 1964 170
Tortoise House project 74
Tower-Shaped Community project 9–11, 77, 121, 163
Toyoda Auditorium project 146
Trans World Airlines Flight Center project 161
transformation 2, 4, 15–16, 46, 51, 62, 76, 103, 121, 192; generational 197; large-scale urban 46; metabolic 77; radical 45; social 76, 78; technological 134; urban 138, 184, 192
TSHS *see* Two-Step Housing System (TSHS)
Tsuboi, Yoshikatsu 146

tsunami 42, 128, 134, 190, 192
Two-Step Housing System (TSHS) 93–5
Tyng, Anne 161
Typhoon Vera 54–5, 116
typhoons 8, 11, 116, 119, 134–5, 142

Unité d'Habitation Marseilles construction site 15
United States (US) 11, 19, 51–2, 165, 186; cities 51; marine technology 11
units 15, 25, 33, 47, 50, 55, 63–4, 79–80, 125, 163–4, 167; architectural 25; changeable spatial 33; flexible 186; identical minimal 68.3-square-meter 125; individual 9, 125; massive megastructure 3; modular 35; new housing 77; non-standard 98; secondary subordinate non-structural infill panels 146; stacking 118
Ura House project 85
urban 20, 42, 53, *70*, 86, 143, 175, 185, 188; amenities 22; conurbations 49; design principles 5, 45; design theories 5; development 2, 45–6, 48, 50, 58, 65, 78, 106, 110; environment 6, 25, 51, 73–4, 81, 121, 128; expansion 23, 45, 52, 54; formations 22, 78; functions 50, 55, 134; futures 5, 63, 131; growth 1, 51, 55, 67, 70, 185; immigration (Tokyo, Osaka, Nagoya) *49*, 55; infrastructures 53, 75, 135, 139, 189; life 48, 62, 76, 161, 166–8; models 45, 51; planning 4–5, 45, 53, 81, 137, 161, 166–8; problems 36, 41, 120–1, 171; projects 4, 51, 70, 177, 197; spaces 1, 3, 19, 54, 59, 121, 184, 188; structures 66, 69, 76, 135, 192; transformations 138, 184, 192; zones 48
Urban Building Law 1919 53
urban forms 1, 4–5, 45, 51, 187–8, 197; bold 54; imaginative 59; radical 45
urban landscape 5, 45, 48, 51; innovative 5; of postwar Japan 45; traditional American 51
urban metabolism 74, 81
Urban Structures for the Future 67
urbanism 2, 4–5, 46, 77, 101, 103, 131, 168–9, 171; aquatic 185; classical 77
urbanization, large-scale 4–5
US *see* United States (US)
Utida, Yositika *96*
utopian 8, 15, 71, 76, 186; architecture 131; images 15; projects 8; world 36

van der Rohe, Ludwig Mies 52
van Eyck, Aldo 69, 101, 103–10; concepts drawn from his sociological and anthropological research on Dogon 106; Municipal Orphanage project 103, 106; working with Fumihiko Maki 104, 106
Venturi, Robert 68

vision 2, 6, 20, 42–3, 64, 101, 126, 128, 138, 162, 170–1; ambitious 49; civic 52; cyclical 134; ecological 175; exploratory 67; failed 154; ideological 51; long-term 190; managerial 179; megalomaniac 139; metabolic 116; new global 51; organic 139; reoriented 43; techno-utopian 102; technological 2
"Visionary Architecture" 3, 8, 161, 163–4, *165*, 166, 170–1
Void Metabolism Exhibition 139, 191
von Liebig. Justus 175

Wachsmann, Konrad 3
water 116, 128, 135, 174, 176, 192; ancient canals 3; pollution 68; reducing 68; services 13, 135; supply 74, 87
waterfront 49–50
Webb, Michael 164
Wendelken, Cherie 131
Westcott, James 114
Wolman, Abel 74
wood-frame construction housing 95, 118
workshops 66, 104

World Design Conference, Tokyo (1960) 1–4, 8, 16, 19, 22, 53, 73–4, 102, 121, 124, 160, 163, 165–8
World Expo (Okinawa 1975) 58
World Expo (Osaka 1970) 2, 4, *56*, *57*, 76
World War I 70
World War II 46, 52–3, 62, 66, 94, 167, 196
Worrall, Julian 184–93

Yadokari Hermit Crab Capsule Lodge project 174
Yamanashi Building *153*
Yamanashi Radio and TV Headquarters, Kofu 29–30, *32*, *34*
Yasutaka Tsuji 160–71
Yatsuka, Hajime 8–20
Yokohama 49, 151
Yoshijima House, Takayama project *152*
Yosizaka House project 85, 98
Yosizaka, Takamasa 84, *85*, 86, *87*, 88–9, 98

Zaha Hadid Architects 70, 138
Zevi, Bruno 167
Zuho-in Zen Monastery, Kyoto *157*